The Legacy
of
King Arthur

The Legacy
of
King Arthur

Chris Barber & David Pykitt

Blorenge Books

First Published 2005

ISBN 1 872730 18 3

© Chris Barber and David Pykitt

Photography by Chris Barber FRGS

Blorenge Cottage, Church Lane, Llanfoist
Abergavenny, Monmouthshire NP7 9NG
Tel: 01873 856114

Printed by MWL Print Group Ltd.,
Units 10/13, Pontyfelin Industrial Estate,
New Inn, Pontypool, Gwent NP4 0DQ
Tel: 01495 750033

CONTENTS

ACKNOWLEDGEMENTS

We are grateful to numerous people whose knowledge and assistance has been indispensable for our research and give particular thanks to the following:

Major George M. Williams, Owain A. M. Williams, Robert M. Williams, Murray A. Mclagan, Paul S. Parry, Mr L. V. Kelly, Selwyn Williams, University of Wales, Lampeter College; Michael Wilcox, Glamorgan Archives Service; John Vivian Hughes, Swansea Reference Library; Claire Smith, Neath Reference Library; Mike Hill, Mold Library, Graham Thomas, National Library of Wales, J. Bryn Jones, Cardiff Central Library, Richard Abbott, Birmingham Central Library; Dawn Birkinshaw, Manchester Central Library and Anthony Beeston, Bristol City Library, Ms Nicholls, Cardiff Castle, and the Rev J. S. Williams, St Basil's Church, Bassaleg.

Michael Blackmore and Paul Davis are thanked for their artwork.

PREFACE

In our previous book *Journey to Avalon*, published in 1993, we revealed that the key to the identity and realm of King Arthur is the fact that the Glamorgan and Gwentian princes of the 5th/6th centuries held territory in South Wales, Cornwall and Brittany. These areas consequently became the main field of Arthur's influence, which explains why they all make claim to this illustrious warrior king to this day.

It is only by understanding that Arthur was the hereditary ruler of the ancient land of the Silures that the truth of the matter can be revealed. Unfortunately, his true identity has been obscured by the romance stories and an academic muddle, which has resulted in a misinterpretation of early Welsh genealogies.

Not only have we have set out to identify the person who provided the basis for Geoffrey of Monmouth's King Arthur, but we have also provided the background to the period following the Norman Conquest of Wales in which the *Historia Regum Britanniae* was written.

Of particular importance to our research was the realisation that Iestyn ap Gwrgan, a direct descendant of King Arthur, was the ruler of Morgannwg at the time of the Norman Conquest of South Wales. This last independent prince of Glamorgan was defeated in battle just outside Cardiff in 1093, but Robert Fitzhamon, his Norman conqueror, allowed Iestyn's son Caradoc to administer a small corner of South Wales, which became known as the lordship of Afan.

Searching in vain for a long lost manuscript, The Register of Neath Abbey, we traced its movements through the centuries and identified relevant antiquaries who had consulted it. The manuscript was last recorded as being in the library of St Donat's Castle in 1725.

St Donat's Castle was purchased in 1901 by a member of a distinguished family residing in the Vale of Neath. We came to realise that this family could be traced to Iestyn ap Gwrgan, the noble descendant of Athrwys ap Meurig, whom we have identified as King Arthur. Remarkably, the descent through the male line has continued unbroken to the present day, and we were thus able to locate a direct descendant. This book is the result of our labours and it reveals the untold story of the legacy of King Arthur.

Chris Barber & David Pykitt
August, 2005

INTRODUCTION

Large numbers of Britons from Wales and Cornwall emigrated to Armorica in the 6th century[1] to escape the Saxon threat, and they took their history and culture with them. Memories of their homeland must have been very important to these settlers and in particular the traditions concerning their much loved hero, Arthur, were preserved to become strongly associated with the country which was now their adopted home.

Their native land of 'Great' Britain (Britannia Magna) was still very much in their hearts, which explains why the country which gave them refuge in time became known as 'Little Britain' (Brittany).

In about 509 Riwal Mawr ('the Great'), the son of Emyr Llydaw, arrived in the Bay of St Briéuc on the north-east coast of Armorica with a large fleet and founded the colony and principality of Domnonia. He rapidly extended his authority over the whole of Northern Brittany and continued to rule as 'dux Britannorum' on both sides of the sea until his death in 524. Also at this time a large contingent arrived from Gwent where the Britons were under considerable threat by the Saxons. These settlers established themselves in the north-west of the Armorican peninsula and named their territory Leon or Lyonesse after the Caerleon in Gwent which they had abandoned. Subsequently, the territory of Leon was annexed by Domnonia in the north-east to form a single kingdom.

Another group of settlers took possession of the Western coast (Finistere) and called their land Cornu (Cerniw) after their homeland, or perhaps because it is shaped like a horn (corn = horn), thrusting forward into the Atlantic. The rest of southern Brittany, including the western part of Vannes was named Bro Weroch, 'the land of Weroch', an area which corresponds to the modern Morbihan.

The leaders of the emigration were largely the princely families of south Wales, although the majority of the immigrants probably came from the Devon / Cornwall peninsula and this is borne out by the fact that the Breton language is related more closely to Cornish than to Welsh. It is evident from the place-names that the holy men known as 'saints' were also important leaders and it is significant that some of the Breton saints are descended from Welsh kings.

Gradually, the newcomers took possession of this sparsely populated country and for two centuries there was a constant flow of settlers. The migration was at its height during the first half of the sixth century and it continued for the next two hundred years with the country remaining divided into mini kingdoms until the 9th century.

Retaining their original language, through the centuries, the Britons were able to hand down their traditions in a way that was impossible amongst other nations who had lost their ancient languages. Thus, we find that the earliest writers of Arthurian Romance refer to Brittany as the source of their legendary knowledge. By the 12th century the legend of Arthur and the belief in his eventual return had taken firm route and it was from the Bretons that the Normans first derived their knowledge of Arthur.

To these exiled Britons, Arthur was their own king, who had led them into battle and whose abdication after the battle of Camlan was also one of the causes of their flight to Armorica. His story was their heritage and the traditions of his life were fondly cherished through the passing centuries. These settlers, poor and exiled, would naturally carry with them the poetry, histories and tales that related to their homeland. Moreover, they would treasure the remembrance of those brave leaders who had defended their native soil and the most popular of these was Arthur.

The part of Britain now known as Wales did not exist as a separate country until the seventh century. Before that time it was merely a part of Western Britain. In 577 it was severed from the Domonii, south of the Severn, by the battle of Deorham, and in 613 that the battle of Chester finally completed its isolation by separating it from Cumbria in the north.

In the middle of the ninth century the Normans over ran the east of Brittany and when the line of Breton Dukes arose a century and a half later they found themselves related to the Dukes of Normandy. In this way a close relationship grew up between the two peoples; and the Arthurian legends passed from the imaginative Bretons into the adapting hands of the Normans.

When William the Conqueror assembled his army to cross over to England, Brittany consisted of large numbers of Bretons who did not object to accompanying him, for they no doubt were excited by the idea of undertaking an avenging expedition against the descendants of those who had opposed Arthur. This large army of nearly seven thousand men landed at Pevensey Bay on the morning of 28 September 1066. Within three weeks William of Normandy had defeated Harold Godwinson in a decisive battle near Hastings and was crowned King of England at Westminster on Christmas day 1066.

After the Conquest, the parallel series of legends that had been growing up in Wales were welded with the Armorican legends under Norman editorship. By the time the Normans had completed their editorship of the traditions, Arthur and his men had ceased to be British or Breton, instead they had become Norman. In the middle of the 15th century, when Malory wrote his *Le Morte d' Arthur*, his hero had ceased to be Norman, but was portrayed as a medieval knight, who conducted himself according to the laws of chivalry of that time. In this way King Arthur was transformed from the half-magical figure of the early Celtic tribes of Wales and Brittany to the lance carrying knight of Medieval England.

Breton entertainers were made welcome at the Norman households where their tales told in French described the adventures of Arthur and in turn these stories were rendered into Welsh by the local bards. The stories, however, were not committed to parchment until the twelfth century.

Geoffrey of Monmouth, the writer who really introduced the world to King Arthur, also may have had a Breton background for he is believed to have been a member of a family of Bretons who came over during or after the Norman Conquest and settled in Monmouth (see page 111). He was obviously conscious of the fact that the Bretons and the Welsh were originally the same people.

By the second half of the twelfth century, Arthur and his knights had become heroes of chivalric romance. During this period French poets on the Continent and in Norman England gave literary form to almost all the well-known Arthurian romances, which must have been recited by wandering storytellers before they were written down. The romancers set their stories in the background of their own day and described the manners and customs of a time when chivalry was flourishing and when women held high place in the royal courts. Within a few years the Arthurian romance stories had passed into the languages of Europe from Italy to Iceland.

Although William the Conqueror vanquished England, it can be questioned whether the Normans ever really conquered Wales. They firmly established themselves in Wales but there was continuous warfare between the two races for more than three centuries.

Between 1160 and 1258 the Welsh laid waste, burned and plundered the Vale of Glamorgan continually, for as descendants of the fierce Silures they had always fought strenuously against any enemy who forcibly took possession of their land. It was not surprising that they resisted the Norman occupation with such determination, for William Rufus had proclaimed, with regard to the Welsh, that he was going 'to destroy utterly all of the people until they would be alive, not so much as a dog.'

An indication of the degree of warfare in the twelfth century is given by the brief sentence relating to Kenfig, when the chronicler notes that Kenfig Castle 'had not been burnt for a year or more.' During the twelfth and thirteenth centuries the Welsh seldom ceased trying to reclaim their own country.

By and large the struggle between the Welsh and the Normans ended in the two nations agreeing to live side by side. From bitter experience, the Norman barons learned that they could never hope to subdue the mountainous parts of the country, as long as the Welsh retained their spirit of independence. After a time they were content to leave these districts under the rule of the native princes. The Welsh on the other hand could not drive the Normans from the fruitful valleys in which they had settled, and were therefore forced to allow these regions to be occupied by the foreigners.

The Normans were very clever people who chose to adapt themselves to the country in which they settled. They did not bring their wives with them but married the women of the country. More than that, when they were settled, they sent for their sisters and married them to the native princes and nobles, so that in a short time all the noble families of both England, and especially south Wales, were of mixed blood.

There is no doubt that the Norman nobility treated the Welsh not as aboriginees of the soil but as an independent nation worthy of respect, and the matrimonial alliances were numerous.

Good examples are the beautiful Nest, daughter of Rhys ap Tewdwr, King of Deheubarth, married Gerald de Windsor; Morgan, the Welsh Lord of Afan, married the daughter of Walter de Sully; Payn Turberville married the daughter of Morgan, the Welsh lord of Coity; Gwladys, daughter of Llywelyn ap Iorwerth, married Ralph Mortimer; Dafydd ap Owain Gwynedd married the sister of Henry II and Llywelyn ap Iorwerth married Joan, the daughter of King John.

From the sixth to the twelfth century, when a great revival of bardism and other forms of literary activity took place, there was a 'Dark Age' period of which Welsh literature preserved few written records. This was a warlike and unsettled period and the ceaseless struggle against the Saxons and the Normans would have left little leisure time or inclination for literary pursuits. Also, many literary documents would have been lost during the long period of sack and pillage. Thus, all we really have are the writings of Gildas, Nennius and Asser, a monk of St David's who fills a gap between Nennius and the next great literary landmark in the history of Wales: the laws of Hywel Dda.

Many of the hill forts dating from the early Iron Age, which had fallen into disuse during the Roman occupation, were re-occupied during the fifth and sixth centuries to play an important part during the defence of Arthur's realm. Archaeology has indeed shown that forts, such as Dinas Powis, Deganwy and Cadbury Castle were occupied during this period. Arthur no doubt held his plenary courts in such forts as Lodge hill at Caerleon-upon-

Usk to coincide with the great Celtic and Christian festivals, but writers of the 12th and 13th centuries saw them as medieval strongholds of their own, and accordingly placed Arthur and his followers in great castles of stone.

Today, the links between Western Britain and Brittany have largely been forgotten, mainly because since the French Revolution Brittany has become an integral part of France.

> 'If it be allowed that a mass of floating tradition was carried by the South British exiles, when in the sixth century they passed over to Armorica, that these traditions were fondly cherished among them, because they told of the former glory of that land to which they could never return, that the imagination of their descendants invested them with a halo of poetic beauty, because these fond recollections were their only heritage, we shall discover not merely the reason why every British tradition up to the sixth century was preserved among them, but a reason, too, why Arthur, merely one of the many brave warriors in the enumeration of the Welsh bards, is the all-powerful monarch and hero of the Breton lay. Arthur, although known in Wales as the monarch of the Silures and the valiant opponent of Cerdic, was but one of the many kings and warriors who fought, though in vain, against the Saxon; but to the Breton exiles he was their own king, who had led them to battle, and whose death was the cause of their flight'.[2]

Arthur's fame has endured for fourteen centuries, but most people assume that he was just a romantic figure. We, the authors of this book, maintain that the identity of King Arthur has been obscured through a series of academic errors with the result that there is a 100 year error which pushed the person who can be identified with this Dark Age king into the wrong century. Our main objective was to trace the bloodline of King Arthur and locate a direct descendant who is alive today.

> 'Of stubborn fact is here no question
> The pearl of every fable is thought
> The truth of every old tradition
> Is in its hidden spirit wrought.'

> John Griffith 1904

One

ARTHUR, KING OF THE SILURES

T he key to the identity and realm of King Arthur is the simple fact that the Glamorgan and Gwentian princes of the 6th century held territory not only in South Wales but also in Cornwall and Brittany. These lands became the main field of Arthur's influence and as a result are the very places where he is best remembered.

Arthur as a name is an anglicised version of a Celtic title which was used by several personalities, who through the passing centuries became fused together into one powerful monarch, whose life seems so incredible and unlikely that he has come to be regarded as a subject of fiction and fantasy.

The earliest reference to Arthur as a king can be found in the *Vita Cadoci* (Life of St Cadoc), which was completed between 1073 and 1086 by Lifris or Lifricus of Llancarfan, who was the son of Bishop Herewald of Llandaff. It is an important document for it preceded Geoffrey of Monmouth's *Historia Regum Britanniae* by two generations.

There is a relevant passage in the *Vita Cadoci* which mentions a grant of land known as Cadoxton-juxta-Neath by a certain King Arthmael to St Cadoc in c.530:-

> 'When the islands became unsafe (Flatholm and Steepholm in the Bristol Channel), owing to the pirates who infested the estuary of the Severn making landing-places, St Cadoc was obliged to look for some other place of retreat. He found one on the banks of the River Neath. He sent gifts to King Arthmael, who thereupon made a grant of this spot, now known as Cadoxton Juxta-Neath, to St Cadoc.[1]

According to the genealogy contained in the Book of Llandaff, the king who was reigning over Morgannwg and Gwent at this time was Athrwys ap Meurig ap Tewdrig. Lifris thus provides us with evidence that Athrwys and Arthmael are one and the same person.[2]

Sir William Dugdale, in his *Monasticon Anglicanum* (Vol III p.190) which he compiled in 1673, mentions Arthur (so spelled) as the king of Gwent, son of Mouric, king of Morgannwg, and father of Morcant. Elsewhere, Arthur is uniformly called Athruis, who was a contemporary of Comergwynus, a bishop of the See of Llandaff. Further investigation reveals that Comergwynus is identical with Athruis's brother Comereg, Bishop of Erging.

Furthermore, Sir William Dugdale states that Morcant, a king in Wales, having treacherously killed his uncle Frioc, after he had in a most solemn manner sworn an inviolable peace with him before the altar, was by Oudoceus, Bishop of Llandaff and nephew of St Teilo, excommunicated. According to the genealogy of the kings of Morgannwg and Gwent contained in the Book of Llandaff, Frioc was the brother of Athrwys ap Meurig and so was Comereg, who is identical with Comergwynus, Abbot of Mochros and Bishop of Erging. Comereg is included in the list of Suffragon, or local bishops, living in the time of St Teilo, Bishop of Llandaff, and is stationed in divers parts of his diocese. He succeeded Ufelwy as Bishop of Erging during the reign of his brother Athrwys, who granted him Llan Cinmarch Church, near Chepstow, with its territory comprising a large portion of Erging. However, a clerical error in the Book of Llandaff has placed Comereg under his Latin name of Comergwynus in eighth position in the list of Bishops of Llandaff when he was in actual fact Bishop of Erging only.

Thomas Carte, writing in 1747, obviously agrees with Sir William Dugdale for he comments that there is little room to doubt but that Arthruis, king of Gwent, who granted the land of St Kinmark to Bishop Comereg, was the Arthur in question.[3]

Writing twenty-eight years later, the Rev John Whitaker in his *History of Manchester* (1775), names Arthur as King of Gwent with his court at Caerwent. In the second volume (p.34) Whitaker writes: "Arthur was the Arth-uir, a great man or sovereign of the proper Silures and therefore the denominated king of Gwent, the Venta Silurum of the Romans, and the British Metropolis of the nation." The name Arth-uir is obviously a variation of Arthwyr - the title given to Arthur, meaning the Bear Exalted.

The Missing Century

Athrwys ap Meurig is not accepted by modern day historians as the King Arthur of legend and history for they claim that the early Welsh genealogies show that he lived in the seventh century and was thus one hundred years too late.

However, through our programme of research, we are convinced that serious errors in the interpretation of the early Welsh genealogies have caused the misplacing of the dynasty of Athrwys ap Meurig and this has resulted in this identification of King Arthur being rejected.

A major problem was initially created by the compiler of the Book of Llandaff, for he failed to realise that there was a gap of approximately one hundred years in the ancient charters. This gap was detected by J.W. James, in his Chronology in the *Book of Llan Dav* 500-900, The National Library of Wales Journal XVI (1969/70). He concluded that the gap between Morgant filius Athruis (Morgan the son of Athrwys) and Morcant pater Iudhail (Morgan the father of Ithel) may be due to the loss of a document, possibly a book of the Gospels, which contained memoranda covering the entire seventh century, and disappeared in a series of calamities hinted at in the Book of Llandaff on page 192; but once the two Morcants are separated by a century, the chronological difficulty disappears.

Furthermore, the compiler was no doubt misled by the *Welsh Annals*, which give the death of St Dyfrig as 612 and the death of Morgan Mwynfawr as 665. St Dyfrig was in fact born c.450 and retired to Bardsey Island about twenty years before his death at the advanced age of 96 years in 546.

As a result, the compiler of the Book of Llandaff made one 'King Morgan' out of two men bearing the same name. The first was Morgan Mwynfawr ('the Courteous') ap Athrwys and the second was Morgan Morgannwg (the father of Ithel), who re-united the kingdom and died fighting the second Battle of Mons Badonicus (Mount Badon), which is recorded in 665.

This confusion led the compiler of the Book of Llandaff to post-date the early kings of Glywysing and Gwent, and consequently the genealogists have stretched the pedigrees in order to accommodate Morgan Morgannwg, who died in 665, but as soon as the two Morgans are separated by a century the chronological difficulty disappears.

Such confusion no doubt caused Professor Hector Munro Chadwick, when he was constructing his genealogy of the dynasty of Gwent, to misplace Meurig ap Tewdrig, king of Glamorgan and Gwent, creating an anomaly which post-dated his son Athrwys by more than a hundred years, thus pushing him into the seventh century. Another error was caused by the late John Morris, who had Athrwys's son, Morgan Mwynfawr, instead of Morgan Morgannwg, fighting the second battle of Mons Badonicus in 665.

The comment has been made that has Meurig's reign was exceptionally long, and that his son Athrwys must have died early in his reign. However, Athrwys did not die young and he no doubt spent considerable time away from Wales, fighting battles, while Caradog Freichfras ruled Gwent during Meurig's semi-retirement. It is certainly true that Meurig was still the nominal king of Gwent and he was still making grants.

Mistakes are so easily made when there is a duplication of names and we can show that two Tewdrigs and two Meurigs have been confused, this being yet another factor which led to Athrwys ap Meurig ap Tewdrig being placed in the seventh instead of the sixth century.

We are in agreement with the Rev Sabine Baring-Gould and John Fisher, in *The Lives of the British Saints*. They were convinced that there were two princes of Morgannwg and Gwent named Meurig and two named Morgan and that the compiler of the Book of Llandaff had confounded them. This view was also supported by the Rev. Arthur Wade-Evans in *The Llancarfan Charter*s (1932). He proved that the Morgan who witnessed the grants of Meurig ap Tewdrig was not his grandson Morgan Mwynfawr, but his brother-in-law Morgan, the son of Gwrgant Mawr, whilst the later grants attributed to Meurig ap Tewdrig were in actual fact made by Meurig the son of Caradoc Freichfras.[4]

The confounding of two Meurigs and two Morgans has helped to stretch the chronology of the early charters contained in the Book of Llandaff. A prime example is a grant made to Oudoceus by Meurig the king, and Judic son of Nud, witnessed by Morgan the king. This Morgan can hardly be the grandfather of Morgan Mwynfawr. There can be only one logical explanation. There were no less than three Morgans making and witnessing grants in the sixth and seventh centuries. They were Morgan ap Gwrgant Mawr, Morgan ap Athrwys ap Meurig, and Morgan Morgannwg, who according to the Welsh Annals died in 665.

According to *The Genealogies of the Welsh Saints*, the daughters of Meurig ap Tewdrig and his wife Onbrawst married sons of Emyr Llydaw. These marriages could not have taken place if the daughters of Meurig had been born a hundred years later. Gwenonwy married Gwyndaf Hen and their sons were Saints Meugant and Henwyn; Anna married Amwn Ddu and their sons were Saints Samson and Tydecho; and Afrella married Umbrafel and their son was St Maglorius. St Samson was ordained by St Dyfrig on 21 February 521 and he attended the third Council of Paris in 557, where he signed his name 'Samson peccator episcopus' among the bishops. St Samson was the nephew of Athrwys ap Meurig. Thus, Saints Dyfrig and Samson and King Athrwys may be positively dated.

It can also be shown that the compiler of the Book of Llandaff made the mistake of confounding Arthur ap Pedr, king of Dyfed, with Arthur ap Meurig, king of Gwent. In the grant of Llan Cinmarch by King Athrwys ap Meurig of Gwent to Bishop Comereg (BLD 165), one of the principal witnesses is Gwernabwy, Prior of Llangystennin Garth Benni, but Gwernabwy also appears as a witness to the grant of Pennalun (Penally in Dyfed) by Nowy ap Arthur to St Dyfrig.

Arthur ap Pedr ap Cyngar ap Gwerthefyr (Vortiporix) cannot be considered as a candidate for the historical King Arthur because his great grandfather Gwerthefyr (Vortiporix) flourished in c.550. Arthur ap Pedr was therefore three generations too late for the time of the historical Arthur.

He must have flourished in the middle of the seventh century. This is yet another example of the compiler of the Book of Landaff failing to notice the hundred year gap in the charters.

It is possible that this gap in the charters contained in the Book of Llandaff may be due to the loss of a document, possibly a book of the Gospels, which contained memoranda covering the entire seventh century, and which disappeared in a series of calamities which are hinted at on page 192 of the Book of Llandaff.[5]

The Life and Realm of King Arthur

In our book *Journey to Avalon* we demonstrated how Cernyw in Gwent has become confused with Cornwall; Silchester with Woodchester and Caerwent with Winchester. Camelot has long thought to be at Cadbury Castle, but we explained why this hill-fort was so-named and also why it has been linked with King Arthur. The romantic idea of Camelot is based on Geoffrey of Monmouth's description of Arthur holding court in Caerleon-upon-Usk, but the actual name was first used by Chretien de Troyes in his *Chevalier de la Charette*.

Countless historians have endeavoured, without any convincing degree of success, to sort out the locations of Arthur's twelve battles, listed by the ninth-century writer Nennius. We have identified a realistic and plausible set of locations, most of which have never been considered before and in all cases we have identified Arthur's enemies.

The Severn Estuary has provided a very important key to the riddle of King Arthur. On the Gwentian side we located the harbour and battle site of Llongborth, the burial place of Geraint, and the location at Black Rock, where Arthur gathered his army before fording the estuary to fight the battle of Badon at Bath. It was at this battle that Arthur's ally Cadwy avenged his father's death at Llongborth by slaying Cerdic of the Gewissei. Cadwy's son Constantine eventually took over from Arthur, when he later abdicated after being wounded at Camlan.

He was taken to the mysterious island of Avalon (known by the Britons as Ynys Afallach), which we have identified as the Isle of Bardsey, just off the far end of the Llyn Peninsula. Here the wounded Arthur was restored to good health in the monastery of his cousin, St. Cadfan, by Modron the daughter of Afallach who in the romance stories has become Morgan Le Fay.

We revealed that the story of Arthur does not end with his dying on the Isle of Avalon. His wounds healed, he sailed across the sea to Brittany, where, like many of his contemporaries, he turned to religion and became highly venerated by the Bretons as St. Armel.

Not only did Arthur (as St Armel) establish several churches in Brittany, but he also participated in one final battle, and, with the assistance of his nephew St. Samson, defeated the usurper Marcus Conomorus (remembered in legend as King Mark). As a result of the battle, the exiled Prince Judwal - the great-grandson of Arthur's one-time ally Riwal Mawr, was restored to the throne of Breton Domnonia. By correctly interpreting an inscribed stone in the church of St. Illtyd at Llantwit Major in Glamorgan we revealed that it commemorates this 6th century battle fought in Brittany by Arthur, Samson and Judwal.

Brittany and Wales have important historical connections, which have been largely forgotten. It is particularly significant that large numbers of immigrants from Gwent and Glamorgan settled in Brittany during the 5th and 6th centuries and they named their territory Léon after the Caerleon in Gwent which they had left behind.[1] The simple fact that Caerleon, Cernyw and Gelliwig in Gwent all have their counterparts in Cornwall and Brittany has caused much confusion in the age-old quest for a solution to the mystery of King Arthur.

Tracing the final years of Arthur's life, we were able to locate his place and date of death. An empty stone sarcophagus stands in a Breton church founded by St. Armel (the Breton name for Arthmael/Arthur). It is recognised as the saint's tomb, but the Bretons seeme unaware that it is the tomb of King Arthur, despite the fact that he is by tradition associated with that locality. A treasured relic kept in the church is a casket containing the jaw-bone of St. Armel , who is none other than King Arthur.

Numerous contemporaries of King Arthur settled in Brittany, so it is hardly surprising that he also spent the last years of his life there. They sailed to this sparsely populated land to escape the threat of the invading Saxons and the peril of the Yellow Pestilence, a form of bubonic plague which was sweeping Britain at that time. In addition these people of royal and noble families settled in Brittany for religious reasons and founded numerous churches and monasteries where in the present-day settlements their personal names and places of origin are still remembered.

We explained why Glastonbury has become confused with Avalon and why the monks in 1191 believed that they had excavated the grave of King Arthur and Guinevere. They in fact more than likely discovered the mortal remains of King Arviragus, who also bore the title Arthwyr, and his queen Genissa, whose name bears a similarity to Guinevere.

The mysterious Island of Bardsey was once known as Ynys Afallach, and is the true site of Avalon. King Arthur was taken to a monastery on the island after the Battle of Camlan.

This now-empty stone sarcophagus can be seen inside the church of St Armel in Brittany. Above the decorated archway, written in French, are the words 'The Tomb of St Armel'. It once held the bones of the mighty King Arthur.

By studying the life of King Henry VII, who saw himself as a descendant of King Arthur, we discovered that he knew the true identity of King Arthur and that a statuette of St. Armel can be seen in King Henry VII's Chapel at Westminster Abbey.

During the eighteenth century it was recognised by several historians that Arthur was the hereditary king of the Silures in South Wales, but the vast majority of present-day historians have chosen to ignore this. We re-examined the early Welsh genealogies and demonstrated that a misinterpretation by learned academics has resulted in the transfer of the Welsh Athrwys (who bore the title Arthwyr) to a later century, thus disassociating him from the King Arthur of legend and history. This re-examination of the source material led us not only to discover the true identity of Arthur, but also to locate his court, the sites of his principal battles, the Isle of Avalon and his final resting place in Brittany.

King Arthur as a war leader and defender of his country was undoubtedly the right man in the right place at the right time, and when he departed he must have been sorely missed. He fell from power during a dynastic revolution, and the great confederacy of British kingdoms, which had been so effective in keeping the Saxon invaders at bay, disintegrated into its component parts. As a result, the subsequent history of the Britons was a succession of defeats until finally all that remained in their possession was the land that we know today as Wales.

The name of King Arthur

The monk Gildas makes a significant statement when denouncing Cuneglassus, a 6th century contemporary of Arthur, when he comments that Cuneglassus was once the charioteer of a person known as 'The Bear'.

The Celtic word for bear is 'arth' and it is thus possible that the name Arthur is a sort of nickname derived from the title Arthwyr.

Many scholars have stated that the name Arthur is derived from Artorius, but if this was so we would expect to find such a form of the name used in Latin texts like the *Annales Cambriae* or the *Historia Brittonum*, yet in these records the name appears respectively as Arthur and Arturus.

It is significant that in Nennius's *Historia Brittonum* Arthur is depicted not only as a military but also as a religious leader. Nennius refers to him as Arturus Miles (Arthur 'the Warrior') and in the *Life of St Efflam*, his contemporary, he is Arturus Fortissimus (Arthur 'the Mighty').

The naming of Arthur in Ancient Manuscripts

Historia Brittonum c.822 (Nennius)	Arturus
Annales Cambriae	Arthur
Vita Cadoci c.1075 (Lifris)	Arthurus
De Rebus Gestis Regum Anglorum c.1125 (William of Malmesbury)	Arturis
Historia Anglorum c.1129 (Henry of Huntingdon)	Arthurus
Historia Regum Britanniae c.1135 (Geoffrey of Monmouth)	Arturo, Arturus
Vita Gildas before 1156 (Caradoc of Llancarfan)	Arthurus
Chronicum Anglicanum 1187-1224 (Ralph of Coggeshall)	Arturi
De Instructione Prucipum 1193-9 (Giraldus Cambrensis)	Arthuri
Historia de Rebus Gestis Glastoniensibus c.1278 (Adam of Domerham)	Arturo

The idea that the name Arthur comes from the Latin Artorius is not very satisfactory and it is our belief that the origin is much more straightforward. It is more likely that the name Arthur is derived from Arthwyr, which was a title or a descriptive term implying a person of high renown or of undaunted fierceness. Arthur as a name is merely another form of Arthwyr and the Latin version of the name is more likely to be Arthurus. In the ancient Book of Llandaff the name Athruis is very likely derived from Arthurus or Arturus.

Further confusion has been caused by the existence of a soldier-saint called Arthmael ('Bear Prince'), or Armel, who lived at the same time as Athrwys ap Meurig and is remembered for the part he played in liberating the Bretons from the tyranny of Marcus Conomorus in the sixth century. He established a persistent legend of a King Arthur operating in Brittany which is remembered to this day. In Breton, a bear is 'arz' and Arth (arz) mael, means bear prince.

'Mael' enters into the composition of many of the old Welsh names of this period e.g. Maelgwyn, Maelog and Maelrhys. Another example is the abbey of St Dogmael (near Cardigan) which derives its name from Dogfael, the son of Ithel ap Ceredig ap Cunedda.

St. Arthmael is portrayed wearing armour in his designation of 'Miles Fortissimus ('Mighty Warrior') in the Rennes Prose (1492) and the Breviary of Leon (1516), in which he is invoked as the armigere (armour- bearer) against the enemies of our salvation. Therefore, Arthmael was a military and religious leader. This again helps to indicate that the soldier saint Arthmael is synonymous with King Arthur. In Latin the name Arthmael is Armagillus which must be derived from armigere, meaning armour-bearer or squire.

According to *The Life of St Dubricius* , contained in the Book of Llandaff, St Dubricius crowned Arthur king when he was fifteen years old. Arthmael was born in 482 and would therefore have been fifteen years old in 497 at the time of the death of Ambrosius Aurelianus, who had nominated Arthur as his successor.

One of the historians who gave support to the identification of Athrwys ap Meurig as King Arthur was the Rev John Whitaker, the foremost historian of Lancashire. In his *History of Manchester* (Vol. II p.34, published in 1775) , he names Arthur as King of Gwent and writes:-

> 'Arthur was the Arthuir, great man, or Sovereign of the Proper Silures and therefore the denominated king of Gwent, the Venta Silurum of the Romans, and British metropolis of the nation.'

William Owen Pughe, in his *Cambrian Biography*, published in 1803, states:

> 'About the year 517, Arthur was elected by the states of Britain to exercise sovereign authority... having been from 510 till then, only a chieftain of the Silurian Britons, being the son of Meurig ap Tewdrig.'

Authorities cited for the identification
of Athrwys, king of Gwent, with Arthmael

1073-86 Lifris *Vita Cadoi*

1120-40 The Registers of Donations to Llandaff Church in the days of the first three bishops - St Dyfrig (c.500-512), St Teilo c.512-563) and St Euddogwy (c.563-570).

15thc *The Register of Neath Abbey*, containing an early history of Morgannwg
The Register of Brecon Priory, containing an early history of Brecon

1502-55 Sir John Price of Brecon - *Historia Britannicae Defensio* (1573) (pages 120-3)

1520-65 Lewys Morgannwg (Llywelyn ap Rhisiart) in his elegy to St Illtud

1572 Sir Edward Stradling of St Donat's Castle (1529-1609) - *The Winning of the Lordship of Glamorgan out of the Welshmen's Hands*

1572-91 Llywelyn Sion of Llangewydd (1540-1615) - *Llyma Enwau a Hiliogaeth Brenhinoedd Morgannwg* ('These be the names and genealogies of the Kings of Glamorgan') page 45

1591 Sir Edward Mansel of Margam (d.1595) - *The Winning of Glamorgan - Another account of the coming of the Normans in a shorter story than before*, page 23

1673 Sir William Dugdale - *The Monasticon Anglicanum*, Volume 111, page 190

1729 The Rev. Dr David Nicholl - *The Antiquities of Llantwit Major*, pages 45-53

1747 Thomas Carte - *A General History of England* Volume I, Book III, page 202.

1759 Lewis's *Dictionary of Wales*

1775 The Rev Whitaker - *The History of Manchester*, Volume 2, page 34

1796 David Williams - *The History of Monmouthshire*

1801 William Coxe - *A Historical Tour of Monmouthshire*

1803 William Owen Pughe - *The Cambrian Biography*

1807 Sharon Turner - *The History of the Anglo Saxons*, Vol 1, pages 101-102
John Hughes - *H orae Britannicae* Volume 2, pages 193-195

1824 John H. Parry - *The Cambrian Plutarch*, page 3

1870 Ebenezer Cobham Brewer *The Dictionary of Phrase and Fable*, p.66

1891 Robert Owen - *The Kymry, their Origin, History and International Relations*, page 77

1911 Owen 'Morien' Morgan *A History of Wales*, page 118

Two

THE LAND OF ARTHUR

The ancient kingdom of Glywysing was an extensive area which stretched from the river Usk in the east to the river Tywi in the west. It was named after its first ruler, Glywys ap Filur, who was a direct descendant of the Roman Emperor Magnus Maximus (known by the Welsh as Macsen Wledig), who as *gwledig* , or commander of forces in the Roman province of Britain, set himself up as Emperor of the West in the year 383.

In the *Life of St Cadoc*, which was written in the eleventh century by a Norman cleric named Lifris, we are told that: 'Formerly in certain borders of the Brittanic country (he means Wales) which was called Demetic (meaning here all south Wales west of the River Usk), there reigned a certain prince named Glywys, from whom all the days of his life the whole monarchy of that district took the name of Glywysing.'[1]

The extent of Glywysing is defined in the *Lives of the Cambro British Saints* (p.336):-

> 'The territory from Ffynnon Hen - that is the old fountain- as far as the mouth of the river Rhymney, and all the territory from the river Gulich to the river Nadauan, from Pentyrch direct to the valley of Nantcarfan; and from that valley to the Gurimi (Gwy-Rhymi), the stream which runs by Cadoxton-juxta-Barry towards the sea.'

Glywys Cernyw, the grandson of Glywys ap Filur, the founder of Glywysing, established a number of churches including Machen (Gwent) and Merthyr Mawr, which was formerly known as Merthyr Glywys.

Apart from its early use in the name of Merthyr Glywys, the name of Glywys is found on two Dark Age memorial stones erected in the same locality. The first of these is the Conbelanus Stone, which in Victorian times was removed from its site on the bank of the Ogmore river and placed inside St Roque's Chapel within the grounds of Merthyr Mawr House. The other stone bearing his name is the 'Artmail Stone', which was discovered at Ogmore Castle (in use as a paving slab) and can now be seen in the National Museum of Wales at Cardiff. Both of these stones provide confirmation of the importance of the area surrounding Merthyr Mawr during the Dark Ages.

The Victorian church at Merthyr Mawr is of little interest to the historian for it was entirely rebuilt in 1848-52, but it stands on the site a very early church.

Behind the church is this fascinating collection of inscribed and decorated stones which were found in the churchyard or on the site of the medieval church. They confirm that it was once the site of a Christian cemetery of some importance.

In the Celtic Church the name 'Merthyr' did not necessarily imply a martyr but referred to a cemetery beside a church or in later Welsh, a 'llan'. Several church-names, now prefixed with 'Llan,' had formerly Merthyr, such as Llanfaches and Llandegfedd in Gwent.

Merthyr Mawr, which is in the vicinity of Ogmore-by-sea, is a name which suggests that here can be found a Christian cemetery of some importance, which in ancient times was probably used as the burial ground of the local ruling family. Certainly, evidence of the one-time importance of this location as an ancient royal burial ground has been provided by the discovery of a 5th - early 6th century stone, which came to light in 1848 when the foundations of the present church were being excavated. It can be seen with other interesting stones in a shed on the north side of the churchyard and is the upper fragment of a slab inscribed: PAUL FILI MA... The inscription is unfortunately not complete for the stone is broken. However, it is reasonable to assume that it belongs to Paul the son of Mar who was the son of Glywys. Other memorial stones dating back to the 6th century have also been found here and these provide strong evidence that on this site once stood a very early and important church.

This broken memorial stone found at Merthyr Mawr Church bears an incomplete inscription which probably refers to Paul son of Mar (grandson of King Glywys).

The ruins of St Roque's Chapel stand within the confines of an Iron Age fortress which may well have been re-occupied during the Dark Ages. The chapel probably occupies the site of the long lost chapel of St John, which was mentioned in 1146 concerning a dispute between Llandaff and Tewkesbury.

Inside St Roque's chapel are two 6th century inscribed stones which were removed from their original positions in the locality, and brought here for safety by Sir John Nicholl in the late nineteenth century. Pictured here is the Conbelanus Cross which has unfortunately lost its entire head. It has interlaced work on the back and sides and the inscription, in miniscules, is in two panels on its face and reads as follows:

'Conbelanus placed this cross for his soul and for those of St Glywys and St Nertat and for that of his brother and for that of his father. It was prepared by me, Sciloc.'

When King Glywys died, his kingdom was divided, according to the custom of gavelkind, among his seven sons, but it seems to have become a single entity again when Einion is described in the Book of Llandaff as King of Glywysing in the sixth-century. The ninth and last king of Glywysing was Hywel ap Rhys, who went to pay homage at the court of King Alfred of Wessex as King of Glywysing. The Book of Llandaff tells us that in 884 Hywel ap Rhys,[2] King of Glywysing, gave the old church at Merthyr Mawr with about 137 acres of land to the Cathedral Church of Llandaff as a penance for a wrong doing. The parish of Merthyr Mawr has remained in the hands of Llandaff Cathedral since that time and the memorial stone of Hywel ap Rhys, who died in Rome whilst on a pilgrimage in 885, can be seen in the church of St Illtyd at Llantwit Major (see page 51).

By the middle of the tenth-century, Glywysing appears to have been incorporated into the kingdom of Morgannwg under the rule of Morgan Hen ('the Aged').

The Royal Palace at Boverton

The village of Boverton, which is situated near Llantwit Major, was once a place of much greater importance than it is today. For five hundred years prior to the Norman invasion it was the site of one of the favourite residences of the rulers of Morgannwg, and can be associated with the ancestors and descendants of King Arthur.

We are told by Nennius, writing in the ninth century, that Ambrosius Aurelianus, the Romano-British Emperor, spent his childhood in the vicinity of Campus Elleti, which the Rev. Arthur Wade-Evans, in his book *Welsh Christian Origins* (1934), identifies with Llanmaes near Llantwit Major. Further support to this idea can be found in the *Mabinogion* which states that Myrddin Emrys (Merlin Ambrosius) came from Maesaleg in Glywysing, which is the ancient name of this territory.

A statement which helps to confirm this location as the seat of the Aurelii family can be found in Wrmonoc's *Life of St. Pol de Leon*. He tells us that Count Porphyrius Aurelianus, who was the father of St. Pol de Leon, was born at the Roman Station of Caput Bovium in the cantref of Penychen in Glywysing. He was a Romano-Briton of high rank who served as a military companion to the King of Glywysing and also held land in Domnonia (Devon).

There has been much controversy over the identity of the Roman settlement of Caput Bovium, with Boverton, Cowbridge and Llantwit Major all being strong contenders for its location. According to the Itineraries of Antonine,[3] it was positioned on the Via Julia Maritima (The Road of Julius by the sea) which was constructed by Julius Frontinus, who first landed in Siluria at Sudbrook near the mouth of the Wye. Here he built the first of his great military encampments, remains of which exist to the present day. From this fortified landing place he built his great military road which was wide enough for ten soldiers to march abreast. It passed through the impressive forts which were subsequently constructed at Caerwent (Venta Silurum), Caerleon-upon-Usk (Isca Silurum), then via Malpas and Bassaleg, to follow the ridge above St. Mellons and on into Morgannwg.

It passed the military encampment of Rat Tabulus at Rumney and continued through Roath; then deviated slightly to the north-west to pass the Heath, where remains of an encampment were once evident. From there it proceeded in a direct line for Caerau, where there are indications of a Roman Station, believed to be the Tibia Amnis, on the summit of a prominent hill. This encampment covered an area of twelve acres and was in the form of a parallelogram, rounded at the angles and defended by one rampart on the north, two on the south and west, and by three on the east. It seems probable that the Via Julia skirted the base of this hill and then headed in a westerly direction for the next station at Bovium,[4] a distance of twenty 'millia passum,' according to the twelfth Itinerary of Antonius. From there the Via Julia continued in a nearly direct line, keeping in site of the Channel, to cross the Ogwr and Newton Downs, past Kenfig to Neath (Nidum), then on to Loughor (Leucarum) and Carmarthen (Maridunum).

Boverton was probably linked with the Via Julia and it is relevant that traces of a Roman road, known locally as the causeway, were found many years ago, about three hundred yards to the north of the village. A subsidiary branch of this road ran to the ancient camp known as Castle Ditches and to the ancient harbour at Colhugh.

In 1798, thirty-eight Roman coins, in a very good state of preservation, were dug up between Eglwys Brewis and Boverton by a local farmer. Twenty six of them can be seen in the National Museum at Cardiff. They include silver denarii of Vespasian, Domitian, Nerva, Trajan, Sabrina Antoninus and Faustina. Coins of Carausius were found in Castle Ditches fort, and at nearby Colhugh coins of Nero and Vespasian were found in 1830.

Local tradition maintains that a royal palace was built near Boverton in the fourth century by Meurig ap Caradog, the brother of Eudaf Hen ('Octavius the Old'), Earl of Gwent, Erging and Ewyas. Meurig was a client ruler appointed by the Romans and he resided in a magnificent villa situated in a field now known as Cae Mead. (see page 37).

It was destroyed during an Irish raid and at the same time a monastery founded by Meurig's sister Eurgain at nearby Cor Worgan (the Choir of Eurgain) was also razed to the ground.

Meurig ap Caradog was succeeded by his son Erbig or Erbic, who is commemorated by a stone cross inscribed with the name 'IRBIC' which can be seen in Llandough churchyard just outside Cardiff. Erbig's son and successor was Erb. The Rev. Arthur-Wade Evans has pointed out that a Welsh personal name of Erb or Erbin is found for St Paul Aurelian's father Count Porphyrius Aurelianus, the identity of whom has baffled scholars. If this is the case then Count Porphyrius Aurelianus may be none other than Erbin, the brother of Ambrosius Aurelianus. The Rev. Sabine Baring-Gould, in *The Lives of the British Saints*, identifies Erbin with Erb, whose successor was Pebiau Clavorauc, who married a daughter of Custennin Fendigaid (Constantine 'the Blessed'), Romano British Emperor 433-443. One of Custennin Fendigaid's sons was Ambrosius Aurelianus and it is significant that Nennius tells us that he spent his childhood at Campus Elleti, which is known today as Llanmaes and is quite close to Boverton. This Romano-British family of Aurelii had been expelled from Arfon in North Wales by the usurper Vortigern (Gwrtheyrn Gwrtheneu) and they settled both in Armorica (Brittany) and close to the Severn in the territory of the Silures.

The name Bovium is probably the Roman form of the Welsh Pen Ychen, an ancient name of this locality. Pen means head and ychen is the plural of ych, an ox. Caput Bovium (Head of the Ox) is the Roman equivalent.[5]

In the late fifth century the co-ruler of Penychen and Gower with Paul of Penychen[6] was Meirchion Vesanus ('Marcianus the Mad'), one of the sons of King Glywys, who inherited this territory on the death of his father. Meirchion was expelled from his petty kingdom along with his son March (remembered in Welsh tradition as King Mark), by King Tewdrig Fendigaid (Theodosius 'the Blessed') who also at one time was in residence at Boverton. This royal palace became a summer residence and it was in due course used by Tewdrig's son Meurig and in turn his son Athrwys (Arthur).

The location of this royal palace is probably where the ivy covered ruins of Boverton Place now stand, for this site has a long history of royal ownership. In the time of Iestyn ap Gwrgan, the building standing here was known as Tre Beferad. Iestyn was the last independent Welsh Prince of Glamorgan and a direct descendant of Athrwys ap Meurig (King Arthur), so it is appropriate that he had one of his courts here. There is also a tradition that Iestyn ap Gwrgan established a mint and foundry in nearby Llantwit Major on part of the land now occupied by the grounds of a house called 'The Hayes'. In the first half of the nineteenth century coins bearing the inscription 'Iestyn ap Gwrgan Twywysog Morganwg' were significantly found near the Town Hall.

Erbic, the son of Meurig ap Caradog, is commemorated by this stone cross which stands in Llandough churchyard just outside Cardiff. Erb (his son) was the Welsh personal name for Count Porphyrius Aurelianus, the father of St Paul Aurelian.

Following the defeat of Iestyn ap Gwrgan in 1091, Robert Fitzhamon seized his lands and it is interesting that he decided to retain for his own use the Grange of Boverton, which consisted of 990 acres of demesne lands. On Fitzhamon's death, this estate was inherited by his daughter Mabel, who married Robert, Earl of Gloucester.

In 1189, Prince John, by virtue of his marriage with Isabel, one of the co-heiresses of Earl Robert's son William, became Lord of Glamorgan for a short period. John thus took up his wife's inheritance which included the Honour of Gloucester, with the castle and Hundred of Bristol and part of the lordship of Glamorgan, but John became dissatisfied with Isabel (also known as Hadwisa of Gloucester), for she failed to provide him with an heir so, when he ascended the throne in 1199, he divorced her and married again.

The ruins of Boverton 'Castle', a late Elizabethan mansion built in the late 1590's by Roger Seys, Queen's Attorney to the Council in Wales and the Marches. It stands on the site of an ancient palace which was used by the ancestors of King Arthur and also his descendants, thus providing a long history of royal ownership.

Isabel retained Boverton Castle as part of her inheritance and some years later when King John was on the run from his enemies she gave him shelter.

The next Lord of Glamorgan was Richard de Clare[7] who took the title by right of his wife Amica, who inherited it on the death of her sister Isabel. The lordship then passed from the De Clares, to the Despensers, the Beauchamps and the Nevilles. Boverton itself fell to the Crown by the marriage of Anne Nevill, daughter of Warwick ('the Kingmaker'), to Richard, Duke of Gloucester, who became Richard III (1483-5).

On April 10 1551, Edward VI granted the lordship of Boverton and Llantwit (with what remained of the lordship of Glamorgan) to William Herbert, Earl of Pembroke, Master of Horse to the king. It was sold by William Herbert, Earl of Pembroke, whose family seat was at Raglan Castle in Gwent, to Sir Rice Mansell for the sum of £10 on 28 March 1536. Mansell bequeathed the property to his son Anthony.

The manor was later granted by Henry VII [8] to his uncle, Jasper Tudor, Duke of Bedford, and then let by Jasper to Griffith Voss, who was related to Matthew Voss, who fought at the battle of Bosworth. There is a story that Jasper Tudor, having killed one of the Herberts of Cardiff, was hidden by Voss at Boverton while he was waiting to be pardoned for his offence. For this assistance, Voss, the tenant of Boverton, is said to have been granted the manor for life. It is recorded that Voss subsequently changed his name to Roger Seys and became Attorney General for all Wales.

The property remained with the Seys family until its extinction in a final heiress who married a Jones of Fonmon. They subsequently had financial difficulties and Boverton was mortgaged for securing the two sums of £8,000 and £2,000 advanced by Sir Henry Goring. The property was then sold for £17,750, in July, 1804, to Vander Hoist, a Bristol Merchant, who in turn sold it to Isaac Harris Wrentmore, who built a pier near Summer House Point. It was then purchased by a Mr Jones, who in 1845 sold it to Sir John Guest, the husband of Lady Charlotte Guest. The property then descended to Lord Wimborne and later became the property of Mr T. Thomas of Cowbridge.

Gradually, the condition of the castle deteriorated, but it continued to be used as a residence during the first half of the nineteenth century until it became so dilapidated that it was dismantled. The stables, which once accommodated sixty or more horses, were demolished and the stalls and fittings of solid oak were sold to various purchasers.

Boverton Place, behind the ruins of the 'castle', is a Tudor mansion which has been successively owned by the Morgan family of Glasbury and the Halls. It later became the house of one of the largest and most valuable farms in the Vale of Glamorgan, which in the 1970s was purchased by Prince Charles, thus continuing the tradition of royal ownership of this site.

The ruins of Boverton 'Castle'

Summary of Boverton's Arthurian Associations

* Caput Bovium (Boverton) was the seat of the reguli who ruled this part of Silurian territory under Roman rule. It later became the royal summer residence of Meirchion Vesanus (Marcianus 'the Mad') and also of Tewdrig Fendigaid (Theodosius 'the Blessed'), King of Morgannwg and Gwent, and of his successor Meurig. Tewdrig was co-founder with Custennin Fendigaid (Constantine 'the Blessed'), the father of Emrys Wledig (Ambrosius Aurelianus 'the Imperator'), of Cor Tewdws (the Choir of Theodosius), the former name of Llan Illtyd Fawr (the great church of St Illtyd), now Llantwit Major. Tewdrig Fendigaid and Custennin Fendigaid were respectively the grandfather of Arthur and the father of Ambrosius Aurelianus.

* In 482 Arthmael (Athrwys, Athruis, Arthur) was born at Caput Bovium. He was educated at the nearby monastic school of Llanilltyd Fawr, where his cousin St Illtyd was Principal.

* In 487 St Paul Aurelian, the son of Count Porphyrius Aurelianus and the cousin of Arthmael, was born at Caput Bovium. He too was educated at Llanilltyd Fawr. According to the Rev Arthur Wade-Evans, the Welsh name for the father of Paul Aurelianus was Erb. If this is the case then Count Porphyrius Aurelianus was none other than Erbin, the younger brother of Ambrosius Aurelianus who reigned over British Domnonia (Cornwall) and was the father of Geraint, who was killed at Llongborth.

* According to W. A. S. Hewins, T*he Royal Saints of Britain from the Latter Days of the Roman Empire* (1929), Paul Aurelian's father, Count Porphyrius Aurelianus, married a daughter of Meurig ap Tewdrig, which made him the brother-in-law of Athrwys (Arthur).

* Meurig's daughter Anna married Amwn Ddu (Annun 'the Black') and became the mother of St Samson, who was also educated at Llanilltyd Fawr. A brother of Amwn Ddu was Umbrafael who married Afrella, another daughter of Meurig ap Tewdrig. It is signifcant that Afrella is the Welsh version of Aurelia.

* St Illtyd was the son of Bicanys, who was the son of Aldwr and nephew of St Garmon. Illtyd's mother was Bicanys' second wife Gweryla, the daughter of Tewdrig Fendigaid. Illtyd was therefore the cousin of Athrwys ap Meurig ap Tewdrig.

* According to *The Mabinogion*, Myrddin Emrys (Merlin Ambrosius, otherwise known as Ambrosius Aurelianus) came from Maesaleg in Glywysing which is undoubtedly the same place as Campus Elleti (Llanmaes), near Llanilltyd Fawr, ('the Great Church of St Illtyd'), now anglicised to Llantwit Major. It was here, according to tradition, that Ambrosius Aurelianus spent his childhood c.433-443.

* It thus becomes obvious that the Roman station of Caput Bovium (Boverton) was the home of the Aurelii, the Romano-British imperial royal family, after their expulsion from Arfon (in North Wales) by the usurper Gwrtheyrn Gwertheneu (Vortigern 'the Thin'), and that Arthmael was a member of this illustrious family, which explains why Ambrosius chose Arthur (Arthmael) as his successor.

* For centuries after, the Manor of Boverton was the residence of the princes of Glamorgan - the descendants of Athrwys ap Meurig (King Arthur) right up until the time of Iestyn ap Gwrgan, the last independent Welsh Prince of Morgannwg in the 11th century. The Norman knight Robert Fitzhamon seized for himself the lordship of Glamorgan, and Boverton Castle became one of his favourite seats. In 1845, Boverton Place was purchased by Sir John Guest, the husband of Lady Charlotte Guest, who translated and published the stories contained in *The Mabinogion*. In the mid 1970's, the property with its adjoining farm was purchased by Prince Charles.

The Monastic College of Llanilltyd Fawr

Wander through the narrow streets of Llanilltyd Fawr and you get the feeling that you have entered a bygone age, with the story of this ancient and attractive little town going back to Roman times.

Evidence of the Roman history of Llantwit Major, to use its anglicized name, has been found in a field on the outskirts of the town, where a large and important Roman villa once stood. Of special interest to us is the possibility that when the Romans left Britain many of their fine buildings and villas were occupied by Romano-British families.

The remains of this important Roman villa were discovered by Prof. J. Storrie in 1888 in a field to the north-west of the present town and between the Wick road and Morfa. In a lease dated the 10th year of Queen Elizabeth I, the field is called Lez Garnes (Llys y Garneddau). In the seventeenth century it bore the name Garne Meadow.

This substantial villa covered an area of two acres with about fifteen rooms, one of them measuring twenty metres by 17 metres. A beautiful mosaic pavement was found during Storrie's excavation, together with coins, pottery and glass.

Among the discoveries were a bath, a sepulchral urn, Samian ware, pottery of various kinds of iridescent glass, wall plaster in tints of vermillion, blue, green, pompeiian red, brown, pink, yellow, orange, blue-black and cream colour, oyster and other shells in abundance. Coins of the time of Maximus, of Victorinus and Constantius Chlorus, as well as Greek bronze coins were also found there. A tessellated pavement in one of the rooms was very impressive and artistic in design. It contained intricate patterns, carried out with great skill, in the colours brown, red, blue, white, light green, and dark sage green. Two thirds of the pavement had been completely broken up, and the skeletons of three horses were found upon it.

Forty-three human skeletons, including adults and children of both sexes, were found. It is interesting that the graves were orientated in the Christian manner in an east-west direction and that they were cut through the mosaic floor of the building, indicating a Christian cemetery of the late 4th century on the site of a ruined villa.

Scattered through the ground were remains of horses, horned cattle, sheep, dogs, swine, cats, deer and stags, many in almost perfect condition. After the excavation the remains of the villa were on view to the public for a considerable time, but then the landowner, following a misunderstanding with those responsible for the excavations, had the site covered over and it is now indistinguishable from other fields in the vicinity.

Disaster struck this courtyard villa in the middle of the fourth century when it was attacked and destroyed, along with St. Eurgain's College, by the Gwyddel Ffichti (Irish Pictish pirates). This event occurred in the lifetimes of Meurig ap Caradog, the brother of Eudaf Hen (Octavius 'the Old'), and his sister St. Eurgain. In the *Genealogies of the Saints* it is stated that Eurgain formed a college for twelve saints at Cor Worgan (the Choir of Eurgain), which flourished until it was raided by Irish pirates. King Tewdrig became its second patron and, in conjunction with Custennin Fendigaid (Constantine 'the Blessed'), restored and re-established the monastery, which then became known as Cor Tewdws (The Choir of Theodosius).

Early in the fifth century the monastic college again suffered at the hands of the piratical hordes, who ravaged the shores of Siluria, and the college of Tewdws remained in ruins for many years until St Garmon came over from Brittany in about 450 AD to preach against wrong teaching in the church and he refounded the college. A young monk named Illtud was made principal and under him the college flourished to become the first university in Britain and among the greatest in Europe.[9] Saints, abbots and bishops of the old British church lectured here and it was visited by the kings and princes of west Britain.

St. Illtud,[10] like St. David, built his sanctuary in a hollow, perhaps hoping that it would not be visible from the sea and attract the unwelcome attentions of the pirates who sailed up and down the Severn Sea (Bristol Channel). From every part of Britain and the Continent pupils flocked to St Illtud's seat of learning. It is reputed that Illtud's students included Saints David, Dyfrig, Teilo, Gildas, Paul Aurelian, Paulinus, Padarn, Samson, Maglorius, Arthmael, Maelgwyn Hir ('the Tall') of Gwynedd, and the bards Taliesin, Talhaiaran, and Elphin, the son of Gwyddno Garanhir. Many high placed members of the Christian church lectured in Illtud's college, and among the students who came here were princes from all parts of Britain.[11] It is said that they were taught philosophy, rhetoric, grammar, arithmetic, logic, Latin, Greek and astronomy.

Illtud's famous establishment was a sort of Oxford and Cambridge rolled into one, and more holy men were sent out from here during the 5th and 6th centuries than from any other similar monastic establishment. Even after the death of Illtud, the college continued to operate with a good reputation right up to the 11th century, when the Normans arrived in Glamorgan. The monastery of St Illtud had flourished for about seven hundred years and it was now dealt a very severe blow by Robert Fitzhamon, when he transferred the ecclesiastical revenues of the property it possessed to Tewkesbury Abbey. Only a small share of the income was allowed to be applied towards the maintenance of the ancient church, college and monastery of Illtud.

Llanilltud Fawr, now anglicized to Llantwit Major, was founded in the 5th century by St Illtud. He established a monastic college, which became the first university in Britain and the greatest in Europe. It is said that his pupils included Samson, who became Bishop of Dol, Gildas the historian, Taliesin the bard, Maelgwyn, who became King of Gwynedd, and Arthmael (King Arthur).

In the churchyard, to the south of the church, is the ancient ecclesiastical cross, probably of Norman origin, but said to mark the spot where in ancient times agreements of various kinds, both ecclesiastical and secular, were arranged and ratified. Here the men of Glamorgan are said to have assembled in 560 to witness the signatures of the Treaty of Peace between King Morcant and Trix his uncle, after which the matter was concluded before the altar of St Illtud.

Subsequently, Robert, Earl of Gloucester, son-in-law of Fitzhamon, restored and helped to sustain the reputation of the college. It thus survived until the reign of Henry VIII when, at the Dissolution of the Monasteries, its profits were bestowed upon the new Chapter of Gloucester Cathedral.

Few places in Wales have roots which stretch so deeply back into the past. The narrow streets of the town now cover the medieval pavings over which famous holy men once walked - St. Patrick, St. David and St. Samson of Dol in Brittany, who was a kinsman of St. Illtud and St Arthmael, and in the surrounding fields are mounds covering the foundations of many ancient buildings.

The college of St Illtud probably stood to the north of the churchyard, and the monastic buildings evidently extended along the brow of the hill to the field known as the 'Old See', where the monastery gatehouse still remains. This is the site of one of the oldest Christian universities in the world,[12] and the original buildings would have been very simple, consisting of bee-hive huts occupied by the monks and seven small churches, all enclosed by palisades. It is said to have possessed seven halls and 400 houses for 2,000 pupils.

In comparison with St. David's church in Pembrokeshire, the existing church of St. Illtyd is small, but its atmosphere is compelling, giving a feeling that you are standing in a very holy place - a sanctuary of peace, simplicity and charm.

The one-time importance of Llanilltud Fawr is confirmed by the number of early Christian monuments which have been preserved in this church for it was once the burial place of royalty.

A ninth-century cross, called the 'Cross of Howell,' has the shape of a wheel on its top and is decorated with patterns on both sides, but of special interest is a Latin inscription which commemorates Rhys, the father of Hywel, who was a king of Glywysing. Translated, the inscription reads:-

'In the name of God the Father and the Holy Spirit
Houelt prepared this cross for the soul of Res, his father.'

The stone was discovered in 1730 and it is of particular importance for Hywel (Houellt), who had it erected, was a direct descendant of Morgan Mwynfawr and thus also of King Arthur. He is mentioned in the Book of Llandaff as having given lands in the vicinity of Merthyr Mawr to the Church of Llandaff in the last quarter of the 9th century as atonement for crimes for which he had been excommunicated. He is supposed to have travelled to Rome to avoid the Saxon conflict. On his arrival at St Peter's, Rome, he was taken ill with sunstroke and died three days later.

41

This inscribed stone which can be seen in St Illtud's Church bears a Latin inscription which has been correctly translated, but, until the publication of our book *Journey to Avalon*, not properly understood. It is only through our investigation into the story of St Arthmael that we have been able to piece together the truth of this matter. It would seem that St Samson erected this stone to commemorate a battle fought in Brittany in which the tyrant Marcus Conomorus was defeated.

The inscription testifies that St Samson made the cross for his own soul and for those of Iuthael (Judwal), the King, and Arthmael (Armel=Arthur). This is confirmation of a successful campaign organised by soldier saints or knights of King Arthur.

About a century ago, the cross of St Illtutus was removed from the centre of the churchyard and placed in the restored chapel. Only the shaft of the cross remains but it stands over seven feet high. It is decorated with an elaborate pattern of ribbons, and in two small panels is a Latin inscription which translated into English reads;

'Samson placed this cross
for the good of his
(Illtud's) soul'

The Cross of St Illtutus

Upon the other side are four small panels surrounded by knotted ornaments. These panels bear the names of Illtud, Samson, Samuel the engraver and Ebisar.

This is one of the most interesting memorials of the Early British Church in existence, and commemorates two holy men whose names are among the most illustrious in Wales.

One would like to think that this cross was erected by Samson, the Abbot of Llanilltud, afterwards Archbishop of Dol in Brittany, to the memory of his relative and instructor, Illtud, the renowned Principal of the fifth century university. Latter day historians have, however, ascribed the carvings and inscription to the eighth, ninth or tenth centuries.

Interior of the Eastern Church

The Samson Cross is the ancient 'crux lapidia', which, according to the *Liber Landavensis*, formerly stood above the grave of Samson, Archbishop of Dol in Brittany. He was previously an abbot and bishop of Llanilltyd Fawr and succeeded Illtud as principal of the monastic college. Comprised of siliceous freestone, it is a large and imposing-looking monolith, standing 3 metres high. On the top is a socket to receive a cross-head, which has sadly long been lost. An oblong panel occupies the whole of the front, and contains a Latin inscription..

There is a tradition that on account for the love and respect that Samson had for Illtud, his former teacher, he gave orders that his body should be brought after death to the monastery of Illtud, and buried there in the cemetery. It is said that at the end of Samson's life, his body was placed in a coffin, 'which moved, and a strong wind raised it, and by divine power carried it in the softest manner to the sea. There it passed over the waves, and arrived like a sailing ship, safe and prosperously in the harbour of Illtyd. The body being received and honourably conveyed was then placed in the middle of quadrangular stones, which were standing upright in the cemetery, a stone cross was fixed thereon.' It would seem that one of the quadrangular stones here mentioned is the pillar now to be seen in the Western Church and the carving and inscription on it may well have been undertaken centuries later.[13]

It was the Welsh bard, Iolo Morganwg, who discovered this stone in 1789. He remembered being told as a boy by Richard Pruden, the village shoemaker of Llanmaes, that a stone, commemorating two Welsh kings, had been buried many years previously in Llantwit churchyard. Iolo, a stonemason, was working one day in the churchyard and he decided to search for the buried stone. He managed to unearth it and with assistance from twelve men raised it out of the ground and placed it against the church wall, where it remained until 1793, when it was taken inside the church.

Inside the church used to be a quaintly carved memorial stone which, according to Leland, was said to mark the burial place of Hywel Dda, the grandson of Rhodri Mawr, who was celebrated as the law-maker of Wales.

> 'Leland, who made his celebrated itinerary through Wales in about 1530, states in his Latin *Collectina* that Hywel Dda was buried in the Church of St Illtutus, or, as the old historian render it, Llaniltud Vawr Church'
>
> Marie Trevelyan
> *The Land of Arthur*

LOUGHOR

In the year 75 AD a military station was established beside the tidal river at Aberllychwyr on the Via Julia, and it was given the name Leucarum. The Itineraries mention it as the fifth Roman station on this great highway.

After the departure of the Romans, this location, known by the Britons as Aber Llychwr, became the site of a royal court which by tradition was the principal seat of Urien of Gorre[14] and his son Owain.

It is important to understand that Urien of Gorre has been confused with Urien of Rheged, and the former can be identified with Gwrgant Mawr ('the Great'), king of Erging, who was ousted from his kingdom by the usurper Gwrtheyrn (Vortigern) in the fifth century. He then established himself on Gower after expelling the Irish who had settled there.

Later, Emrys Wledig (Ambrosius 'the Imperator') reinstated Gwrgant Mawr as King of Erging, but he still retained Gower with his court at nearby Aber Llychwr (Leucarum). It is of particular significance that the famous son of Urien of Gorre was Owain or Yvain, the Knight of Leon, who was the father of Count Gwythyr of Leon, whose daughter, Gwenhwyfar (Guinevere), Arthur married. The relationship between these two important families is an integral part of the story of King Arthur and the colonisation of Brittany.[15]

It was during the reign of Arthur's father, Meurig, that Urien conquered Gower by expelling the Irish and it would seem that when Arthur came to power he bestowed upon Urien the kingdom of the country of Gorre, comprising the territories of Gower, Cydweli, Carnwyllan, Iscennen and Cantref Bychan. His royal residence was at Aber Llychwr (Loughor), where he constructed a fortress called Aberllywyr, probably on the spot where the ruins of the later Norman castle now stand.

Tradition is strong that on occasions King Arthur held court in Goyr (Gower) and a passage in the 'Life of St Illtud' speaks of Arthur's court in Glamorgan, but does not name it:-

> 'In the meantime the magnificent soldier, Illtud, hearing of the magnificence of his cousin, King Arthur, desired to visit the court of so great a conqueror. He left what we call Further Britannia (Brittany), and arrived by sailing, and here he saw a great company of soldiers, being honourably received in that place, and being rewarded as regards his military desire. His desire to receive guerdons being also satisfied, he withdrew very pleased from the royal court. Journeying he came to Paulentus (Paul of Penychen), King of the Glamorgan folk, accompanied by his very honourable wife, Trinihid.'

The above commentary would seem to locate one of Arthur's courts somewhere in southern Glamorgan. Its location is revealed in the 'Life of St Cenydd,' written by John of Tynemouth:-

'In the days of King Arthur, the prince of Letavia (Llydaw), now Brittany, was Deroch, who, by incestuous fornification, polluted his own daughter. Summoned by King Arthur, as a tributary, to come to his court to celebrate the Feast of Christmas in Goyr, he took with him the woman, and she gave birth to a child, who was born a cripple and baptised Cenydd.'[16]

Urien is reputed to have been buried in the coronation chapel of St Aaron at Caerleon and his son Owain appears to have succeeded to the lordship of Gorre with his main residence at Aber Llychwr. The *Stanzas of the Warriors' Graves* state that Owain, son of Urien, was buried at Llanmorfael (Loughor), so one might suppose that he lived at Loughor during most of his life.

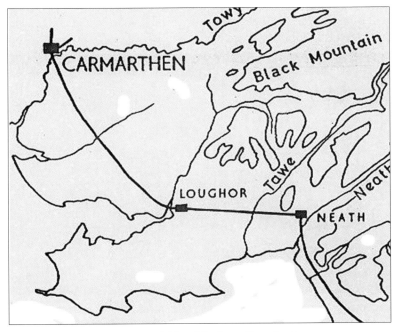

Location of Aber Llychwr (Loughor)

Urien of Gorre is usually confused with Urien of Rheged, who ruled the kingdom of Rheged in the north of Britain from his court at Carlisle. This was a district which reached as far as the Clyde. Some writers have confused the two Uriens and have the northern Urien of Rheged, who fought the Angles of Bernicia in the latter half of the sixth century, coming southwards and driving the Goidels from the districts of Gower and Cydweli, but the Urien who did this was Urien of Gorre.

Jane Williams, in her History of Wales, was certainly confused for she wrote: 'Urien Rheged, a Cymru of North Britain, who spending his youth as an emigrant in Demetia, led the forces of that extensive region against the rebellious interlopers who had formerly been reduced to slavery and drove them entirely out of the country. He thus obtained the sovereignty of all the lands lying between the two rivers Towy and Tawe, comprising Gwyr, Cydweli, Carnwyllion, Iscennen and Cantref Bychan, and gave to this territory the name of his paternal inheritance in North Britain.'

Geoffrey of Monmouth, in particular, is confused by the two Uriens, while Malory in his *Le Morte d' Arthur* writes of 'King Urien of the land of Gorre,' but seemingly does not know the location of Gorre. Cadell, the son of Urien, was with Cadoc at Llancarfan and an extinct 'capella' under Llancarfan was named Llangadell after him. He may also have been the founder of Sully in Glamorgan.

Loughor Castle was erected on the crest of a natural spur, over the SE corner turret of the Roman fort, by Henry de Beaumont, Earl of Warwick, in about 1099. It was considered a very important castle at that time for it commanded the ferry across the estuary. In 1115 the castle was attacked by Gruffydd, the son of Rhys ap Tewdwr, and razed to the ground.

Three

AFTER ARTHUR

The abdication and departure of King Arthur was a decisive event in the general fate of the island of Britain. Every idea of uniting the powers of the island seems to have vanished with him. We are told by Geoffrey of Monmouth that Arthur as king or general of all Britain was succeeded by his kinsman Constantine (Custennin Goronog, son of Cadwy), the king of Domnonia. In the kingdom of Gwent, Arthur would have been succeeded by his son Morgan Mwynfawr (Morgan 'the Courteous').

In 560 the princes of North Wales assumed the right to the British throne. Lluyd, in his Breviary, describes the Britons as confined to the provinces of Cambria, which underwent a division into six principalities, one of which was Morgannwg, under the government of Morgan Mwynfawr.

During Morgan's reign the Saxons made predatory incursions in small parties into the eastern and southern part of his kingdom but he was generally successful in resisting these attacks. It would seem that the shores of the Severn were particularly bothered by Saxon raiding parties and in 586 Creoda, an Angle chief, forced the Britons beyond the Wye and founded the kingdom of Mercia.

There is a tradition that Morgan Mwynfawr, alarmed by the westward advance of the Saxons, moved his court from Caerleon-upon-Usk to the western side of his domain, taking up residence first at Rhadyr Brigin (near Cardiff - possibly on the site of Castell Coch) and later at Margam (near Port Talbot). Records show that Margam was formerly called Morgan, which became Margan and then Margam. The name Morgan was used until the 17th century.

The territory from the Neath or the Tawe rivers to the Rhymney river, a mile east of Cardiff, became known as Gwlad Morgan, or Morgan's Country (after Morgan Mwynfawr), but originally the whole area as far as the River Wye bore the name Morganwig (Morgan's Wick).

Morgan Mwynfawr died in about 570 and was succeeded by his adopted son Rhyhawd, who was known as Eil Morgan. In the next few years the power of Morgannwg and Gwent was eclipsed by Cynan Garwyn of Powys, who seems to have threatened Arthur's old principality of Cernyw. The *Trawsganau Cynan Garwyn* records the Powysian monarch's victories over Gwynedd, Dyfed, Brycheiniog and Gwent and reports that he effectively threatened Cernyw. Unless these threats were conveyed across the Severn Sea, they must have been made while Cernyw was accessible by land, either before the West Saxon advance to the Severn in 577, or after the fall and death of Ceawlin in 591 or 593 respectively. This suggests that, after Maelgwyn's death in 547, Powys sooner or later replaced Gwynedd as the paramount state in Wales and that the West Saxon advance was directed against this paramountcy as it affected Severnside.

The grandson of Morgan Mwynfawr was Einydd, who reigned for twenty-three years and was said to be a popular sovereign who gave considerable wealth to the churches in his domain. However, he did not live long and was succeeded by Morgan Morgannwg.

Morgan Morgannwg, the great-grandson of Morgan Mwynfawr, re-united the kingdom but died fighting at the second battle of Badon in the seventh century. From the *Annales Cambriae* we learn that this battle was fought in the year 665 and that 'Morcantius' (Morgan) was slain. This information is confirmed by Nennius, who also states 'Bellum Badonis Secundo 665 - the battle of Badon for the second time, Morcant dies.' The most likely site for this battle is Mynydd Baedon in Glamorgan, where a number of entrenchments and mounds can still be seen. This location is significantly just a few miles to the east of Margam where Morgan is said to have had his court.

Morgan Morgannwg was succeeded by his son Ithel who in turn was succeeded by his son Rhys, who drove the Saxon settlers from Wales and built a church at a place now known as Peterstone-super-Ely.

When Rhys died his brother Arthfael II came to the throne and he is reputed to be buried beneath the altar of Roath Church. The next ruler was Meurig whose principal residence is said to have been at Llantwit Major. To him is attributed the founding of a castle on the Usk at Caerleon and another on the banks of the river Rhymney, at a place called Meigen al Ceincoed. It is said that he was a very cruel man and was ultimately killed by the men of Morgannwg who threw him from a high cliff into the sea.

Meurig was followed by his son Brochmael who during his reign had several disputes with Cyfelawg, the Bishop of Llandaff. Brochmael is said to have established many churches and also built the first royal fortress at Cardiff, thus establishing it as a royal city.

He was succeeded by his son Gwriad who is said to have resided at Cardiff. When he died from yellow fever, which was prevailing at that time, he was probably buried in his church at Llanweirydd (Gwriad's Church), which is now known as Caerau.

The next in line was Gwriad's son, Arthmael III, who in turn was followed by his son Rhys who caused a number of ships to be built to enable the Welsh to meet the Danish invaders on even terms.

This stone, known as the Houellt Cross, is about 2 metres high, with a disc head and shaft carved from a single piece of gritstone. The inscription in half-unical script with no punctuation or letter spacing refers to Hywel and Rhys, kings of Glywysing in the ninth century.

Rhys is commemorated with a stone cross which can be seen in St Illtyd's church at Llantwit Major. It was erected by his son Hywel and bears the following inscription:-

> 'In the name of God the Father and the Son and the Holy Spirit, Hywel prepared this cross for the soul of Rhys his father.'

Hywel the son of Rhys, King of Glywysing, died in 885. He was succeeded by his son Owain, who in turn was followed by Morgan Mawr (the Great). This king is sometimes referred to as Morgan Mwynfawr II and also Morgan Hen (the Old). He married Elen, the daughter of Rhodri Mawr.

Morgan had a dispute with Owen, the son of Hywel Dda, about the territory of Ystrad Yw and Ewyas, which he eventually referred to the arbitration of the English King Edgar, and the bishops of Llandaff and St. David's. Edgar selected twelve wise-men to adjudicate the case in accordance with the law of Morgan Mwynfawr; that is twelve men from Deheubarth, the country of Owen, and twelve from Glamorgan, the country of Morgan. The King himself presided in Council at their deliberation and it was decided that Morgan had fully established his claim to Ystrad Yw and Ewyas, which were both restored accordingly.

In 918 Ethelfleda, Queen of Mercia, led an army into Morgan's territory but she was defeated and killed. At a later date, the Danes made a fierce raid on his kingdom. They sailed across the water from Cornwall and swept through Morgannwg destroying a large number of churches and monastic colleges.

On the death of Morgan Morgannwg in 974 the kingdom was ruled by Idwallon and Ithel until 1001, when Gwrgan became Prince of Morgannwg. He is said to have been a wise ruler who introduced several important laws. During his reign, in 1029, a band of Irish pirates attacked the Glamorgan coast, but the Welsh led by Gwrgan arose in large numbers and defeated the invaders. He is also remembered for giving a large common, in the northern part of Morgannwg, to his subjects, for the pasture of cattle and sheep, and also for the growth of corn. This has been called after his own name, *Hirwaun Wrgan*, or Gwrgan's long meadow. Gwrgan died in 1042.

The next ruler was Gwrgan's brother Hywel and when he died his nephew Iestyn ap Gwrgan came to the throne. He was a quarrelsome man who had frequent skirmishes with the princes of Dynefwr. They ruled the greater part of South Wales and Iestyn and his sons were keen to extend their own territory.

Four

RHYS AP TEWDWR,
KING OF SOUTH WALES

In 997, Tewdwr Mawr[1] was killed in battle, whilst fighting under his uncle Meredydd, Prince of Deheubarth[2], against Idwal, King of North Wales. The death of Tewdwr Mawr left his two infant sons, Rhys and Rhydderch, at the mercy of their enemies. Subsequently, the eldest, Rhys ap Tewdwr, at the age of twenty, was expelled from Deheubarth by the three sons of Bleddyn ap Cynfyn (Madog, Cadwgan and Rhirid), who were by now the joint rulers of Powys. Rhys sought refuge in Brittany, where he lived for the next sixty years, until news came of the death of his second cousin, Rhys ab Owain, the brother of Mareddud ab Owain, who had by that time usurped the sovereignty of Deheubarth.

As the only prince left of the line of Hywel Dda (the Good), Rhys ap Tewdwr was the rightful claimant to the throne of Deheubarth. By now he was nearly eighty years of age, but with the courage of a man half his years, he was determined to return to the land of his ancestors to claim the throne of Deheubarth.

Gwynedd (North Wales), at this time was illegally held by Trahaiarn ap Caradog, who had contributed to the downfall of Rhys ap Owain. He was now determined to expand his domain by taking possession of Deheubarth. Before seizing Gwynedd, he had been just a minor ruler of the the petty kingdom of Arwystli on the southern border of Powys.

Gruffydd ap Cynan, a youth of twenty, was the rightful ruler of Gwynedd and, like Rhys ap Tewdwr, he resolved to win back the realm of his fathers. Gruffydd had been born in Ireland, where his father Cynan, the rightful King of Gwynedd, had settled during the ascendancy of Gruffydd ap Llywelyn. In exile, Cynan had married Ragnaillt, daughter of Olaf, King of Dublin, the son of King Sitruic 'of the Silken Beard,' and Gruffydd was born of this union. When he came of age, his mother encouraged him to make an attempt to recover his rightful inheritance. The King of Dublin generously agreed to assist him by providing ships manned by Irish and Danish warriors, to help him conquer Gwynedd.

Setting sail from Ireland, Gruffydd and his followers landed at Abermenai, a port on the western end of the Menai Strait, near Caernarfon. Assistance was then sought from Robert of Rhuddlan, who consented by sending sixty of his best soldiers to help Gruffydd in the coming struggle. It was not long before other men of Gwynedd came to join them, for Trahaiarn was regarded as an alien ruler, being a native of Powys.

A battle took place at a location called Gwaet Erw (The Bloody Acre), and a defeated Trahaiarn was driven back to Powys, but Gruffydd's success was short lived for he soon offended his new subjects by keeping too many of his mother's countrymen, the Irish, as a personal bodyguard. Large numbers of his followers deserted him within a few months and, without their support, he was defeated in a second battle against Trahaiarn, fought at Bron-y-erw, near Clynnog Fawr in Arfon. However, Gruffydd managed to escape from the affray and returned to Ireland where he remained for the next six years.

Gruffydd mounted a second expedition which failed. He then set sail from Ireland a third time in 1081 with a fleet carrying a strong force consisting of Irishmen, Danes and Britons. This time, instead of making for Gwynedd, he landed at Porthclais, near St. David's, for he was anxious to secure the assistance of Rhys ap Tewdwr, who had been successful in reclaiming the throne of Deheubarth.

Rhys at this time was having problems curtailing the ambitions of some of the minor princes and chieftains of South Wales, so the prospect of combining his forces with those of Gruffydd was very acceptable to him. Side by side, they led their combined army to do battle with Trahaiarn, who had by now secured the assistance of his cousins Caradog and Meilyr.

On the edge of the Preseli Mountains in West Wales, a fierce battle was fought which is remembered in Welsh history as the battle of Mynydd Carn[3]. Meilyr and Caradog were both slain and Trahaiarn, was according to the *Brut*, '...pierced in the centre until he was on the ground biting with his teeth the long grass, and groping about to come upon his weapons; and Gweharis, the Irishman, made bacon of him as a pig!'

Gruffydd and his followers, armed with two-edged axes and flails, pursued the vanquished army, 'through groves and glens and marshes, and mountains throughout that night, by the moon, and throughout the following day.'

This battle certainly had an important effect on Welsh history, for it put an end for ever to the continued strife for the crown, waged for so long by rival families in both north and south Wales. It secured the sovereignty in the legitimate line which for several reigns had been held by usurpers. Gruffydd took over the crown of Gwynedd and Rhys strengthened his possession of Deheubarth, which he was to rule for the next twelve years.

The restoration of Gruffydd ap Cynan and Rhys ap Tewdwr to power led to a great rise in the creation of Welsh literature. Gruffydd brought back from Ireland a revised interest in culture and introduced reforms to the organisation of the bardic order. Likewise, Rhys brought back from Brittany many of the old traditions, which had been preserved by the descendants of the Cymric exiles who had settled there in the time of Arthur. Rhys was the leading Prince in the south of Wales for fourteen years and he was the last man who can really be regarded as the king or prince of the ancient kingdom of Deheubarth.

Further battles fought by Rhys ap Tewdwr

Rhys ap Tewdwr now had to deal with a problem prince in Glamorgan, who threatened his position as ruler of southern Wales. During Rhys's long exile in Brittany, the family of Iestyn ap Gwrgan, Prince of Glamorgan, had aspired to expand their territory by taking control of Deheubarth. Acting decisively, Rhys anticipated the designs of his rival and struck the first blow by marching into Glamorgan and destroying Iestyn's fortresses at Boverton, Dindryfan (Dunraven) and Dinas Powys.

In 1087, just as Rhys no doubt thought that he had overcome all his enemies, Cadwgan, Madog and Rhirid, the three sons of Bleddyn ap Cynfyn, marched out of Powys with a large force and attacked Deheubarth. The aged King Rhys, being unprepared to meet them in battle, was forced to flee to Ireland, where he quickly raised a band of Irish mercenaries and returned to Deheubarth. News of his landing quickly spread and loyal supporters flocked to join his army.

A battle was fought at Lechryd (in Pembrokeshire) which resulted in the death of Madog and Rhirid and the flight of Cadwgan. Rhys paid off his Irish mercenaries and once more resumed the rule of Deheubarth. However, it was not long before a new storm menaced his unhappy fortunes. In 1088, Llywellyn and Einion, sons of Cadifor ap Collwyn, Lord of Dyfed, took up arms and persuaded Gruffydd ap Meredydd to join their cause. Their combined forces marched against the aged Rhys, who met them at Llandudoch, near the mouth of the River Teifi, and a long battle was fought, during which the rebels were well and truly defeated. Llywellyn, the younger son of Cadifor, was slain while Gruffydd ap Meredydd was taken prisoner and then killed as a traitor. Einion fled to Glamorgan and sought the protection of Iestyn ap Gwrgan.

Having struggled against one band of enemies after another, Rhys by now must have thought that his problems were at last over and that he would be able to enjoy his remaining years in peace, but a much more serious enemy was soon to emerge as a result of the Norman Conquest. William the Conqueror, having completed his campaign in England, now had his eye on Wales.

In 1081 William had entered Deheubarth in peace, under the guise of making a visit to St. David's. Although he was undoubtedly a deeply religious man, it is hardly likely that he would have been prepared to travel such a long distance just to visit the shrine of a Welsh saint. It is interesting that the Saxon Chronicle says 'the king led an army into Wales, and there he freed many hundred men.' This suggests that William came to make terms with Rhys ap Tewdwr and at the same time gain freedom for captured Norman soldiers. The Welsh Prince and the Norman king probably met at St. David's and came to an agreement that as long as William I and Rhys ap Tewdwr lived there would be comparative peace in South Wales. In the Domesday Book it is recorded that Rhys was paying the sum of £40 a year rent to King William, and this was no doubt for Deheubarth. The agreement recognised Rhys as King of Deheubarth, but the terms meant that in reality he was a vassal to the throne of England.

History is clouded by tradition with regard to the events leading up to the Norman Conquest of South Wales. Most of what has been written is of doubtful authenticity but certainly makes fascinating reading.

It is said that Einion ap Collwyn, now at the court of Iestyn ap Gwrgan in Glamorgan, persuaded the prince to strengthen his resources by seeking the assistance of some Norman adventurers. We are told that Einion made an offer to procure the Normans' assistance on the condition that he could in due course take Iestyn's daughter in marriage.

To this request, Iestyn agreed and also promised to bestow on her a large part of his territory as a dowry. We are told by Caradog of Llancarfan that the gift was to be the lordship of Meisgyn (Miskin).

His future prospects thus assured, Einion travelled to Bristol, where he solicited the aid of the Norman knight Robert Fitzhamon, who agreed to return with Einion to Wales, accompanied by twelve military adventurers and a powerful force of soldiers. According to tradition, the 'magnificent twelve' were, William de Londres, Richard Grenville, Robert St. Quentin, Richard Siward, Gilbert Humphreville, Roger Berclos, Reginald Sully, Peter le Soor, William de Esterling and John St. John.

Fitzhamon's army was said to consist of 12 knights, 24 squires and 3,000 men. Landing at Porthkeri, in Glamorgan, in 1093, they joined forces with the army of Prince Iestyn and marched into Deheubarth where they sacked and pillaged the territory of Rhys ap Tewdwr with merciless ferocity.

History has blended with romance to provide two versions of the story of how Rhys ap Tewdwr fought his last battle.

The traditional story

A terrible battle between Rhys ap Tewdwr and the combined forces of Iestyn ap Gwrgan and Robert Fitzhamon is reputed to have been fought in the hills above Hirwaun on the border of Breconshire. The name Hirwaun originates from Waun Hir ('Gwrgan's Long Meadow'), which was a large common between Merthyr and the Vale of Neath which Gwrgan gave to his peasants in perpetuity for raising corn and breeding livestock.

Local names, such as Maes y Gwae (The Field of Blood), Carn y Frwdr (Battle Cairn) and Bryn-y-beddau (Hill of Graves) are said to commemorate the battle.

The tradition is that Rhys ap Tewdwr was captured and delivered into the hands of Iestyn ap Gwrgan and Robert Fitzhamon and that the defeated King of Deheubarth was killed at Ynysgrug. His body, after being decapitated, was reputedly buried a mile away at Penrhys (Rhys's Head) which is said to recall the spot where he was decapitated.[4]

There is also a tradition that, in about 1130, Robert, Earl of Gloucester, the grandson of Rhys ap Tewdwr, founded Penrhys Monastery for the repose of the soul of his ancestor,[5] but this is disputed. The name 'Pen Rhys' is contained in early manuscripts of Llantarnam Abbey, but is not necessarily associated with Rhys ap Tewdwr. Pen meaning head, summit or chief, is a common element in Welsh place names and in Wales, as in other countries, stories are often invented to explain certain place names.

The traditional story is completed with the claim that, after this victory at Hirwaun Wrgan, the Normans marched into the Vale of Glamorgan and at 'Milltir-aur' (the Golden Mile), near Colwinston (supposedly named after Einion ap Collwyn), they received their promised payment. The golden coins were laid side by side along this road, thus representing a mile of gold. In 1093, this would have been a fantastic sum and gold coins would certainly have not been sufficiently numerous in those days for such a method of payment to be possible. On receiving their reward for services rendered, Fitzhamon and his men are supposed to have made their way back to England overland.

The accepted version of the death of Rhys ap Tewdwr

Present day historians dismiss the traditional story of Rhys ap Tewdwr's last battle as merely folklore and the version given by Theophilus Jones in his *History of Brecknockshire* (1805 Vol I , 1809 Vol II)) is the one featured in current books on the history of Wales.

Brecon Castle was established at the confluence of the Usk and Honddu rivers by Bernard Newmarch utilising stone from the Roman fort known as Y Gaer.

Brecon Cathedral stands on the site of a priory established by Bernard Newmarch as a cell of the Benedictine Abbey of Battle in Sussex. The present building was begun in the 13th century and it has been described as 'half chuch and half castle.'

We are told that Rhys went to the aid of his brother-in-law, Bleddyn ap Maenarch, King of Brycheiniog, when his domain was threatened by the advancing Normans under the command of Bernard de Newmarch.

Bernard de Newmarch was a member of the prominent Norman family of Aufay. On his mother's side he was descended from Gilbert de Saint Valérie, who married a daughter of the Duke Richard. Bernard accompanied the Conqueror to England, and his name figures as a witness to many of William's early charters. He married into a French family which had settled in Herefordshire prior to 1066.

Advancing into east Brycheiniog, Bernard, before the end of 1088, had made considerable progress, with the settlements of Hay, Glasbury and Talgarth, now in his possession.

It is probable that Bronllys Castle was established as a motte and bailey at the junction of the rivers Dulais and Llynfi as a base for his further advances along the course of those two rivers. He seems to have taken the Llynfi route through Llandefaelog, Llanwern and Trostre to Aberhonddu (Brecon), which he reached in 1091.

Rhys ap Tewdwr is believed to have marched to the old Roman fort of Y Gaer, just outside Brecon, to assist Bleddyn ap Maenarch, and encamped with his men at a place called Y Glydwi, between the fort and the site of the later town of Brecon. Bernard de Newmarch and his army had taken up their position on the summit of Pen y Crug Iron Age hill fort.

Rhys then headed to an area north-west of Pen y Crug and here at the place now appropriately called Battle, the Welsh force was defeated by the Normans. Rhys is said to have been decapitated on the common above near a well since called Ffynnon Pen Rhys, situated near Battle village.[6]

Having routed the Welsh forces and slain both Bleddyn ap Maenarch and Rhys ap Tewdwr, Bernard Newmarch gave orders for a castle to be established beside the Usk at Brecon, with stone brought from the old Roman fort (Y Gaer). The location was of strategic importance for it was the most westerly Norman outpost, guarding routes to the north and west.

From his new castle at Brecon, Bernard Newmarch[7] controlled the four cantrefs of old King Brychan, and for the next four hundred years the area of Brycheiniog and Buellt (which later became known as Breconshire) became part of the marcher land which extended in a broad band of border country from the mouth of the Dee to the Severn estuary.

The Welsh Chronicle states that : 'Rhys ap Tewdwr, King of South Wales, was killed by the French (i.e. Normans) who inhabited Brycheiniog, and then fell the kingdom of the Britons'. This is certainly an appropriate statement for the defeat of Rhys ap Tewdwr and the entry of the Normans into South Wales marks the beginning of the first stage in the complete

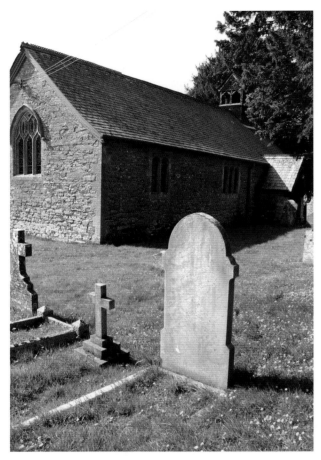

Battle Chapel, 2 miles NW of Brecon, stands near the site of the battle where Rhys ap Tewdwr and Bleddyn ap Maenarch were defeated by the Normans. It is significant that not long afterwards this chapel of Brecon Priory, itself affiliated to Battle Abbey, was erected here. It is possible that as Battle Monastery marked the site of Harold's death, so also did Battle Chapel commemorate Rhys ap Tewdwr.

'Whether he fell in a fair fight or by treachery is uncertain; all that is clear is that his death opened the flood-gates of Norman rapocity in South Wales, and that its trickling rills now united in one great deluge that swept the country from end to end.'

J. E. Lloyd

downfall of ancient British power in the Principality. From that time onwards the Normans rapidly gained territory and became masters of the whole of Wales.

Rhys's young queen[8] was at Dinefwr Castle when news of the disastrous defeat reached her. She escaped with her infant son Gruffydd by sailing to Ireland. Nest, the beautiful daughter of Rhys ap Tewdwr, did not flee with her mother and was soon taken prisoner by Bleddyn ap Cynfyn of Powys, who handed her over to Robert Fitzhamon.

For nearly twenty years Rhys ap Tewdwr had been able to hold back the Norman advance and even make terms with William the Conqueror, thus preserving his kingdom of Dehebarth. He was the last completely independent ruler of South Wales and when he was killed in 1093 his kingdom was split up among the various claimants.

The door had also been opened for the Norman invaders to take over the whole of Wales. Rhys ap Tewdwr's son, Gruffydd,[9] made several attempts to regain his ancestral lands and win back his father's crown. A large number of Welshmen from the south gathered around him, but it was just a momentary blaze and his campaign came to nothing. He eventually made peace with Henry I of England and settled in the upper valley of the Cothi, with his wife Gwenllian, a daughter of Gruffydd ap Cynan.

Princess Nest

Princess Nest, the daughter of Rhys ap Tewdwr, was famous for her beauty and it would seem that no man could see her without falling head over heels in love. She first had an affair with Henry I when she was his ward after the death of her father, and a son born to her was named Robert (Fitzroy), no doubt as a compliment to Robert Fitzhamon.

Her first husband was Gerald de Windsor, Castellan of Pembroke, by whom she had four children, one of these being Angharad, who married William de Barri of Manorbier Castle in West Wales and became the mother of Gerald of Wales (Giraldus Cambrensis).

A fascinating story, concerning Nest, tells of the time when her husband Gerald built a new castle at Cilgerran in the Teifi Valley. He brought his wife and children to live there and on Christmas Day, 1109, a great feast was held to which many of the local Welsh nobility were invited.

One of these Welshmen was Owain ap Cadwgan, who was the nephew of Princess Nest, and on seeing her for the first time, became infatuatedwith her beauty and charms. Soon after, he returned to the castle one night with a small band of followers. They tunneled beneath the castle wall, set fire to the place, and in the confusion Owain carried off his aunt Nest and her children, whilst her husband Gerald made a very undignified escape down a privy. Owain took Nest and the children to a very remote hunting lodge, owned by his family, at a romantic location, called 'World's End', high in the hills above Llangollen.

Cadwgan was greatly disturbed when he heard of his son's actions, for Gerald de Windsor was high in the king's favour and the abduction of Nest and her children would result in much trouble. He did his best to persuade Owain to return Nest and her children, and in due course the latter were sent back to their father, but Nest was for the time being retained.

Hearing of Owain's misdeed, the king's steward at Shrewsbury sent for Ithel and Madog, sons of Rhirid ab Bleddyn of Powys, and persuaded them by large promises to make an attempt to seize Owain, or, failing that, to expel him and his father Cadwgan from Britain.

Owain and Cadwgan made their escape and took refuge on a ship at Aberdovey. Owain sailed for Ireland, while Cadwgan went secretly to some land in Powys which he possessed in right of his wife. Some time later, Owain made peace with the king and, on the payment of one hundred pounds, Cadwgan was allowed to return to his possessions in Ceredigion, on the condition that there should be neither communication nor friendship between him and his son.[10]

When Gerald de Windsor died, Nest married Sir Robert FitzStephen, Constable of Cardigan Castle, and they had several children. In total, Nest is reputed to have given birth to seventeen children. It was Nest's sons (in particular Robert FitzStephen) and grandson who led the way to the conquest of Ireland, yet in later years her descendants fought as famously for Ireland as ever they had fought against it.

> 'There are many princesses in history, but there is not one of them who could have been so fair and sweet as Nest. It seemed as if no man could see her without falling in love with her. The fame of her loveliness and charm went through the land, causing long war and bloodshed about her.'
>
> Owen Rhoscomyl 1905
> *Flame-Bearers of Welsh History*

Five

GWENLLIAN THE WARRIOR PRINCESS

When Henry I died in December 1135, the Welsh rose in revolt against foreign rule and threatened a national uprising. Consequently, Gruffydd, the son of Rhys ap Tewdwr, decided to ride to North Wales and seek reinforcements from his father-in-law, Gruffydd ap Cynan, Prince of Gwynedd. He was accompanied on this journey by his young son Rhys.

During Gruffydd's absence, Maurice de Londres, the powerful lord of Cydweli, decided to take action before the Welsh gathered strength. Faced with this threat, Princess Gwenllian, the wife of Gruffydd ap Rhys, bravely marched from Cantref Mawr against the Norman lords of Cydweli (Kidwelly).[1] Accompanied by her young sons, Morgan and Maelgwyn, she marched at the head of a small but determined force on the Norman castle. She halted with her soldiers beside the river Gwendraith at the foot of Mynydd y Garreg, about two miles from Cydweli Castle. Her plan was that if Maurice de Londres came out of his castle with his soldiers to meet her small force then the Normans would have to fight their way across the river.

However, it proved to be a poor strategy, for Gwenllian's force was caught unawares by a large number of Normans who attacked from behind. As her men bravely fought off this surprise attack, the Normans from the castle crossed the river and the Welsh were quickly surrounded.

The battle was over in a very short time for Gwenllian's men were easily overwhelmed and the brave Welsh princess was wounded severely. Her young son Maelgwyn was killed by her side, while feebly endeavouring to shield his heroic mother from the blows of the enemy. Both Gwenllian and her other young son were captured and Lord Maurice immediately gave orders for the Welsh princess to be beheaded in his presence. The site where this sad event took place is on the eastern bank of the Gwendraith Fach river and it is known as Maes Gwenllian (Field of Gwenllian).

Meanwhile, in North Wales, Gwenllian's father, Gruffydd ap Cynan, who was now in his 80th year, was understandably disinclined to take up arms himself, but he agreed that his sons, Prince Owen and Prince Cadwaladr, should accompany Gruffydd ap Rhys at the head of 2,000 horsemen and 600 foot soldiers to deal with the problems in South Wales.

This carved stone slab, standing near the great gatehouse at Cydweli Castle, is a memorial to Princess Gwenllian, who lost her life in a battle fought in 1136 on the field below the castle which is still known as Maes Gwenllian.

In due course, this impressive army joined up with bands of Welshmen in the south, and the Norman castles of Aberystwyth, Dinerth and Caerwedros were sacked and destroyed. Next to be attacked was Cardigan Castle, which was defended by Sir Robert FitzStephen, second husband of Princess Nest, formerly the wife of Gerald De Windsor, and the daughter of Rhys ap Tewdwr.

A fierce battle was fought on Crug Mawr near Cardigan, during which Gruffydd ap Rhys defeated Robert FitzStephen, Robert FitzMartin, and William and Maurice FitzGerald. The Welsh force drove the Normans eastwards and as they crossed Cardigan bridge over the Teifi it collapsed, causing many of the Normans to be drowned. The remainder fled in the direction of Glamorgan, to be dealt with by the sons of Caradoc ap Iestyn, who came out of Aberafan with their forces to meet the retreating enemy and slew 3000 of them. The survivors made for Gower. This act of retribution by the Welsh was told and retold for generations after, and Ceredigion remained under Welsh control for the next one hundred and fifty years.

By 1137, both Gruffydd ap Cynan and Gruffydd ap Rhys were dead,[2] and the reins of government passed into the hands of their sons, Owen Gwynedd and Rhys ap Gruffydd (better known as 'the Lord Rhys'). Half a century after the death of his mother Princes Gwenllian, Rhys won back his father's lost kingdom and ruled as Prince over the whole of southern Wales.

Maurice de Londres, who killed Princess Gwenllian at Cydweli, died in 1149 and was buried at Ewenny Priory, which he founded at the beginning of the 12th century for a community of Benedictine monks from St Peter's, Gloucester. This was the first Norman monastic house to be established in Glamorgan. While the main gateway and a substantial portion of the curtain wall can still be seen, the main point of interest is the nave of the monastic church which survived the Dissolution to serve as the parish church of Ewenny.

St Michael's is the best example of a fortified ecclesiastical building in Britain, and the tower is of massive proportions for it was built at a time when the Norman invader had yet to secure a footing in the Vale of Glamorgan. The windows in the thick walls were small and few, and today, with the exception of a west window and the north aisle, the church is pure Norman throughout. It is more like a cathedral than a church with its magnificent chancel, transept and side chapels.

Not only did the De Londres family make extensive gifts to St Peter's Abbey, Gloucester, for the foundation of Ewenny Priory, but they also made grants to Tewkesbury and Neath Abbeys. In doing so, they greatly diminished their possessions in Ogmore and then moved further west to become Marcher Lords of Cydweli.

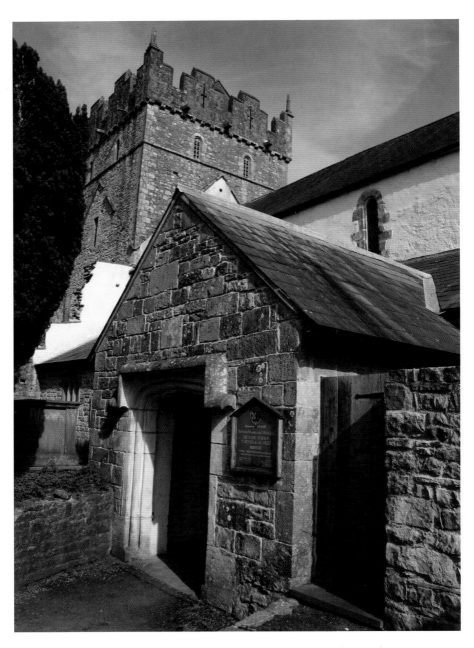

Ewenny Priory Church was founded by Maurice de Londres,
who murdered Princess Gwenllian at Cydweli

Maurice's father William de Londres[3] was the most powerful of Robert Fitzhamon's knights. He built Ogmore Castle in about 1162, and also held the sub manor of Dunraven. It is believed that the wife of William de Londres was a daughter of Caradoc ap Iestyn ap Gwrgan, and, by this marriage, William obtained the detached portion of Llangeinor, which afterwards formed part of the lordship of Ogmore. He later acquired the greater lordship of Cydweli, together with the holding of Oystermouth in Gower.

While it is generally believed that Ewenny Priory was founded by Maurice de Londres, as stated on his tomb, the original grantor was his father William de Londres. It is said that he and his son Maurice founded Ewenny Priory in about 1100 as an offering to the church to recompense their murder of a monk.

In the transept of Ewenny Church are three sepulchral slabs commemorating members of the De Londres family. The main one is that of Maurice de Londres, the founder of the priory and the murderer of Princess Gwenllian. The slab is a fine example of early 13th century craftsmanship, and was obviously erected some time after his death. It is beautifully carved and displays an elegant floreated cross between two lines of Norman/French verse in Lombardic capital letters:-

ICI / GIST : MORICE : DE : LVNDRES : LE : FVN
DVR : D (I)EV : LI : RENDE : SON : LABVR : AM.

('Here lies Maurice de Londres, the Founder.
God reward him for his service, Amen)

Maurice de Londres generously gave several churches to the monastic order. However, he was also guilty of numerous evil deeds. The Pope denounced him in a Bull as a 'despoiler of Church lands,' and accused him of having robbed and defrauded the mother-church of Llandaff. Perhaps this caused Maurice to repent and make amends with his generous gifts.

In front of the farther chapel doorway lies an incised slab in three pieces, with a fragment missing. It bears the inscription:-

+ HIC IACET W (ILLECMUS) DE LON (DRES).

Three members of the family were named William so which one this stone commemorates is uncertain. It possibly commemorates the grandson of Maurice de Londres, who was the third William to hold the lordship of Ogmore.

Memorial slab to Maurice de Londres, founder of Ewenny Priory in about 1100

The third memorial to the De Londres family is incised with the full length figure of Hawise de Londres (d.1274). Unfortunately, the head and shoulders are missing. She was the daughter and heiress of Thomas de Londres (d.1196), and great-great-granddaughter of William de Londres, the first Norman to hold the lordship of Ogmore. Hawise was the sixth and last of the line and she married at least twice. Her first husband was Walter de Breose, who died in 1234, and she next married Patrick de Chatworth, who was killed in battle against the Welsh in West Wales. One of her most famous descendants was Henry, Earl of Lancaster, who became Henry IV.

This tomb-slab of Hawise was found in 1893, buried near the porch of the Priory church. It was being used as part of a stone bench and the upper part had been cut off to enable the slab to fit into the angle of the walls. She is depicted wearing a pleated dress and pointed shoes. Her feet rest on a floreated design springing from a sixfoil flower. Around the edge of the slab is a Norman-French inscription which is now hard to decipher, but translated it probably reads:-

'Remember and pray for the soul of
the noble Lady Hawise de Londres.'

The 13th century canopied niche in the south transept once contained the broken effigy, believed to be that of Sir Payne Turbervill, and now lies upon a base in the middle of the transept.

Did Princess Gwenllian write the early tales of the Mabinogion?

Dr Andrew Breeze in his book *Medieval Welsh Literature* (published by Four Courts press, Dublin 1997) has suggested that Princess Gwenllian, the daughter of Gruffydd ap Cynan, King of Gwynedd, was the author of the *Four Branches of the Mabinogi* (Tales of Youth), which is considered to be the greatest work of Welsh literature and one of the finest pieces of Celtic mythology. The oldest copy is preserved in the *White Book of Rhyddderch*, which dates from about 1300 and is held at the National Library of Wales, Aberystwyth.

Dr Breeze emphasises that the author of this work shows a detailed knowledge of courts and the royal attitude of the twelfth century. He believes that the stories were written by a woman and suggests that Princess Gwenllian dictated the tales to a scribe in about 1128, whilst she was residing in Deheubarth.

This is certainly a fascinating theory and Dr Breeze considers that the author of this work must have been familiar with the ceremonies and luxuries of court life. The tales stress royal descent and status and such reference would be natural for the daughter of a king and the wife of a prince.

He points out that Gwenllian was the daughter of a successful king while her dispossessed husband, Gruffydd ap Tewdwr, was a less successful ruler. It would, therefore, be natural for Gwenllian to portray the glories of her husband's former territory in an attempt to revive the fortunes of Deheubarth.

It is relevant that the poet Hywel ab Owen Gwynedd, who died in 1170, was a natural son of Gwenllian's brother and the style of his poetry closely resembles the *Four Branches of the Mabinogi*. It is appropriate that Gwenllian's own son, the Lord Rhys, instigator of the Cardigan Eisteddfod of 1176, also had an interest in poetry, so they were obviously a family with an inclination towards literature.

> ' All the evidence we can point to indicates her authorship of the the Four Branches. Though circumstantial, it amounts to a very strong case.'

Andrew Breeze 1997

The Lord Rhys

Rhys ap Gruffydd[4] was born in 1132 in the commote of Caeo, in a remote corner of Cantref Mawr, which at that time was all that remained of the family possessions.. He was just four years of age when his mother was killed at Cydweli and he lost his father just two months later.

By 1155, Rhys ap Gruffydd was the sole representative of the ancient dynasty of Deheubarth and he established his main court at Dinefwr Castle in the heart of the fertile Tywi Valley, near Llandeilo.

Rhys was obliged to submit to Henry II in 1164 and he did homage to him at Woodstock, giving hostages for his future fidelity. However, he was unable to submit to the insults offered to him for very long, and in 1165 he joined the other Welsh princes in an uprising against the king.

After maintaining his independence by force of arms during the next seven years, Rhys made an honourable peace with Henry in 1171, when the king was passing through South Wales on his way to Ireland. He received Henry at one of his courts and made a political submission, which resulted in his being allowed to retain the whole of his dominions. From this time Rhys was a vassal to the English king but he condescended to accept the title and office of Chief Justicar of South Wales.

In 1174 Henry was engaged in a critical struggle with his rebellious sons and barons. Rhys gave him valuable support and even sent a contingent of valuable troops to help the king.

Through the diplomacy of Rhys ap Gruffydd, the Welsh princes were induced to attend the great Council held at Gloucester on 29 June, 1173. Among those named as being present and doing homage to Henry II were Morgan ap Caradog of Glamorgan, Gruffydd ab Ifor of Senghenydd, Sitsyllt ab Dyfnwal of Gwent-uth-coed and Iorwerth ab Owain of Caerleon.

Rhys was a patron of bardism and music and he sponsored court poets such as Gwynfardd Brycheiniog, Cynddelw Brydydd Mawr and Seisyll Bryffrwch, who all in their poetry referred to him as 'Yr Arglwydd Rhys' (The Lord Rhys)[5]. In 1176 he convened a National Eisteddfod at Aber Teifi (Cardigan), which was held in his new stone castle. He offered two chairs (with valuable gifts as well), the one to the poet and the other to the musician who performed most skillfully before him. We are told that it was a young man from his own court who won the prize for music, but the bardic chair went to a poet from Gwynydd.

The Lord Rhys was also a generous patron of the Church he endowed the monastery of Whitland (mother-house of the Cistercians in Wales), and was the main benefactor of Strata Florida Abbey.

Little remains of Cardigan Castle which was the first recorded Welsh masonry castle to be built (1171) and it became the most important stronghold of the Lord Rhys. The first recorded eisteddfod was held there at Christmas 1176, after a year of proclamation in 'Wales, England, Scotland, Ireland and the other islands.'

Dryslwyn Castle stands on a hill overlooking the River Towi and it was once held by the powerful Lord Rhys.

Dinefwr Castle was once one of the most important royal seats of Wales. It is built on the site of a much earlier fortress, and occupies a strategic position on a hillside, overlooking the river Tywi near Llandeilo.

In July 1189, following the death of Henry II, Rhys attacked and captured the castles of Laugharne and Llanstephan and ravaged Pembrokeshire and Rhos. He succeeded in seizing all of Dyfed that he did not already possess. His actions resulted in his cousin, Giraldus Cambrensis, being sent into Wales by the English court to promote peace, but two years later Rhys captured Nevern Castle from William FitzMartin, the son of Martin of Turo, the first Norman ruler of Cemais. FitzMartin, was in fact Rhys ap Gruffydd's son-in-law for he had married his daughter Angharad.

Rhys ap Gruffydd undoubtedly stemmed the tide of the Norman's advance into Wales and succeeded in restoring the ancient kingdom of Deheubarth, which had been partitioned by the Norman warlords. He was indeed a worthy grandson of Rhys ap Tewdwr, who in 1081 had fought so hard to regain the throne of Deheubarth.

Towards the end of his reign there was considerable tension between his sons over who should inherit the kingdom. The succession of the chosen heir, Gruffydd ap Rhys (d.1201), was strongly opposed by his half-brother, Maelgwyn ap Rhys (d.1236). However, it was eventually agreed that the patrimony of Deheubarth should be shared by Rhys ap Gruffydd's sons and grandsons, and nineteen years after his death the lands were divided in the presence of Llywelyn Fawr.

On 28 April 1197, Rhys ap Gruffydd died of the plague at the age of 65, and was buried in the newly constructed church of St David's. Prior to this time, the abbey of Strata Florida had been the chief burying place for the princes of South Wales, but Rhys no doubt chose to be interred at St David's because he had been a great benefactor to the re-building of the cathedral by Peter de Leia.

His tomb is believed to be the one which can be seen in the south choir aisle and he is depicted as a knight in 14th century armour. A similar tomb and effigy can be seen in the opposite aisle, which is thought to be that of the Lord Rhys's son Rhys Gryg, who was laid to rest here in 1233. Being of 14th century design, these tombs were erected about one hundred and fifty years after their deaths., probably by members of the Talbot family, who were their descendants.

'Rhys ap Gruffydd was the man who by his unceasing efforts and fine sense of patriotism kept alive the tradition of Welsh independence and nationality.'

A.L. Poole

This fourteenth-century tomb effigy in St David's Cathedral is reputed to represent Rhys ap Gruffydd - 'The Lord Rhys' (d.1197). He founded Strata Florida Abbey where many of his dynasty of princes are buried.

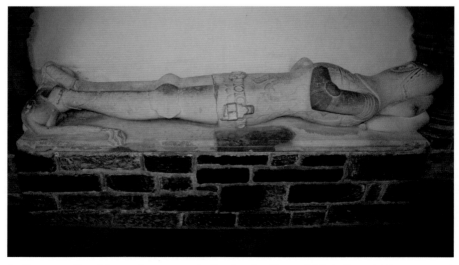

In the opposite aisle can be seen a similar tomb effigy which is thought to represent Lord Rhys's son Rhys Grug, who was buried here in 1233.

Six

IESTYN AP GWRGAN AND THE NORMAN CONQUEST OF GLAMORGAN

Much romance has been written about Robert Fitzhamon's conquest of Glamorgan and the way in which he divided the best of his territory amongst his twelve knights. It is quite feasible that he took advantage of the ongoing quarrel between Rhys ap Tewdwr and Iestyn ap Gwrgan, but it is certainly not easy to separate fact from fiction concerning the details of the events which took place.[1]

When Gwrgan, the father of Iestyn, died in about 1042, he was succeeded by his brother Hywel, the third son of Morgan Hen ('the Aged'). Hywel passed away in 1043 and he was succeeded by Iestyn ap Gwrgan, who reigned over Morgannwg for the next fifty years.

Iestyn's first wife was Denis, the daughter of Bleddyn ap Cynfyn, Prince of Powys, and, through this marriage, Iestyn associated himself with the powerful Gwyneddian family. His wife also provided him with eight sons.

Following the death of Denis, Iestyn married Princess Angharad, daughter of King Elystan Clodrydd, whose rule extended over Lower Powys, the country between the Wye and the Severn. This marriage resulted in the birth of four sons, who were named Caradoc, Madoc, Morgan and Rhys. There was also a daughter named Nest, which seemed to be a popular name at this time.

 The traditional story tells us that, after the defeat of Rhys ap Tewdwr, Iestyn refused to honour the agreement that he had made with Einion ap Collwyn to give him his daughter Nest in marriage. Einion then decided on revenge and urged his Norman friend Robert Fitzhamon to evict Iestyn from his territory.

In 1093 the Normans defeated Iestyn in a battle fought at Mynydd Bychan (Little Mountain). Known today as 'The Heath,' it is a suburb of Cardiff, and the location of a large University Hospital, but in the eleventh century this was a vast area of heath land extending from the north of Cardiff as far as Llanishen Fach Farm.

It is said that the battle lasted a whole day and hundreds of men on both sides were wounded or killed. Local folklore maintains that so much blood was shed in the fighting that a certain brook in Rhiwbina ran red with blood and became known as Nant y Waendlyd (Bloody Brook).

According to one account, Iestyn was slain in the battle and his followers took the body of their prince to a hill about a mile away. Here they sat him on his horse in a deep hole, with various possessions around him. Stones and earth were then heaped over his burial place to form the mound which is known today as the Twmpath. It is an unlikely story for the mound is really the remains of a motte castle, which was subsequently constructed by the Normans.

Another tradition maintains that Iestyn escaped from the battle and crossed the Severn to seek sanctuary at Glastonbury, then Bath and finally Keynsham Priory, where he became a monk. Keynsham is situated in the Avon Valley, about mid-way between the cities of Bath and Bristol, but this priory was not founded until 1169, by William of Gloucester, so it would not have existed in Iestyn's time and it is possible that two locations have been confused.

In the 'Book of Aberpergwm' it is stated that Iestyn ap Gwrgan found sanctuary 'in the monastery of Llangenys in Gwent,[2] where he is reputed to have died at the unbelievably advanced age of 129!

The invasion of Glamorgan by the Normans was inevitable, for in 1070, with the fall of Chester, the conquest of England had been virtually completed and, following the conquest of the Marches, a definite policy regarding Wales must have been in preparation. By this time, the Normans had already taken possession of Abermynwy (Monmouth) and a part of Brycheiniog (Breconshire), and there is evidence that William Rufus, the son of William the Conqueror, was waiting at Alveston (between Bristol and Gloucester) for the outcome of Fitzhamon's expedition into Wales.

There is a tradition that the Twmpath at the foot of the Wenallt is the burial mound of Iestyn ap Gwrgan, who in one version of his demise is reputed to have been slain in a battle half-a-mile away, near Tyn-y-coed. Excavation of the mound in 1849 by the Cambrian Archaeological Association revealed nothing of interest.

Lineage of Iestyn ap Gwrgan

Macsen Wledig (Maximus 'the Imperator') d. 388
Anhun Dunawd (Antonius Donatus) b. c. 365 d.388
Tathal
Teithrin*
Teithfallt
Tewdrig Fendigaid ('the Blessed') b. c.400 d. 470.
Meurig
Athrwys (Arthur) b. 482 d. 562.
Morgan Mwynfawr ('the Most Courteous')
Rhyhawd (Eil Morgan)
Einydd
Morgan Morgannwg d. 665
Ithel (Iudhail)
Rhys
Brochmael
Gwriad
Arthmael
Rhys
Hywel d. 885
Owen d. 931
Morgan Mawr, ('the Great') also called Hen ('the Aged') d. 974
Idwallon
Ithel
Gwrgan d. c.1042
Iestyn, the last independent Welsh prince of Morgannwg,
overthrown in 1093.[3]

*Apparently Teithrin died early and his widow married Nynniaw ap Erb. It was through this marriage that Iestyn ap Gwrgan claimed descent from Llyr Lledieth ('Half Speech'), the ancestor of the Royal Tribe of Morgannwg:

Llyr Lledieth ('Half Speech')
Bran Fendigaid ('The Blessed')
Caradog
Meurig
Erbig
Erb
Nynniau
Teithfallt

The Twelve Knights Hotel at Margam perpetuates the myth of the conquest of Glamorgan in 1091 by twelve Norman knights under the leadership of Robert Fitzhamon.

The twelve knights who are reputed to have accompanied Robert Fitzhamon were:- William de Granville, his brother, Paganus de Turberville, Robert St Quentin, Richard de Syward, Gilbert de Humfreville, Roger de Berkerolls, Reginald de Sully, Peter Le Soor, John Le Fleminge, Oliver de St John and William de Esteringe, whose ancestors came out of Dansk and came into England with the Danes, and afterwards became known as the Stradlings. The names of some of these twelve knights are certainly familiar, but their entry into Glamorgan probably did not take place until some time after the arrival of Robert Fitzhamon and they have certainly left their names on the map. Reginald Sully, for example, inherited the manor of Sully, and the village of Flemingston bears the name of Sir John Fleming.

According to the traditional story, Porthkerry was the inlet on the Glamorgan coast, in which Fitzhamon and his men landed, but it is more likely that his ships sailed into the Usk estuary for his troops to embark on the coast of Wentlooge. Here, his right flank would have been protected by the Norman forces which already occupied Gwent. From the Usk he would have advanced to the Rhymni river and then continued west until he landed beyond the River Neath but proceeded no further.[4]

Robert Fitzhamon was the benefactor of Tewkesbury Abbey, which today is the largest parish church in England.

This image of Robert Fitzhamon looks down from one of the marvellous choir windows of Tewkesbury Abbey. It was his son-in-law, Robert Fitzroy, who completed the building and raised the impressive tower.

Robert Fitzhamon was certainly an important knight, who, as Lord of Cruelly in Normandy,[5] had come into England with William the Conqueror in 1066. He was rewarded for his fidelity by William Rufus in 1089, with extensive possessions in Gloucestershire. Now a wealthy landowner, he established his headquarters at Gloucester and also built a house at Tewkesbury. These strategically important lands were granted to Fitzhamon at a time when preparations were undoubtedly being made for further advances into Welsh territory.

The old Roman fort at Cardiff was taken over by Robert Fitzhamon as his headquarters. He built a wooden stockade on top of the ruined walls and a large artificial mound, surrounded by a ditch, was constructed within the enclosed area. Timber buildings were then erected on top of the mound and water was diverted from the river Taff to fill the moat, which was bridged at one point to provide access.

In addition to Cardiff, Fitzhamon took as his share of the conquered lands the towns of Cowbridge and Kenfig; and as demesne lands Miskin, Glyn-Rhondda, Tir-y-Iarll and Boverton. He now governed a territory extending from the Usk to the Tawe, which throughout the medieval period was to remain in the separate lordships of Glamorgan and Gwynllwg.

Robert Fitzhamon did not seem to have spent much time in his Welsh lordships for he took more interest in Tewkesbury. So generously did he endow the town's Benedictine abbey that he became regarded as its founder. He gave it considerable grants including the possessions of the ancient Welsh religious institutions of Glamorgan, such as Llanilltyd Fawr, Llancarfan and Llandough, while other lands were granted to the Benedictine abbey of St. Peter at Gloucester. Fitzhamon's vassal knights also made gifts to these two abbeys as well as to other monastic establishments outside his lordship.

Although his headquarters were at Cardiff, he did very little for the place. In the only extant charter relating to the place, he granted the monks at Tewkesbury an arm of the Taff at Cardiff for a fishery. In addition he gave them St. Mary's Church with its properties, the Castle Chapel, and lands and tithes in Cardiff, a meadow and a village on the Taff.

Robert Fitzhamon was foremost a soldier who in 1105 was appointed general of the King's army and immediately ordered to undertake a campaign in Normandy. His military career came to a sudden end at the battle of Tenchbrai, on 28th September 1106, when he received a spear wound in his temple. He was not killed outright but lived in a state of imbecility until he died in March of the following year.[6] His body was laid in the Chapter House at Tewkesbury Abbey and from there moved to the presbytery by Abbot Robert in 1240.

In 1397, three centuries after his death, a chantry was erected over Fitzhamon's tomb by Parker, the eighteenth abbot. Enriched with handsome tracery and oak-leaf cresting, the chantry has fan-vaulting and is paved with its original tiles showing the Norman knight's arms. Unfortunately, the vault was pillaged at the Dissolution and the contents carried away.

The tomb of Robert Fitzhamon stands in a bay on the north side of the Choir. He died in 1107 and was first buried in the Chapter House of the monastery, but his body was removed to the present position in 1241. The Chantry itself was built by Abbot Parker in 1397.

Seven

THE NORMAN KINGS

Williamn the Conqueror died in 1087 and, according to his wishes, his lands were divided among his three sons. He gave England to William Rufus, Normandy to Robert, and the maternal inheritance to Henry. Thus, as ruler of England, William I was succeeded by his second son William Rufus ('the Red Faced'), who was twenty-seven years of age and rather corpulent with an unscrupulous nature.

Seven years into his reign William II was faced with a great anti-Norman rising in Wales, which was led by Gruffydd ap Cynan in Gwynedd and Cadwgan ap Bleddyn, the Prince of Powys. On two occasions, William Rufus had to invade Wales to lend support to his barons, and during this period nearly every castle in Wales was virtually destroyed. His problems were finally sorted out by Hugh Lupus, Earl of Chester, and Hugh of Montgomery, Earl of Shrewsbury, who forced Gruffydd and Cadwgan to flee to Ireland. However, they returned during the following year (1099) and agreed terms with the Normans, with the result that Gruffydd would rule over Anglesey and Arfon; Cadwgan would hold Ceredigion and part of Powys, while the remainder of Wales was to remain in Norman hands.

The thirteen year reign of William Rufus came to an end on 2 August, 1100, whilst on a hunting expedition in the New Forest. The king went in pursuit of a stag and was followed by a knight, Walter Tirel. William shot an arrow at the stag but missed and called out to Walter to shoot, which he did, accidently killing the king. Tirel later denied that he was even present and as nobody cared for William the matter was not investigated. It was Robert Fitzhamon who covered the corpse with his cloak and carried it on his horse to Winchester for burial. Henry, William's younger brother, who was also taking part in the hunt, immediately made his way to Winchester and seized the keys of the royal Treasury. His elder brother, Robert, was crusading in the Holy Land at this time, so, without delay, Henry[1] seized upon the opportunity to have himself elected King of England by a few supporters who claimed to represent the Great Council.

The body of William Rufus was interred at Winchester Cathedral with very little ceremony. The clergy even denied it religious rites and he was buried beneath the crossing of the tower, which collapsed the following year.

Henry's brother, Robert of Normandy, returned to his duchy from Jerusalem the following year, and he was soon persuaded by disloyal barons to make an attempt to seize the crown of England. Landing at Portsmouth with a strong force, he marched on London and the two brothers met at Alton, where Robert surprisingly chose to negotiate. By the treaty of Alton (1101), he agreed to accept a pension of three thousand marks.

Normandy, however, remained a threat to Henry, for it became a meeting place of many of his disaffected barons, whom his brother Robert was unable to control. In 1105, Henry invaded the duchy and took Bayeux and Caen. The following year his Anglo-Norman army decisively routed Duke Robert at Tinchebrai and Normandy was annexed. Robert was brought to Wales, where he spent the rest of his life in captivity at Cardiff Castle.

This effigy of Robert Curthouse, Duke of Normandy, can be seen in Gloucester Cathedral. He is depicted as a fearless crusader, clad in armour. Imprisoned by his brother Henry I in Cardiff Castle for 28 years, he died in 1134.

Henry I was the first Norman king to be born on English soil, and he pleased his English subjects by marrying Edith, daughter of Malcolm III (of Scotland) and of St. Margaret, sister of Edgar the Atheling, thus uniting himself with the old royal house of Alfred the Great. It is recorded that Henry I was a well educated man, who had learned to read and write Latin and also studied English language and law. His learning earned him the sobriquet of 'Beauclerc' (fine scholar) and he ruled over England as complete master for thirty-three years. The Anglo-Saxon Chronicle states that: 'He was a good man, and was held in great awe. In his days no man dared to wrong another. He made peace for man and beast.'

Gruffydd ap Cynan, whilst professing allegiance to Henry I, managed gradually to extend his rule over most of Gwynedd. His increasing power, and a suspicion that he was supporting the lawless Owen of Powys (son of Cadwgan) in a revolt, induced Henry I to invade Gwynedd in 1114 and compel Gruffydd to pay a heavy fine. The king's actions had the desired effect, for the remainder of Gruffydd's reign was peaceful and he remained neutral during Henry's second invasion of Wales in 1121. This campaign was provoked by Gruffydd ap Rhys in Deheubarth and in particular by the growing power of Maredudd, the last of the three sons of Bleddyn in Powys, which at that time was the strongest principality in Wales.

The seal of Henry I

By now Henry was in the autumn of his life and a sad man, for his heir and only legitimate son, William, had been drowned the previous year, along with his entourage, in the White Ship, whilst returning from Normandy. Henry was so afflicted by his personal loss that it is said he never smiled again. His only legitimate surviving child was Matilda and he was anxious that she should succeed him. He held a great court in Windsor Castle and compelled his barons to take an oath of fealty to Matilda, acknowledging her as Queen of England and Duchess of Normandy.

During one of his frequent visits to Normandy, in 1135, Henry I died at St Denis-le-Fermont, near Gisors, on 1 December, 1135, after eating too plentifully of lamphreys (eels). He was sixty-five years of age.

The king's body was brought back to England by his illegitimate son, Robert Fitzroy, and he was buried at Reading Abbey, which Henry had founded. Sadly, neither the tomb of Henry I nor the abbey exist today, and the site is now a car park.

Robert, Earl of Gloucester and Lord of Glamorgan

Robert Fitzroy, despite being born out of wedlock, was Henry's favourite son,[2] and he in turn had been devoted to his father. In 1119 he served with Henry at the battle of Brenneville, and in 1122 was at the taking of Byton Castle. In 1127 he was among those who swore in Henry's presence an oath of allegiance to his daughter Matilda in 1127.

Fitzroy was known by several titles, including Robert of Caen, which was his birthplace, and Robert 'the Consul', which was a term denoting the King's Counsellor, or 'one with whom the king consults'.

However, he was best known as Robert, Earl of Gloucester, owing to the fact that when he married Mabel, the daughter of Robert Fitzhamon, in 1122, and the main part of her inheritance in England was Gloucester. Accordingly, Robert took on the titles Earl of Gloucester and Lord of Glamorgan.

Soon after becoming Lord of Glamorgan, one of Robert's first acts was to recognise and confirm the possessions of the sons of Iestyn ap Gwrgan, the last true Prince of Glamorgan. He also allowed Ifor Bach, the Welsh lord of Senghenydd, to retain his patrimony and powers in the hill country to the north of Cardiff. Throughout Robert's lordship, the natural Welsh were allowed to retain their local customs without interference, for he was undoubtedly a man of great moderation, culture and learning. He was most sympathetic in all his dealings with the Welsh, and he quickly gained their respect.

Robert was also most generous in all his dealings with the Church, for he gave liberally to Ewenny Priory and financed the re-building of Llandaff Cathedral. In 1130, he is reputed to have established a monastery at Penrhys where a doubtful tradition maintains that his grandfather Rhys ap Tewdwr was beheaded in 1088.

Not only was Robert, Earl of Gloucester, an eminent statesman, but, like his father Henry I, he was also very interested in literature. He was a generous friend of many scholars and his close connections with both South Wales and Normandy resulted in his taking a close interest in the legendary tales of Wales and Brittany. His fascination with Celtic history was no doubt inherited from his Welsh mother, Princess Nest, the beautiful daughter of Rhys ap Tewdwr.

Robert's enlightened patronage of scholars and poets is shown by the fact that William of Malmesbury, probably the most distinguished scholar of his day, dedicated to him his *History of the Kings of England*. It is very likely that it was upon Robert's request that Geoffrey of Monmouth and Walter, Archdeacon of Oxford, embarked upon a quest for the source material relating to King Arthur, which resulted in Geoffrey's *Historia Regum Britanniae*..

The impressive twelve-sided keep of Cardiff Castle was built early in the 12th century by Robert, Earl of Gloucester. At the same time, he erected substantial curtain walls on the south and west, while the remaining sides were defended by the banks of earth, which covered the ruins of the walls of the Roman fort.

Robert Consul's Glamorgan residence was Cardiff Castle, which had previously provided a base for Robert Fitzhamon, who had strengthened the old fortress of Iestyn ap Gwrgan and surrounded the town with walls. However, it was Robert Consul who established a much grander castle here of which today the only remnants are the ancient keep and portions of the Curthouse tower.

Standing on an impressive 13 metre high mound, the keep is a spacious tower of twelve nearly equal sides. It is 10 metres in height and about 26 metres in diameter with walls 2 metres thick. Robert also built the curtain walls to the south and west of the castle on top of earlier Roman masonry, dating back to the first century when a fort was established here by Aulius Didius.

The Curthouse Tower can be seen beside the main entrance to the castle from High Street. It is also known as the Black Tower and is famous as the reputed prison of Robert Curthouse, Duke of Normandy, the eldest son of William the Conqueror. He was brought here from Devizes by his brother Henry I and placed under the custody of Robert the Consul for twenty-eight years until his death in 1134.

Cardiff Castle was restored by the third Marquis of Bute between 1867 and 1890. The architect was William Burgess, who not only extended the apartments, but also created their unique decorated interiors.

Cardiff Castle, as it is seen today, is the masterpiece of the Marquis of Bute and his architect William Burgess. It is indeed a magnificent structure with an ornate Clock Tower, restored curtain walls, and a set of private rooms used by the Bute family when they were in residence.

The Clock Tower, in particular, contains a beautifully decorated suite of rooms which were intended for use by the Lord of the Castle. At the head of the stairs leading from the Grand Entrance is the large Banqueting Hall, which is considered the finest room in the castle, and was designed by William Burgess to be a tribute to the life and deeds of Robert the Consul.

The fireplace is surmounted by a representation in stone of the Castle Gateway and its towers. A mounted warrior, Robert Consul, is riding forth to battle. His uncle, Robert, Duke of Normandy, is seen behind the bars of his prison; while Robert Consul's wife, the Countess Mabel, is depicted waving a handkerchief. The Empress Matilda, and a priest (possibly intended for Geoffrey of Monmouth, the celebrated chronicler, who was chaplain to Robert Consul), stands on the embattled tower to bid the warrior God-speed, while six heralds proclaim the departure of their lord.

The Banqueting Hall occupies the upper part of the Great Hall and is the largest of the stately rooms in Cardiff Castle. Of special interest is this ornate fireplace depicting Robert Consul ridin g forth to battle.

Twenty-two frescoes, decorating the walls of the room, representing scenes from the lives of Henry I and Robert the Consul. They follow his career from his wedding in about 1110 to his funeral in 1147. The frescoes were painted by Mr. H.N. Lonsdale and commencing from the north end depict the following events:-

1. Marriage of Robert, Earl of Gloucester, son of Henry I, to Mabel, daughter and heiress of Fitzhamon (about 1110).

2. Contention between Robert and Stephen, nephew of Henry I (who should take the oath of allegiance to Matilda first, in which contention Stephen was upheld).

3. Henry I, on his death bed, enjoining Robert to be faithful to Matilda, the King's daughter (1135).

4. Robert, after the death of Henry I, pledging himself to Stephen (1136).

5. Messe (1138).

6. A single figure carrying spears with a legend that the trumpet and war-cry are heard, also a heron swallowing a frog, and a dog about to attack a heron, to signify that every creature lives upon his neighbour.

7. Robert and Matilda arriving at Arundel when he brought her to England. They landed near that place (1138).

8. Stephen's candle extinguished at Mass, an incident said to have happened just before the battle at Lincoln, and taken as an omen.

9. Stephen taken prisoner at the Battle of Lincoln (1141).

10. Stephen taken as a prisoner to the Empress.

11. Stephen in prison (1141).

12. Agreement between Matilda and Henry, Bishop of Winchester (Stephen's brother).

13. Matilda received as Queen at Winchester, April (1141).

14. Matilda leaving London in fear of treachery (1141).

15. Fighting at Winchester, in which Robert is taken prisoner. David of Scotland fighting for Matilda, and the escape of Matilda (1141).

16. Agreement as to liberating Robert and Stephen in exchange (All Saint's Day, 1141).

17. Matilda escaping from Oxford, clad in white, over the frozen river.

18. Prince Henry, afterwards Henry II, landing in England, being brought from France by Robert (1142).

19. Robert attacking the Convent of Wilton (fortified by Stephen) - below nuns are seen lamenting (1143).

20. Prince Henry being instructed at Bristol Castle.

21. Robert and Stephen fighting at Faringdon Castle. Robert is said to have burnt the Castle, but some authorities state that Stephen took it and razed it to the ground (1144).

22. Funeral of Robert at Bristol (1147).
    A priest chanting.

When Henry I died on 1 December, 1135, at St Denis-le-Fermont, near Gisors, after a reign of 35 years and four months, his peaceful administration was turned into nearly two decades of feudal chaos. The oath of allegiance sworn by the barons to acknowledge Matilda as his successor was scornfully ignored by the Great Council, who chose Stephen of Blois and Boulogne, the king's nephew and grandson of the Conqueror, to be the new King of England.

Matilda's claim was dismissed out of hand, for not only was she a woman, but she was also married to an Angevin who were the hereditary enemies and rivals of the Normans. Stephen, on the death of Henry I, had seized the royal treasury at Winchester, which amounted to a hundred thousand pounds. He used the money to obtain equipment and provision troops in anticipation of the troubles that were to come.

England thus entered a period of civil war with the succession to the throne in dispute between Matilda and Stephen. Throughout these troubles, Robert, Earl of Gloucester, loyally supported his sister Matilda, thus fulfiling the oath given by him and other barons to Henry I to guarantee the succession to Matilda. He fought on her behalf at the battle of Lincoln, having led into the field a large body of Welshmen; this being the first time that the Marcher Lord of Glamorgan was so supported.

King Stephen

Stephen's reign was one of considerable confusion and lawlessness which caused a great deal of misery and discontent. Out of regal control, the barons built numerous strong castles and waged private wars to satisfy their own ambitions.

After arriving in England in 1139, Matilda made several attempts to gain the throne of her father and several barons caused further problems by supporting her against King Stephen. In 1138, King David of Scotland invaded England on Matilda's behalf, but was defeated at Northallerton in the battle of the Standard, which was named after a mast erected on a wagon carrying the banners of three saints.

In 1141, Stephen was captured in the battle of Lincoln and sent to Bristol Castle, but was released some months later in exchange for Robert of Gloucester, who had fallen into the hands of Stephen's supporters. Matilda was subsequently besieged in Oxford Castle, from which, camouflaged in a white cloak, she escaped over the snow in the winter of 1142.

Robert, in 1147, founded the great Cistercian abbey of Margam, endowing it with lands lying between Kenfig and Afan. He died at Bristol in October of that year and was buried under a tombstone of green jasper in the Priory of St James, his own foundation (1129) at Bristol. He was laid to rest in the choir where his effigy carved in wood, though probably not of contemporary date is still preserved.

Robert's eldest son William, a man already advanced in years, succeeded him in his titles and honours. His other sons were Roger, Bishop of Worcester, who died at Tours in France in 1179; Hamon, who died at the Siege of Toulouse in 1159, and Philip. Countess Mabel survived her husband by ten years, dying in 1157.[3]

The tomb of Robert Consul can be seen in the choir of the Benedictine Priory of St James, which he founded in 1129. This church is the earliest example of Norman architecture in Bristol and it stands on the north east side of the city.

Civil War continued for several years without any decisive result. Geoffrey Plantagenet of Anjou succeeded in capturing Normandy and Matilda eventually retired there in 1148. During the following year, her son Henry, who had been granted the government of Normandy by his father, crossed to England to take up his mother's cause, but, on the death of Geoffrey of Anjou in 1150, he returned as heir to Normandy and Anjou. In 1152, he married Eleanor of Aquitaine, and thus became master of all the territory between the Loire and the Pyrenees, an area covering more than half of France.

Henry of Anjou invaded England again in 1153, with a large army, and King Stephen, whose only son had just died, offered just feeble resistance. He made peace by the Treaty of Wallingford, by which Henry of Anjou should succeed to the English Crown on Stephen's death. He did not have long to wait, for Stephen died the following year after a short illness and with him ended the rule of the Norman kings in England. His rule of nineteen years had been disastrous. The Crown, unjustly snatched from the heir who had the right to wear it, had brought him neither profit nor happiness. When he died, in 1154, of appendicitis, at the age of 57, the English had been under Norman rule for nearly ninety years, during which time they had suffered every kind of injustice and wrong and had been brutally oppressed by their cruel masters. Stephen was buried at Faversham Abbey (which he had founded) alongside his wife and son Eustace, who had predeceased him.

William, the Second Earl of Gloucester
and Lord of Glamorgan

William, the second Earl of Gloucester, succeeded his father in 1147 and his mother in 1157 and held the lordship for thirty-six years.[4] He is first mentioned in the foundation charter of Neath in 1129, and next as governor of Wareham Castle, during his father's absence in Normandy, in 1142, when he was attacked by Stephen and the castle taken.

Unlike his father, William was devoid of much energy and, as a result, his mother Mabel took more part than he did in running the affairs of Glamorgan. Countess Mabel, after the death of her husband, seems to have acted with considerable authority in Glamorgan. Her earliest charter as a widow, given probably in 1147, is a confirmation of St Peter's of Gloucester. Mabel also gave to St Augustine's, Bristol, sixty acres of land in the marsh of Rhymney; and in Earl William's charter to Neath, he adds the assent and consent of Mabel, his mother. Countess Mabel died in 1157.

A famous incident during Earl William's life took place one night in 1158 when Ifor Bach (Ifor ap Meurig), the Welsh lord of Senghenydd,[5] took revenge on William of Gloucester for appropriating some of his territory, thus breaking his father's pledge that Welshmen should not be molested in the land which they held. Ifor entered Cardiff Castle by erecting ladders to scale its 12 metre surrounding walls and, despite the armed garrison, 120 strong, succeeded in capturing Earl William, his wife and their young son Robert. He carried them off to the hill country to the north of Cardiff and they were not released until William had agreed to return everything which had unjustly been taken from the Welshman.

A period of calm followed this incident; but in 1160 Earl William took part in an expedition against Rhys ap Gruffydd on the western borders of the lordship. In the following year Rhys retaliated by burning the Grange of Margam.

William sought his place in heaven by making generous benefactions to Margam Abbey and he also rebuilt the church of St Mary and St Thomas at Cardiff, which had been erected by his father.

He died on the night of St Clement's, 23 November 1183 (the anniversary of his own birth), and was buried at Keynsham Abbey, which he had erected to the memory of his only son, Robert, who had died some years previously at Cardiff. William left three daughters, Mabel, Amica,[6] and Isabel as co-heirs of the lordship, but the lordship of Glamorgan fell into the custody of the Crown and remained so for six years. Henry II became the guardian of the three co-heiresses and, when he died in 1189, the wardship passed with the crown to Richard I.

Eight

THE PLANTAGANET KINGS
AND ARTHUR OF BRITTANY

King Stephen was succeeded by Matilda's son, Henry, who was twenty-one years of age and the great grandson of William the Conqueror. He was crowned Henry II at Westminster Abbey on 19 December, 1154, and ascended to the throne with a clear and unquestioned right. Both Englishmen and Normans, weary of the strife and bloodshed of the previous twenty years, welcomed his arrival in England with a new feeling of optimism for the future.

Blessed with a dynamic personality, Henry was strong-willed, impatient, observant and tenacious. He worked with a restless energy and it was not long before the old hatred between Saxons and Normans began to fade, with law and justice asserting their power against violence and wrong.

The barons of England were soon made to understand the determination of this young Angevin king, who proceeded to demolish the unlicensed castles built in Stephen's reign, and there was only feeble opposition, for it soon became apparent that Henry was intent on restoring order out of chaos.

Henry II's accession to the English throne also altered the political map of Europe and the House of Plantaganet became the most powerful in Christendom. The Counts of Anjou had been named 'Plantaganet' from their family badge, a sprig of broom, (the genista or genêt: hence, plante-á-genêt). By marriage and inheritance, Henry's possessions were enormous, for he was not only King of England, but Lord of Western France from the Channel to the Pyrenees; being Lord of Normandy, Maine and Anjou, and also of Aquitaine through his marriage to Eleanor, Duchess of Aquitaine, formerly wife of Louis VII, King of France.[1]

In 1166, Henry acquired direct rule over Brittany through the betrothal of his young son Geoffrey to the infant duchess Constance of Brittany, the daughter of Duke Conan IV. In 1187, Constance gave birth to a son who was named Arthur, whom the Bretons welcomed as their promised deliverer from foreign rule. It was the Breton hope that Arthur, the long-awaited leader, would return again to lead his people. Henry II no doubt had plans to bring Brittany under Plantaganet rule through his grandson, for he had succeeded in providing Brittany with an heir named Arthur,[2] who was both of the line of the English kings and also the legitimate descendant of the Breton ruling house.

Henry II from his tomb at Fontrevault

During his reign, Henry II paid several visits to Wales and in 1163, when he invaded South Wales to subdue Rhys ap Gruffydd of Deheubarth, an ancient prophecy was recalled. It had been foretold that when a 'freckled man of might' should cross the ford of Pencarn, on the River Ebbw (on the outskirts of Newport) in Gwent, it would be an event of ill omen for Wales. The result of his visit was indeed the surrender of Rhys ap Gruffydd at Cardigan.

Henry eventually gave up all attempts to conquer Wales. His decision was partly due to his lack of success and partly to his wars in France. In 1171 he decided to visit Ireland to demonstrate his overlordship and on his return from the 'Emerald Isle' he wisely appointed Rhys ap Gruffydd as his 'Justice' in South Wales, endowing him with some authority over the lesser princes and making him responsible for their good behaviour. From that time Rhys was called 'Yr Arglwydd Rhys' or the Lord Rhys.

Henry II was a great patron of literature and his court became a centre for all the learned men of the day. He was not only surrounded by political advisers and lawyers, but also by historians and chroniclers such as Robert FitzNeal, Roger de Hovedon, Gervasse of Canterbury, Gerald of Wales, John of Salisbury, Walter Map, Geoffrey of Monmouth, who dedicated the third edition of his Historia Regum Britanniae to Henry II, and also the Norman writer Wace who translated Geoffrey's book into French and introduced the Round Table into the story. Owain Cyfeiliog, Prince of Powys, who was well known for his ready wit and constant loyalty to Henry II, was also a frequent visitor to the Court.

It is also believed that the famous French poet Chrétien de Troyes was a regular visitor to the Court, for it is obvious from his poems that he spent time in England and was familiar with Windsor Castle. Marie de France also enjoyed the patronage of the English Court and dedicated her lays to Henry, who was quite possibly her half-brother.

The version of the Tristan poem, composed by the Anglo-Norman Thomas between 1185 and 1200, was also written under the patronage of some member of the Angevin House, perhaps, Queen Eleanor[3] who was a great patroness of the poets. In addition to her vast possessions, Eleanor had inherited a great love of literature from her grandfather, William IX, Duke of Aquitaine and VIIth Count of Poitiers. He was the first troubadour poet of whom we have any knowledge and he took a special interest in the Arthurian legends.

One of Eleanor's daughters was Matilda, whom her father Henry had married to the Duke of Saxony in 1160, and she too was a patroness of literature who caused the Tristan story to be translated into German for the benefit of the members of her Court.

Another of Eleanor's daughters, also named Eleanor (or Leonore), was given by her father, Henry, in 1170, in marriage to the King of Castile, Alfonso VIII. She too was intimately connected with the Arthurian stories for she caused the introduction of these legends into Spain.

Queen Eleanor and Henry II
From the tomb at Fontevrault

Geoffrey Plantagenet

Eleanor's son Geoffrey seems also to have been interested in the Celtic legends, for he gave his child the name of Arthur.[2] The boy's mother, Constance of Brittany, no doubt for sentimental and perhaps political reasons, hoped that their son might yet succeed to the throne as King Arthur.

Four sons were born to Henry and Eleanor, who they named Henry, Richard, Geoffrey and John. All four were united only in their discontent because their father allowed them very little power and insufficient wealth. Prince Henry, the eldest son, died in 1183 and his brother Geoffrey passed away three years later. As Richard was now heir-apparent and would succeed to England and Normandy, Henry II suggested to King Philip Augustus that Prince John should marry his daughter Alice, and should receive Richard's Duchy of Aquitaine.

King Philip seized this opportunity of causing trouble between father and son. He told Prince Richard of his father's plan and suggested that they formed an alliance against the King of England. In 1188, Richard and Philip Augustus took to arms and drove Henry II from Le Mans (Maine), to his birth place, and forced him to capitulate at Angers (Anjou). Henry II ceded the Auvergne, the most easterly province of Aquitaine, gave an indemnity to the French king and acknowledged Richard as his heir.

Before long Henry learned that his favourite son, John, had joined the rebels and his resultant grief no doubt led to his early death on 6 July, 1189. He died at Chinon and was buried ten miles from there at Fontevrault Abbey, the favourite monastery of Queen Eleanor of Aquitaine.[3]

Richard I (1189-1199)

Richard born at Beaumont Palace, Oxford, on 8 September 1157, was aged thirty-two at his accession. He was crowned by Archbishop Baldwin in Westminster Abbey on 3 September 1189. Although born in England, he only actually lived there for six months of his ten year reign. By education he was totally French and was concerned with England solely as a kingdom from which he could derive revenue for his crusading expeditions. To this end he used every possible device; bishoprics and offices of state were sold to the highest bidder and he sold many royal manors and numerous charters to towns.

Richard I from his tomb at Fontevrault

Leaving his mother Eleanor as regent of the realm, Richard set out in 1190 for the Holy Land with about forty ships. He was joined by Philip Augustus, King of France, at Marseilles and the two crusaders sailed together to Sicily, where they were delayed during the winter while Richard settled a private quarrel with Tancred, the Norman King of that country.

In June 1191, Richard landed in Palestine and his forces, with those of Philip of France, succeeded in raising the siege of Acre, which had lasted for two years. Richard then began an offensive against Saladin, the Sultan of Turkey. He defeated the Moslem forces at the battle of Arsuf and captured Jaffa in 1192. He then advanced to within two days' march of Jerusalem, but was advised against an assault because his troops were not numerous enough to hold the city even if he had captured it. Richard therefore decided to make a temporary peace with Saladin, who allowed the Christians to keep their conquests, including Jaffa, and to have free access to the Holy Sepulchre.

Leaving Palestine, Richard had every intention of one day renewing his efforts to re-capture Jerusalem, but on his return journey he fell into the hands of his enemy Leopold of Austria while crossing the latter's territory. In order to obtain his freedom, Richard had to pay the enormous ransom of a hundred and fifty thousand marks, which, according to feudal law, was raised from his tenants-in-chief, who had to pay heavily. In 1194, Richard landed in England, but within a short time he crossed the Channel again to Normandy to make war on Philip of France, who had attacked the Duchy in his absence. The remainder of Richard's life was spent waging war in France, subduing revolts by his brother John and crushing rebellions in Poitou. He remained popular in England despite his continual money exactions for his Crusade and his French war. Undoubtedly, his courage was much admired and he was known among his contemporaries as Coeur-de-lion ('the Lion -Heart').

It was while besieging the castle of one of his vassals at Cháluz, in Limousin in the duchy of Aquitaine, that he was wounded by an arrow, fired by Peter Basilus on 26 April, 1199. The wound turned gangrenous and he subsequently passed away at the castle and was buried at Fontevrault Abbey at the feet of his father Henry II. His heart was buried at Rouen Cathedral and his entrails in Charrox, Poitou. Also buried at the early 12th century abbey of Fontrevault are Eleanor of Aquitaine and King John's wife, Isabella of Angouléme.

By 1291 the Christians had lost their footing in Palestine and Jerusalem was not in Christian hands again until 1917, when General Allenby marched into the Holy City at the head of British troops.

Richard I left no son to succeed him, for his marriage to Princess Berengaria of Navarre had brought him no children. The next heir to the throne, therefore, was young Arthur of Bretagne, the son of Richard's late brother Geoffrey; for, according to the feudal law, the son of an elder brother succeeded to an inheritance before a younger brother. Richard had, in the early part of his reign, solemnly declared young Arthur to be his heir, but in a will he made a year before his death he named his brother John as his successor. It is thought that his will was made on the persuasion of his mother, the old dowager Queen Eleanor, who detested Constance of Bretagne, the mother of young Arthur.

King John (1199-1216)

John, the youngest son of Henry II, was said to be cruel, treacherous and very selfish. He was betrothed at the age of ten to his second cousin Hawise, , daughter of William the second Earl of Gloucester and grand-daughter of Robert Consul. Hawise, with her sister Amica, was co-heiress to the great earldom of Gloucester.

Ten years after his marriage to Hawise, John acceded to the throne and was crowned at Westminster Abbey on 27 May, 1199. Having grown tired of Hawise, who had given him no children, and, in spite of threats from the Church and the anger of his barons, John divorced her to take as a new wife Isabella, the daughter of Audemor, Count of Angoulême. She was just twelve years old when she was crowned Queen of England.

Portrait of King John - from his tomb at Worcester

In 1202 John is believed to have murdered his nephew Arthur of Brittany in order to gain control of Anjou. He was the son of John's deceased elder brother, Count Geoffrey of Brittany. The murdered Prince Arthur was buried in the Cistercian abbey of St André-en-Gouffern in Normandy.

Hawise, John's ex-wife, took up residence at Boverton Castle in Glamorgan, and there is a tradition that the king went there in order to hide from his barons, who were pestering him to sign the Magna Carta. He no doubt decided that his pursuers would be unlikely to think that he would seek shelter in the home of his divorced wife. [4] John persuaded Hawise to conceal him and a story is told that, when news went around the village, the stranger who called himself Gerald Fitzalan was, in fact, their king, they re-named the Plas at Boverton, Trebrenin - 'The Place of the King'.

After about a year, John decided to face the barons and ultimately signed their Charter at Runnymede in 1215. This was drawn up by the barons to safeguard their privileges. Its object was to guarantee their feudal rights by protecting their lands and revenues against the exorbitant demands of a king who had lost considerable revenue with the loss of his Continental possessions. It is of interest that the Vale of Glamorgan supplied strong supporters to the final draft of the Magna Carta, which is reputed to have been drawn up at Beaupre Castle, near St Hilary, the residence of Sir Philip Bassett, who became Lord Chief Justice of England in the reign of Henry III.

King John died at Newark Castle on 18th October, 1216. His intestines were entombed at Croxton Abbey, but in accordance with his will his body was buried in Worcester Cathedral before the altar of St Wulfstan, the 11th-century bishop, who had been canonised in 1203. John's heir, Henry III was just nine years old when he succeeded to the throne.

King John's tomb in Worcester Cathedral

Nine

LLANDAFF CATHEDRAL
AND ITS ANCIENT CHARTERS

Llandaff is said to be the most ancient Episcopical see in Britain remaining on its original site. Many of the English sees, after their first buildings fell into decay, were removed to cities of greater importance, while the Welsh sees remain to this day in the places where they were originally founded. There is a tradition that the first church at Llandaff was founded within half a century of the Roman evacuation of Britain, when King Meurig endowed it with large possessions.

At the time of the Norman Conquest, the Bishop of Llandaff was Herewald, who is said to have been a Welshman, educated in England and consecrated in 1056 in the time of Gruffydd ap Llywelyn. Herewald's son, Lifris, based at Llancarfan, became Archdeacon of Morgannwg.

Herewald's episcopate was very long, but during its latter years purely nominal due to his age, while the new Norman lord Marcher, Robert Fitzhamon, was the true master. Herewald died in 1104 at the age of one hundred, and three years later Urban (Gwrvan), archdeacon of Llandaff, was appointed to the vacant position. He was consecrated by Anselm, Archbishop of Canterbury, for by this time the Welsh Church had lost its independence and become subject to the jurisdiction of Canterbury. Urban thus became the first bishop of a Welsh diocese to profess obedience to Canterbury.

On taking up his appointment, Urban found the bishopric in a deplorable condition with its revenue much reduced by the bad management of his predecessors. The financial situation was so bad that instead of being able to afford the maintenance of twenty-four canons there were scarcely sufficient funds for the support of two, but worst of all the church, which was just 9 metres long, 5 metres wide and 7 metres high, had suffered so much during the Norman invasion that it was in danger of collapse.

Bishop Urban made his grievances known to Pope Calixtus II at the Council of Rheims in 1119 and obtained from him circular letters to the King, the Archbishop of Canterbury, and his own diocesans, earnestly exhorting them to contribute towards the much needed repairs of his church. Urban decided to rebuild the church on a new site, but before commencing its erection he decided to obtain the relics of the sixth-century

Llandaff Cathedral, near Cardiff, is said to be the oldest bishopric with a continuous history in the country, for a religious establishment existed here soon after the introduction of Christianity to these islands.

St. Dyfrig (Dubricius), the reputed founder of the See, who had been buried on Bardsey Island. According to Geoffrey of Monmouth, it was Dyfrig who crowned Arthur and he was said to be 'so remarkably pious that by merely praying he could cure anyone who was ill.'

The grave of St. Dyfrig was located, and with the consent of Gruffydd ap Cynan, King of Gwynedd, was opened on Friday, 7 May 1120, in the presence of David, Bishop of Bangor, Gruffydd ap Cynan, King of Gwynedd, and a large gathering of clergy and local people. Dyfrig's relics were removed[1] from his stone sarcophagus and reverently placed in a convenient vessel to be carried back to Llandaff, where they arrived sixteen days later.

It is recorded that during this time there was a severe draught in Morgannwg, for it had not rained for seven weeks, but on the day that Dyfrig's remains arrived in Llandaff it began to rain heavily. The rivers Taff and Ely rapidly filled and their waters rolled in torrents to the sea. The faded and dying vegetation in the surrounding countryside quickly revived and the threat of famine, thus removed, was regarded as a favour obtained through the prayers of Bishop Dyfrig himself.

The relics of Dyfrig were washed in the presence of Bishop Urban, Esni the Dean, the canons, and Isaac, the Bishop's chaplain. The bones were then placed in three basins and we are told that strange things immediately began to happen. As the bones touched the water it began to bubble as if a red-hot stone had been thrown into the basins. Then a bone of the saint's arm was seen to move around at the bottom of the water and apparently this went on for an hour or so, before it slowly came to rest. The relics, now still, were then placed in a tomb positioned before the altar of St. Mary, facing to the north.

Bishop Urban started to build his new church on 14 April 1121 and in size it was nearly as large as the present cathedral. It is believed that the beautiful Norman arch in the choir is one of the remaining parts of his work. The building was constructed in hewn stone and measured 100 metres in length, 26 metres in breadth and 10 metres in height. Urban dedicated his new church to the first bishops of the diocese - Dyfrig, Teilo and Oudoceus, as well as St. Peter, thus uniting the old Celtic traditions with the new Latin sentiments, introduced by the Normans.

Having demolished the old church, Urban moved the tomb of St. Dyfrig into the new building and placed it on the right hand side of the altar. The effigy of the saint, which can be seen today, was carved in the fourteenth century and it was moved, yet again in 1857, to its present position in the north aisle of the presbytery and choir.

The tomb of St Dyfrig in the north aisle of the presbytery and choir

The tomb of St Teilo on the south side of the presbytery

At one time the tomb of St Dyfrig was considered so holy that it was customary to take the most solemn oaths upon it. The effigy is of Early Decorated workmanship and it is carved to show a bishop in Mass vestments and wearing a mitre.

St Teilo had also been buried in the old church and Urban had his remains moved into the new building and deposited in a tomb on the south side of the presbytery, where it attracted generation after generation of pilgrims. The sick were brought before it and on this spot solemn compacts were concluded or ratified as late as the seventeenth century. Today, the supposed sepulchre of St Teilo is still to be seen on the south side of the choir and the effigy is of 14th century period.

Bishop Urban certainly led a busy life for not only was he a builder and an ecclesiastical reformer but a traveller as well. His name is found among those of the bishops attending the church councils of Rheims in 1119 and of Westminster in 1125 and 1127. He also negotiated an agreement with Henry I's famous son, Robert, Earl of Gloucester, which ensured the stability of his bishopric and a steady revenue.

However, it was another matter to establish the definite territorial limits of his see, for there were boundary disputes with both St David's and Hereford. During his long episcopate, Urban endeavoured to establish a claim to ecclesiastical jurisdiction over an area extending from the Wye to the Tywi, and he tried to provide an historical basis for his territorial claims through the compilation of the *Liber Landavensis* (Book of Llandaff). He claimed that the See of Llandaff had once been an Archbishopric, and it is significant that Geoffrey of Monmouth supported his claim in his *Historia* by describing St Dyfrig as Archbishop of Caerleon.

Urban fought hard for what he conceived to be his rights and those of his see, and when he failed to obtain support from the English bishops, who were no doubt somewhat indifferent to the matter, he decided to take his case to Rome. He visited the sacred city in 1128 and 1129. Fresh disputes broke out and in 1130 he once more made his way to Italy to plead the claim of Llandaff to include the district of Archenfield within its territory. This was his final journey and he died at Pisa, in his 57th year, whilst on his way to Rome to visit Pope Honorius II.

The position of bishop of Llandaff was then left vacant for six years before Uchtryd was appointed to fill the position, having been archdeacon since 1126. He was looked upon with great disfavour by the stricter churchmen and was later branded by Giraldus Cambrensis as a man who led a scandalous life; but in fact he was a Celtic bishop, uninfluenced by the dictates of the Roman Church on the celibacy of the clergy, and had married. His daughter Angharad, by her union with Iorwerth ap Owain ap

Caradog of Caerleon-upon-Usk, had allied him with the great Welsh families of Gwent. Above all, he was a vigorous defender of his See.

A nephew of Uchtryd was Galfrid ap Arthur whose assumed name was Geoffrey of Monmouth. He was denominated Geoffrey of Monmouth, from his having been born in that place and he perhaps received his education at the Benedictine monastery of Monmouth.

The *Liber Landavensis* (Book of Llandaff),[2] also called Teilo's Book, is a chronicle dealing with the early history of the diocese of Llandaff. It was written between 1120 and 1140 and goes back about 500 years. It contains the lives of some of the early occupants of the See, records of Celtic saints, charters, legends, etc. In particular it contains a *Life of St Teilo*, in which it is stated that the author of the '*Life*' was Galfrid, brother of Urban, Bishop of Llandaff. It is double the length of the *Life of St Dubricius*, and its writer has done his best to set forth the excellences of his hero, and had adorned his composition with all the ornaments and devices of rhetoric which were at his command.

The *Liber Landavensis* also bears testimony to the brutal savagery prevalent in the sixth and subsequent centuries, and shows how the Church endeavoured to modify these evils, which it could not completely stop. Princes who were feuding with one another would come to Llandaff and in the presence of the bishop, before the altar with the relics of saints before them, would swear that there should be firm peace kept between them. King Morcant (Morgan) and his Uncle Frioc chose Llanilltyd Fawr as the place they would take this oath, and there in the church of this celebrated monastery, in the presence of Bishop Oudoceus and the three great abbots of the diocese, Concen, Sulgen and Congen, they swore to end their quarrel. Yet for all this, Morcant treacherously slew Frioc. The record states that Morcant was excommunicated but afterwards repented of his crimes and gave land to the See and obtained absolution.

Guidnerth, King of Gwent, quarrelled with his brother over matters concerning the kingdom and slew him. Bishop Oudoceus placed him under a sentence of three years, at the end of which he was sent as a penance on a pilgrimage to Dol in Brittany.

Merthyr Mawr (see page 27) came into possession of the church of Llandaff through a treacherous murder perpetrated by Hywel, son of Rhys. A man named Gwallwn had risen against Hywel, seeking to take from him by violence the land of Antivei. Bishop Cerenhir mediated between them, and they swore to keep the peace on the holy Gospels at the altar of Dubricius, Teilo and Oudoceus at Llandaff, but afterwards Hywel broke his oath and murdered Gwallwn, for which he was excommunicated for nearly a whole year. At last he sought pardon 'with naked feet and many fears', and as a penance he gave to the church Merthyr Buceil and Merthyr Mawr, with other adjacent lands.

During the Celtic period the Church of Llandaff received large endowments, and the records of the *Book of Llandaff*, as also those of the *Life of St Catwg*, preserve details of such transactions, whereby a gift of land was made to the Church. A landowner would deliver the gift, if the ceremony was performed out of doors, by placing the deed or gift on the hand of the bishop or abbot. Pepiau did this when he gave Maenour Garth-benni to Dubricius, and also Bronnoguid did likewise with his three sons when they gave land to Abbot Conige of Nant Carvan. If, however, the ceremony was performed in a church, the donor made his gift at the altar, 'placing his hand upon the four Gospels' in presence of the bishop or abbot and witnesses.

Tithes are not mentioned in the *Book of Llandaff* until the time of the Normans. In the *Life of St Catwg*, however, a rule is given that whosoever shall pay tithes must divide them into three parts and give one to the Confessor, one to the altar, and one to those who pray for him.

These ancient records tell of times when money was little used and the cow was the standard of value. A sixth-century landowner buys a villa 'for a sword whose hilt was gilded and valued at the price of twenty-five cows.' He gives a friend a horse of the value of four cows and another a sword of the value of four cows. A foster-son of King Morcant gives a clergyman his gilded sword Hipiclaur. It would appear that it was a very precious sword, for it was valued at seventy cows. In the time of Bishop Berthguin, a benefactor of the See of Llandaff bought an uncia of land for twenty-four cows, an Englishwoman, a valuable sword and a powerful horse.

'A very good horse,' we find, was worth as much as twelve cows, but an ordinary one was only worth three or four; a hawk used in hunting might be worth twelve cows, but an inferior hawk was worth six, and a useful dog which killed birds with the hawk was worth only three. As time goes by, values are given in ounces of silver as well as in cows, and finally less simple times came when cows are no longer mentioned.

The original author did not finish his work for besides blank pages at the end, he left gaps here and there, which have been filled in by later hands, without any regard to chronological sequence. Later scribes have contributed a few important details and the last entry is by Bishop Field, who added his name to the list of bishops in 1619.

Although it was not completed before the early part of the twelfth century, the *Book of Llandaff* makes a brave show of presenting the early history of the See. However, much of it was written with the purpose of authenticating the claim of Llandaff to churches and lands situated outside the limits of the diocese in St David's and Hereford.

The compiler of the *Book of Llandaff* made a serious error when he took the incorrect year of 612 from the *Annales Cambriae* for the death of St Dyfrig (Dubricius), and as a result there is an error of 100 years which has caused much confusion.

St Dyfrig was born c.450 and consecrated bishop by St Garmon (Germanus), Bishop of Man, who died in 474. He ordained St Samson deacon and priest and later consecrated him bishop at Llanilltyd Fawr on the Festival of St Peter's Chair on 22 February 521. He died and was buried on Bardsey Island on 14 November 546. He can be positively dated by the historical record of St Samson's consecration as bishop by St Dyfrig on 22 February 521.

Furthermore, St Samson can be positively dated for he attended the third Council of Paris in 557, where he signed his name 'Samson peccator episcopus' among the bishops. He died in 565.

Of vital interest is a genealogy contained in the *Book of Llandaff* providing the pedigree of the kings of Gwent and Erging. It is significant that Sir William Dugdale, in his Monasticon Anglicanum (vol.III, p. 190) observed that, in one instance in the grant of Lann Cinmarch, near Chepstow, occurs the name ARTHUR, so spelled, as the king of Gwent, son of Mouric, king of Morgannwg, and father of Morcant. Elsewhere in the manuscript, he is uniformly called Athruis and is contemporary with Comergwynus (Comereg), Bishop of Erging.

Sir John Whitaker, in his *History of Manchester*, vol II (1775), utilized the registers of donations to Llandaff Church in the days of the first three bishops - Saints Dyfrig, Teilo, and Oudoceus - and writes: 'Arthur was the Arth-uir, great man or sovereign of the proper Silures, and therefore the denominated king of Gwent, the Venta Silurum of the Romans and the British metropolis of the nation.'

The original manuscript of the *Book of Llandaff* was in the keeping of the Church of Llandaff until shortly before 1655, at which time, William Dugdale, in the first volume of his *Monasticon Anglicanum* refers to it as being in the possession of John Seldon the antiquary. It was in Seldon's library at his death in 1655 and was then transferred with his collection to the 'publique library at Oxford.' In 1659 John Vaughan of Trawscoed obtained the loan of it for Robert Vaughan of Hengwrt, who made a transcript of it. He sent the original to Robert Vaughan, who did not send it back to the Bodleian Library. On his death it passed into the hands of Robert Davies of Llanerch, near Denbigh. He died in 1710 and from him it passed to his descendants. His great-grandson John Davies died in 1785 without issue and his Welsh estates were divided between his two sisters. The *Book of Llandaff* (with other manuscripts) was then taken to Gwysaney and remained there until it was acquired by the National Library of Wales.

Ten

GEOFFREY OF MONMOUTH AND THE
HISTORIA REGUM BRITANNIAE

Geoffrey of Monmouth was either born in that town or brought up in the priory, and it would seem that he was the son of a Breton family who settled there after the Norman Conquest. From 1075, Monmouth was held by the Bretons, first by Gwethenoc (Wihenoc), who was a son of the nobleman Caradoc of La Boussac, an estate a few miles east of Dol. His wife was probably the daughter of Juthael, Archbishop of Dol from 1039 to 1076, and his nephew was William Fitz Baderon,[1] who held the custody of Monmouth Castle at the time of the Domesday Survey. Both Gwethenoc and Fitz Baderon were notable benefactors to the Breton abbey of St Florent de Saumur.

At this time, monastic life in Monmouth was centred around the ancient church of St. Cadoc, who was a saint already known to the Breton followers of Gwethenoc, for several churches had been founded by him in Brittany as well as in Wales.

Soon after 1075, the chapel at Monmouth Castle was dedicated by Herewald, Bishop of Llandaff, in the presence of Caradog ap Gruffydd, the local Welsh prince. By 1083, Gwethenoc had established a priory in Monmouth. He was a close friend of William of Dol, abbot of the Breton monastery of St. Florent de Saumur, who no doubt inspired him to bring Breton monks to his new priory at Monmouth. After handing over the lordship of Monmouth to his nephew William Fitz Baderon, Gwethenoc retired to the abbey of St Florent de Saumur and became a monk.

Geoffrey of Monmouth was born in about 1090, when William Fitz Baderon was lord of Monmouth, a position he held for no less than forty years. We are told by Caradoc of Llancarfan, who was a contemporary of Geoffrey, that 'Galfrai was the son of Arthur, the domestic chaplain of William ap Robert' (William, Earl of Gloucester). He also tells us that Galfrai 'was the foster son of Uchtryd, Archdeacon of Llandaff, being his brother's son; an archdeanery was bestowed on him on account of his learning. He was the instructor of many nobles.'

We can assume from this statement that Geoffrey of Monmouth was the son of Arthur, the private priest to William, Earl of Gloucester, the son of Robert Consul, who became Geoffrey's patron, and that he was brought up as the foster-son of Uchtryd, his paternal uncle, who was then Archdeacon of Monmouth and later Bishop of Llandaff.

'Geoffrey's Window', overlooking Priory Street in Monmouth, was installed in this remnant of the Benedictine priory about three centuries after his time, but it was once thought that he used the room behind it as a study and wrote his famous book there!

Geoffrey was most likely born in Monmouth and educated at the priory which explains his connection with that town.[2] He then came to live at Llandaff and was perhaps looked after by his uncle Uchtryd on the death of his father.

It is not known exactly when Geoffrey moved to Oxford, but he certainly lived there from 1129 to 1151, for his signature appears in the list of witnesses appended to six different twelfth-century charters dealing with religious foundations in the Oxford area during that period. It is interesting that in two of these charters Walter, Archdeacon of Oxford, appears as co-signatory and in three others the statement witnessed is a grant or agreement made by Walter himself. It is possible that Geoffrey was one of the six canons of St. George's College of secular canons while his friend Walter was the provost.

The first signature of Geoffrey in 1129 was on the foundation charter of Osney Abbey which Walter the Archdeacon also signed. Geoffrey next witnessed a charter in January 1139 in connection with the dedication of Godstow Abbey and he signed as 'mag. Galf Arturus'. In 1150 he signed as 'magistro Galfrido Artour'[3] and in 1151, a few months after Walter's death, as 'Gaufridus episcopus Sancti Asaphi.' Later that year, Geoffrey signed a charter of Robert de Chesney, Bishop of Lincoln, as 'Gaufridus electus Sancti Asaphi.'

During Geoffrey's long residence in Oxford he wrote three works which have come down to us today. These were his *Historia Regum Brittaniae*, the *Prophetiae Merlini*, which he later incorporated into it; and the *Vita Merlini*, which first appeared in about 1151 as a very involved Latin poem of over 1,500 lines, purporting to represent the life and prophecies of Merlin. This work was dedicated to Robert de Chesney, one of Geoffrey's Oxford associates.

Geoffrey's source material

In the first chapter of Geoffrey's *Historia Regum Brittaniae*[4] he tells us that, 'Walter, Archdeacon of Oxford, a man learned in foreign histories, offered me a very ancient book in the Brittanic tongue, which in a continued regular story and elegant style related the actions of all the famous Britons down to Cadwallader. At his request, therefore, I undertook the translation of that book into Latin.'

He again refers to this mysterious source book at the end of his history when he comments:-

> I leave the history of the later kings of Wales to Caradoc of Llancarfan, my contemporary, as I do also the kings of the Saxons to William of Malmesbury and Henry of Huntingdon, but I advise them to be silent concerning the kings of the Britons, since they do not have that book written in the Brittanic tongue, which Walter, Archdeacon of Oxford, brought out of Britannia.

Geoffrey dedicated his *Historia* to Henry I's natural son, Robert, Earl of Gloucester, and called him 'a second Henry', which is some indication of the admiration that he had for the king who died before he had completed the book. He wrote: 'Let it be held to be thine offspring, as thou thyself art an offspring of the illustrious Henry, king of the English.' In a later copy of his work the dedication was changed to 'Stephen, King of England, nephew of the illustrious Henry, king of the English.'

It becomes obvious that Geoffrey made use of all the material that he could lay his hands on and he incorporated into his work many of the traditions which were in vogue at that time. He certainly consulted the *De Mirabilibus Britanniae* which constitutes the seventh section of Nennius's *Historia Brittonum*, for it contains certain wonders, which Geoffrey has adroitly absorbed into different parts of his work. The composition of the *Liber Landavensis* (Book of Llandaff) is attributed to a period when Geoffrey was in residence at Llandaff, and significantly the text in places very much reminds one of the *Historia Regum Britanniae*. A relevant example is Geoffrey's reference to St. Teilo 'as an illustrious priest of Llandaff,' and comments that he was St. Samson's successor as archbishop of Dol in Brittany. It can hardly be a coincidence that both Geoffrey of Monmouth and the *Liber Landavensis* associate St. Teilo with both Llandaff and Dol. Thus, it is highly probable that Geoffrey derived his knowledge of St. Samson from the 'life' in the *Liber Landavensis*. Another example of the similarities between these two works is that in both books St. Dubricius is described as an archbishop.

The *Liber Landavensis* gives an account of the lives and fortunes of the Bishops of Llandaff over a period of nearly five hundred years, ending in about 1132. The main body of the book consists of the 'lives' of the first three bishops of Llandaff, Dubricius, Teilo and Oudoceus; charters attributed to the lifetime of each of these saints, and charters and other records covering all the bishops of Llandaff from the age of the saints to the consecration of bishop Urban in 1107.

The natural conclusion is that Geoffrey knew the *Liber Landavensis* or at least material from which it was composed. Since Geoffrey's *Historia* was certainly completed by 1139, we can probably date the later stages in the compilation of the *Book of Llandaff* as 1134-38; but we must allow for the possibility that what Geoffrey used was not the final article.

The *Liber Landavensis* preceded Geoffrey of Monmouth's *Historia* and is wholly free from the legends about King Arthur, with which a few years later it would have been filled. The more one examines the subject the more one finds reason for attributing the composition of the *Liber Landavensis* to the time of Geoffrey of Monmouth's residence at Llandaff.[5]

Gwenogvryn Evans in his edition of the *Liber Landavensis* states that in his opinion Geoffrey is the author of a considerable part, if not most, of that work, and he comments that there is in particular a similarity in the style and language of the *Historia Regum Brittaniae* with those of the *Life of St. Teilo*.[6]

'The text bears throughout the impress of so marked an individuality that I am convinced that it is the work of one man, whom I suspect to be no other than Geoffrey of Monmouth.'

J. Gwenogvryn Evans

According to the Gwentian Brut, Gruffydd ap Arthur was brought up as a foster son by his paternal uncle Uchtryd, Archdeacon of Llandaff. The Brut also tells us that towards 1140 an archdeaconry was conferred upon Geoffrey in the church of St. Teilo, where he was the instructor of many scholars and chieftains. In that same year his uncle Uchtryd was made Bishop of Llandaff.

Uchtryd served as Bishop of Llandaff from 1139 to his death in 1148, and Caradoc of Llancarfan, who was a contemporary of Geoffrey of Monmouth and must surely have had his facts right, tells us that Geoffrey was appointed Bishop of Llandaff [7] in 1152, but died at mass in the cathedral before being consecrated.

It has been stated that early in 1151, just before the death of Walter, Archdeacon of Oxford, Geoffrey was elected Bishop of St Asaph and was consecrated by Archbishop Theobald in February 1152. However, it is possible that Geoffrey of Monmouth has been confused with Gruffydd ab Arthur, Archdeacon of Monmouth, also called Godfrey, who was consecrated Bishop of St Asaph on 24 February 1152 and Abbot of Abingdon in 1165, which he held with the bishopric until 11 July, 1175, when in a general council at London his clergy complained that he was constantly absenting himself from his diocese, and he was compelled to resign his bishopric. The real Geoffrey of Monmouth 'Galfrai ap Arthur,' was elected bishop of Llandaff in 1152, and died in the same year.

Geoffrey of Monmouth as the nephew and adopted son of Uchtryd,[8] Bishop of Llandaff, may well have participated in the compilation of the *Book of Llandaff* in its **original form** under his uncle's patronage. If this was the case then the sequence of events in Geoffrey's life would have been as follows:-

c1090	Born at Monmouth and educated at the priory.
c1105	Living at Llandaff under the care of his uncle Uchtryd.
c1129-1139	At Oxford
c1136-8	*Historia Regum Britanniae* published
1147	Death of Geoffrey's patron, Robert, Earl of Gloucester
1148	Death of Uchtryd, Bishop of Llandaff
1153	Geoffrey is present as a witness to the final agreement between Stephen and Henry, which confirmed Henry's succession in December. 1153.
1155	Death of Geoffrey at Llandaff as recorded in the *Brut y Tywysogion*

An examination of Geoffrey's *Historia Regum Britanniae*

Compiled as an epic in prose, Geoffrey's *Historia* is divided into twelve books, and Geoffrey begins by telling the story of the ancient British race from the days of Brutus to the death of Cadwaladr, but a considerable part of the book is devoted to an account of the life and deeds of King Arthur, and it is in this work that the main traditions of the Arthurian epic are established for the first time. The *Historia* was started in about 1130 and the first version completed shortly after the death of Henry I in December 1135. It was certainly compiled before 1139, for in that year Henry, Archdeacon of Huntingdon, accompanied Theobald, the new Archbishop of Canterbury, on a journey to Rome, where Theobald was going to receive the pallium from the Pope. On the way they stayed for a brief time at the Abbey of Bec, in Normandy. In the Abbey library, Robert of Torigny (afterwards Abbot of Mont St Michel) showed Henry 'a great book' - *libergrandis* - by one 'Gaufridus Arturis', containing a history of the early kings of Britain.

In a letter, subsequently written to one Warinus (pub. in Rolls Series, Chronicles of Stephen iv, p.65), Henry gives a short abstract of the work. This abstract, in one or two passages, differs somewhat from the extant texts of the History, which suggests that it may have been an early draft of Geoffrey's final work. It is interesting that a different version of Arthur's final battle is given in Henry's abstract. Here Arthur is described as engaging in a hand-to-hand combat with Modred, in which he himself is so sorely wounded that he fell, 'although the Britons deny his death, and still continue to look for his return. '

William of Malmesbury had mentioned Arthur in his writings some years before Geoffrey even began his *Historia*. William commented on this man 'about whom the idle tales of the Britons rave.' So we may assume that Geoffrey, either himself or through others, heard these tales from the native Welsh, and, with a literary instinct for romance and drama, decided to include them in his narrative, but with many embellishments. He no doubt manipulated his material to make the story of King Arthur more attractive to his Norman masters and also to make it appeal to the romantic tastes of his less exalted readers.

Geoffrey claimed that his source material came from a book 'written in the Britannic tongue, which Walter, Archdeacon of Oxford, brought out of Britannia.' This could mean that it was written in either Welsh or Breton and Geoffrey claims that his own work is a direct translation into Latin from his source book. However, there is no doubt that he gathered together several old manuscripts which covered the history of the earliest days of the Cymry and set out to re-write them in one complete work.

It would seem that Geoffrey was confused by his muddled source material, but it is open to conjecture whether it was by accident or design that he weaved a series of major errors into his entangled story. It is our opinion that by careful analysis one can still get at some of the truth of the matter and straighten out certain aspects of his statements.

Geoffrey has been called a fabricator and a liar but to his credit the most important point to remember is that but for his *Historia Regum Britanniae* the world might have completely forgotten about King Arthur. Following the publication of this work, in less than half a century, the romances of King Arthur had gained an extraordinary popularity on the Continent. For six centuries after it was written, the *Historia* was accepted by the majority of readers as accurate history, while the medieval poets found in its contents a wealth of material which they used as inspiration for writing beautiful and fascinating tales and verses relating to the deeds of King Arthur.

While Geoffrey had his followers there were also a number of contemporary writers who not only made fun of him but vigorously denounced him as a fabricator, who not merely collected folk tales, but freely invented stories under the guise of Merlin.

William of Newburgh, a Yorkshire monk, speaks of Geoffrey as 'a saucy and shameless liar,' and, a few years later , Giraldus Cambrensis makes a particularly sarcastic comment about Geoffrey's *Historia*. He speaks of a Welshman at Caerleon, named Melerius, who 'having always an extraordinary familiarity with evil spirits, by seeing them, knowing them, talking with them, and calling each by his proper name, was enabled through their assistance to foretell future events....He knew when anyone speaks falsely in his presence, for he saw the devil as it were leaping and exulting on the tongue of the liar...If the evil spirits oppressed him too much, the Gospel of St. John was placed on his bosom, when, like birds, they immediately vanished; but when that book was removed, and the History of the Britons by Geoffrey Arthur was substituted in its place, they instantly reappeared in greater numbers, and remained a longer time than usual on his body and on the book.'

> 'If Geoffrey of Monmouth's historical sources were thin on verifiable fact, they were generous on passion for the old, lost Britain. And that is the story of which Arthur is the hero.'
>
> Graham Fife 1990
> *Arthur the King*

Sorting out Geoffrey's Muddle

'After the death of Utherpendragon, the leaders of the Britons assembled from their provinces in the town of Silchester and there suggested to Dubricius, the Archbishop of the City of the Legions, that as their King he should crown Arthur, the son of Uther.'

It would appear that in stating that Arthur was the son of Uther, Geoffrey misinterpreted a passage in Nennius's *Historia Brittonum* . The term applied to Arthur by Nennius was 'mab uter' ('the terrible son') which did not mean that he was the son of Uther, but perhaps that he was cruel from his childhood.

We are told by Geoffrey that Uther Pendragon fell in love with Igerna, the wife of Gorlais, Duke of Cornwall, while they were guests at his court. Gorlais left the court in a rage and refused Uther's command to return. Uther then invaded Cornwall, and Gorlois sent Igerna away to Tintagel Castle for safety. Uther managed to gain entry to the castle and made love to Igerna with the result that Arthur was conceived.

If we substitute Gwawr for Eigyr (Igerna), Meurig for Uther Pendragon and Glywys for Gorlois then the following hypothesis seems plausible as an explanation for what really took place:-

Meurig ap Tewdric (Uther Pendragon) fell in love with Gwawr (the daughter of Ceredig ap Cunedda Wledig), the wife of King Glywys, while they were guests at his court. Glywys left the court in a rage and refused Meurig's command to return. Meurig invaded Glywysing and Glywys sent Gwawr to Caput Bovium (Boverton) for safety. Meurig managed to gain entry to Glywys's court and made love to Gwawr. Thus, Arthmael (Athrwys/Arthur) was conceived.

Pedigree of Glywys contained in the 'Life of St Cadoc'

Macsen Wledig
Owain
Nor
Solor*
Glywys

*in the Jesus College MS20 Glywys's father is called Filur.

A late pedigree of Gwrlais ascribed to Iolo Goch (c. 1320 -1398)

Macsen Wledig
Owain
Mor
Selor
Gerdan
Pandwlff
Sartogys
Gwrlais

Whoever originally constructed the pedigree of Gwrlais seems to have known that Glywys was known as Glywys Cernyw, and that there were close connections between Glywysing and Cornwall. It can be shown that Glywys and Gwrlais belonged to the lineage of Solor ap Nor, and they were in fact contemporaries. Therefore, there are too many generations in Iolo Goch's pedigree of Gwrlais.

The wife of Glywys of Glwysing and mother of Gwynllyw was Gwawr ferch Ceredig ap Cunedda Wledig while the wife of Gwrlais was Eigr ferch Gwen ferch Cunedda Wledig. It can thus be shown that both Glywys and Gwrlais married grand-daughters of Cunedda Wledig.

Evidence for the existence of Glywys and Arthmael

St Glywys Cernyw, the grandson of King Glywys of Glywysing, before his death is said to have entered the 'desert' (gone into retirement?) at Clivis in Newton Nottage, Glamorgan ; formerly Merthyr Glywys. This place appears as Merthir Gliuis in the *Book of Llandaff*. The site of the martyrium is unknown, but the cult of St Glywys is recorded later in the immediate locality of Merthyr Mawr.

A stone was erected at Merthyr Mawr to Conbelan for the soul of St Glywys and at Ogmore (Aberogwr), another sixth-century monument records the gift of a field by Arthmail to God and to Glywys and to Nertat and to Fili the Bishop.

The Arthmael Stone at Ogmore Castle

119

Geoffrey of Monmouth's fictitious King List

Geoffrey appears to have extracted the names for a succession of kings from the Charters of Llandaff, but he placed them in chronologically impossible positions. He needed the names of the kings who succeeded Arthur and made use of the kings so bitterly criticised by Gildas, who in fact reigned simultaneously in Britain, but arranged them so that they reigned one after the other.

Brut y Brenhinedd	Latin equivalents in Geoffrey's 'Historia'
51. Morudd ap Dan	Morvidus son of Danius
52. Gorbonion ap Morudd	Gorbonianus son of Morvidus
53. Arthal ap Morudd	Arthgallo son of Morvidus
54. Elidir War ap Morudd	Elidurus Pius son of Morvidus
55. **Arthal ap Morudd**	**Arthgallo son of Morvidus**
56. Rhys ap Gorbonian	Regin son of Gorbonianus
57. **Margan ap Arthal**	**Marganus son of Arthgallo**
58. Einion ap Arthal	Ennianus son of Arthgallo
59. Idwal ap Owain	Iduallo son of Iugenius
60. Rhun ap Peredeur	Runo son of Peredurus

Looking at kings 55 and 57 one can detect Arthur in the form of Arthgallo with his son Morgan as Marganus eventually succeeding him. Elsewhere in Geoffrey's list of kings, Arthmael appears as the fifty-fifth king of Britain after Brutus.

(56) Rhys ap Ithel, King of Glywysing is mentioned in the *Book of Llandaff*. (58) Einion is mentioned in the *Life of St Oudoceus* as Einion, King of Glywysing, who gave land on the banks of the River Wye, near the brook Caletan (now Llandogo) to St Oudoceus. (59) Idwal is a king mentioned in the *Book of Llandaff* as a contemporary of Bishop Berthwyn and King Morgan ap Athrwys. He is probably the same Idwallon in the time of Bishop Oudoceus and King Morgan ap Athrwys. In this way Geoffrey of Monmouth took the names of some of the genuine kings of Glywysing and compiled his own fictitious king list.

It is interesting to compare names given in the *Brut y Brehinedd* (the Welsh version of Geoffrey's *Historia Regum Britanniae*) with the equivalent names in the *Book of Llandaff*.

Brut y Brenhinedd	Book of Llandaff
Arthal ap Morudd	Athrwys ap Meurig
Rhys ap Gorbonion	Rhys ap Ithel ap Morgan
Margan ap Arthal	Morgan ap Athrwys
Einion ap Arthal	Einion
Idwal ap Owain	Idwallon

It is significant that both the *Brut y Brenhinedd* and the *Historia Regum Britanniae* name Arthmael as the fifty-fifth king of Britain after Brutus. Arthal (Arthgallo), the father of Margan (Marganus), became the fifty-fifth king of Britain and thirty-second from Brutus, when he ascended the throne for the second time. Thus, we have Arthmael as the fifty-fifth king of Britain. He was eventually succeeded by his son Margan (Morgan). We may compare Arthgallo with Arthegal, who appears in Edmund Spenser's *The Faerie Queene*. He was the uterine brother of Prince Arthur and he married Britomart, a warrior maiden who was the daughter of Arthur's foe, Ryence, king of Deheubarth. She became the progenitress of a line of kings which superseded both the Saxons and the Normans - the Tudors. Arthegal ruled Guerinus, so he may be identical to Artgualchar, Earl of Guerensis, who attended the plenary court held by Arthur in the City of the Legions in Geoffrey's *Historia*.

We may also compare Geoffrey's King Margan ap Maglawn, who was slain at Maes Mawr (now Maes Margan) and was buried in a place where the monastery of Margan (Margam) now stands, with Mar ap Glywys, who received Margan (now Margam) as his patrimony. There is a distinct possibility that the inscription on the so-called 'Paulinus' stone found at Merthyr Mawr should read Paulinus fili Mar and was erected in memory of Paul ap Mar ap Glywys.

Arthur's court at Caerleon upon Usk

Geoffrey gives a glowing account of the crowning of Arthur at Caerleon and the grand feast that took place there at Whitsun and it becomes obvious that he is drawing upon the events and politics of his own time to create a parallel between his story of Arthur and the Norman kings. It is relevant that in the time of William Rufus the Easter feast was held at Winchester, the Whitsun feast in London and the Christmas feast at Gloucester. Geoffrey's description of Arthur's coronation ceremony and the festivities that followed were no doubt an adaptation of the crowning of King Stephen at Lincoln, which Geoffrey may have witnessed.

When Geoffrey was describing Arthur's court at Caerleon-upon-Usk, he required more names for the list of guests than were provided in the Welsh Arthurian traditional tales, so to increase the number he selected more names at random from the Welsh genealogies.

Geoffrey made Dubricius Archbishop of Caerleon in order to enhance the dignity of Arthur's court, ignoring the fact that there were no archbishops in Britain during those times. He was no doubt aware of Bishop Urban's claim that Llandaff had been a former archbishopric and this gave him further cause to introduce a Caerleon archbishopric into his narrative.

The Coronation of King Arthur

'Since the plenary court was being held in his own diocese, Dubricius made ready to sing mass in celebration of the moment when the King should place the crown upon his head. As soon as the King was enrobed, he was conducted with due pomp to the church of the metropolitan see.'

Geoffrey of Monmouth
History of the Kings of Britain

122

The name of Guinevere

Geoffrey refers to Arthur's queen as Guanhumara and calls her the daughter of a Cornish nobleman. In the Welsh texts she is called Gwenhwyfar ('White Spirit') which Malory converts into Guinevere.

> 'She was descended from a noble Roman family and had been brought up in the household of Duke Cador. She was the most beautiful woman in the entire land.'
>
> Geoffrey of Monmouth
> *History of the Kings of Britain*

Arthur's Weapons

Geoffrey provides a description of Arthur arming himself with weapons that were all given names that he obviously extracted and adapted from the Mabinogion story of 'Culhwch and Olwen'. He wrote:-

> 'And Arthur himself, having donned a helmet of gold on which was engraven the figure of a dragon. And on his shoulders he placed the shield called Pridwen; upon it was a picture of the blessed Mary, mother of God, which kept him continually in remembrance of her. Then girding on Caliburn, his excellent sword forged in the island of Avallon, he graced his right hand with his lance, which was called Ron, and a hard and huge lance it was, well adopted for slaughter.'

In the *Mabinogion* story, Arthur's shield is called 'Wynebgwrthucher', his sword 'Caledfwlch' and his lance 'Rhongomynt'. The Celtic name for Arthur's sword was Latinized into Caliburn and the name of the lance just shortened to Ron.

Geoffrey obviously had a ear for classic poetry and generally softened the old British words, so as to adapt them to the language in which he was writing. The word Caled-fwlch (meaning 'hard-notch') had no doubt been first given treatment by the bards of Brittany, translated into French and then Latinized by Geoffrey. The sword is first called Excalibur (Cut Steel) in Walter Map's *The Death of King Arthur*. In later years both Sir Thomas Malory and Alfred Lord Tennyson call the sword Excalibur and such a name is now firmly established as an essential ingredient in the traditional story of Arthur.

The Battle of Mount Badon

Geoffrey places Arthur's greatest victory at Bath, which in Roman times was called Aquae Sulis, and he attributes the foundation of that place to King Bladud who made hot baths there dedicated to the goddess Minerva.

In Geoffrey's later poetry about Merlin he has him prophesying that 'the baths of Badon shall grow cold, and their salubrius waters engender death.' Geoffrey can only have been alluding to the waters of Bath and it is significant that the adjacent valley on the Avon was once known as Nant Badon. The Welsh word for a bath is 'baddon' pronounced 'bathon', so it seems quite probable that the hill, at whose base was situated the finest Roman bath in Britain, would be called by the Welsh: 'Mynydd yr Baddon,' and in Latin 'Mons Badonicus'.

Gildas, writing in the time of Arthur, tells us that Mons Badonicus was near the mouth of the Severn which is a reasonable description of the hill at Bath, but absolutely shuts out Badbury Rings, as some writers have suggested as the site of Mons Badonicus.

We are told by Geoffrey that the name of the leader of the enemy force is 'Cheldric,' who was in fact Cerdic, and that he was slain by Cador (Cadwy). Geoffrey seems to forget that Cheldric is killed here for later on he talks of him as an ally of Modred (Medraut).

Geoffrey extends Arthur's conquests across Western Europe. Ireland, Iceland and the Orkneys, Norway, Dacia and Gaul all come under his sway and he finally marches on Rome itself. So imposing a figure does Geoffrey's Arthur become that William of Newburgh complains that he has made the little finger of Arthur stouter than the back of Alexander the Great!

The Battle of Camlan

When dealing with Arthur's final battle, Geoffrey addresses his remarks to his patron Robert, Earl of Gloucester:

> 'About this particular matter, most noble Duke, Geoffrey prefers to say nothing. He will, however, in his own poor style and without wasting words, describe the battle which our famous king fought against his nephew. Once he had returned to Britain after his victory; for that he found in the British treatise already referred to. He heard it, too from Walter of Oxford, a man most learned in all branches of history.'

Geoffrey provides very few clues to the actual site of Arthur's thirteenth battle, yet West Country tradition has established it near the town of Camelford, which is conveniently just six miles from Tintagel. The name of the town is supposed to be derived from Camlan and the battlefield is said to be near Slaughter Bridge, which spans the river Camel, about half-a mile to the north.

There is no doubt that this place has been identified as the site of the Battle of Camlan because of the similarity of the names Camel and Camlan and because of its close proximity to Tintagel Castle.

Camelford is in fact the site of a battle fought in 721 when the Saxons were defeated by the Britons. Also, Egbert, King of Wessex, fought a battle here against the West Britons in 823. It is conceivable that memories of these battles have been handed down in a confused form, and owing to the similarity of the names Camlan and Camelford have been associated with Arthur.

It is relevant that Cornwall at the time of the Norman invasion was ruled by a Cornishman named Cador, who was Earl of Cornwall. William of Normandy deposed him but his son Cadoc was later re-instated. In 1104, Cadoc's daughter, Avice, married Reginald Fitz Henry, the son of Henry I, who inherited the earldom through his wife.

Contemporary Authors

The identity of Geoffrey of Monmouth's colleague, Walter, Archdeacon of Oxford, is confusing for there were in fact three archdeacons of Oxford in the twelfth century who were called Walter: (a) Walter Calenius[9] (or Walter of Walingford in Berkshire - the place of his birth), who was still living in 1151, (b) Walter de Countances, archdeacon in 1183 and (c) Walter Map or Mapes, archdeacon in 1197 and still living in 1208. The first and third of these Walters have often been confused by writers on this subject.[10]

It was the manuscript of Walter Calenius that Geoffrey of Monmouth translated, while Walter Mapes of Llancarfan was the celebrated writer whose *Histoire de Roy Artur* was the principal source for Sir Thomas Malory's *Le Morte d' Arthur*.

Geoffrey speaks of Archdeacon Walter (Calenius) as accomplished in the art of oratory and foreign history and states in his own *Historia* that his work is a translation of 'an old book written in the British language' supplied by Walter himself.

Undoubtedly, Walter Calenius is traceable as holding the post of archdeacon of Oxford from at least 1115 and possibly from 1104 to 1151, so it is understandable that he is often confused with Walter Mapes, who was archdeacon of Oxford at a later date.

Walter Mapes was of Welsh stock and called himself a marcher of Wales. He has been claimed as a native of Pembrokeshire and also Herefordshire, but he was in fact born at Llancarfan in the Vale of Glamorgan. At the time of the Conquest, this village had come into the possession of his father Blondel de Mapes, who arrived in Glamorgan with Robert Fitzhamon in 1088.

Blondel took possession of the lands of Gweirydd ap Seisyllt and married the Welshman's only living daughter. They had two sons, Herbert and Walter. Herbert, the eldest, died without heirs and, when Walter inherited the family estate, he built the village of Trewalter (Walterston) with a mansion for himself. He restored most of the land in his possession to the original owners and rebuilt the church of Llancarfan and it is likely that the existing chancel arch may well have been part of his work during the reign of Henry II.

After receiving an excellent education in Paris, he returned to England in 1162 and became attached to Henry II's court, holding a position as clerk of the king's household. He was with the king at Anjou in 1183. In 1197 he was made archdeacon of Oxford, and in 1199 and 1203 was an unsuccessful candidate for the Sees of Hereford and St David's respectively. According to Giraldus Cambrensis, Walter Mapes was a friend of Henry II who much admired him for his learning and courtliness.

Throughout his life he seems to have taken an interest in Welsh folklore and was himself a prolific writer. He has been credited with the original Latin versions of the Arthurian legends *Lancelot, Queste del Saint Graal* and *Mort Artu* . He wrote the Romance of the Quest of the Holy Grail in 1170 and thus introduced the heroes of romance, Lancelot, Owain, Gawain, Caradoc, Galahad and Percival. He conceived the character of the pure and stainless knight Sir Galahad, assigning to him the worthiest position in the Arthurian list of knights. It is possible that he based this character on the immaculate saint-knight Catwg, the founder of Llancarfan Church. Walter Mapes's story of the quest for the Grail (a Christianised rendering of a Celtic myth) was a Latin translation of an original Welsh prose under the title *Y Seint Greal* attributed to Bledri ap Cydifor (Bledri Latimer).[11]

William of Malmesbury was born in about 1090 in Somerset and he became a monk in Malmesbury Abbey, which today is still famous for its library of beautiful medieval manuscripts. He later became the abbey librarian and this position obviously gave him access to some useful sources. It is of interest that he mentions King Arthur in his *Historia Regum Anglorum* (History of the English Kings), which appeared in 1143, about four years after the publication of Geoffrey of Monmouth's *Historia Regum Brittaniae* During a visit to Glastonbury, the Benedictine monks had told William tales of a great hero who crushed the Saxons, and, having already heard the Welsh legends, William came to the conclusion that this famous hero must be Arthur. He wrote: 'This is that Arthur of whom modern Welsh fancy raves. Yet he plainly deserves to be remembered in genuine history; for he long preserved his dying country.'

Strongly critical of Geoffrey's *Historia* when it appeared, he later wrote:-

'Everything this man (Geoffrey) wrote about Arthur and his successors, or indeed about his processors, from Vortigern onwards, was made up, partly by himself, partly by others, either from an inordinate love of lying or for the sake of pleasing the Britons.'

In a passage of his *Gestum Regum* , William of Malmesbury speaks of Gwalchmai, or Walwen as he calls him, and says that:-

'Some years ago (1086) in the province of Wales called Ros there was discovered the tomb of Walwen, who being the son of Arthur's sister was not unworthy of him. He ruled in that part of Britain which is still called Walweitha: a very valiant knight, but he was driven from his kingdom by the brother and nephew of Hengist; first getting satisfaction, however, by inflicting great harm upon them. He shared deservedly in the glory of his uncle, because they deferred for many years the ruin of their falling country. The sepulchre of Arthur is nowhere known; whence ancient songs fable that he will come again. But the tomb of the other, as I have just said, was discovered in the time of King William upon the shore of the sea, fourteen feet in length; where it is said by some that he was wounded by enemies, and shipwrecked; by others, that he was killed by his countrymen at a public feast. The truth, therefore, remains in doubt, but neither of them was unworthy of his fame.'

Gwalchmai was the son of Gwyar and Anna (the sister of Arthur whose second husband was Gwyar). Gwalchmai is celebrated in the Triads as one of the 'three golden-tongued knights in the court of Arthur'. His name was latinized into Walganus and Walwyn, which in turn was changed by the French into Gawain. He was said to have been killed in the beginning of the civil war between his uncle Arthur and Medraut his half-brother. Castell Gwalchmai (Walwyn's Castle), Haverfordwest, Pembrokeshire, is said to have been named after Gwalchmai.

William of Malmesbury worked under the patronage of Robert, Earl of Gloucester, who was also the patron of Henry of Huntingdon and Caradoc of Llancarfan. Geoffrey of Monmouth became the fourth member of this exclusive set of writers, and he was no doubt motivated by his obvious feelings of patriotism and perhaps jealousy of the success of the chronicles of William of Malmesbury and Henry of Huntingdon.

Geoffrey's *Historia* certainly became a potent fount of literary inspiration. Geoffrey Gaimer, in 1154, immediately translated it into Anglo-Norman verse, to be followed by Maistre Wace, a native of Jersey, who was born in about 1100 and obtained the favour of the Norman kings. He was the author of two long romances in Norman-French, the famed *Le Roman de Brut* , or *Geste des Britons* , and the almost equally famous *Roman de Rou* . The former work was a free metrical rendering, published in Henry II's reign, of Geoffrey's *Historia* , completed some twenty years after Geoffrey's work was published but with some new material. The fact that Wace's version was written in Norman-French made the material of Geoffrey's *Historia* more accessible to those who were unable to speak Latin

Wace was educated in part in Paris and lived at Caen in Normandy, where he held a regular position at the court of Henry III. He dedicated his *Brut* to Eleanor of Aquitaine.

Of particular interest is the fact that he was the first writer who mentioned 'the table Round, of which the Bretons tell many a fable.' (*Le Roman de Brut*).

He commented that: 'Arthur made the Round Table, so reputed by the Britons, that when his fair fellowship sat to meat, their chairs should be high alike, their service equal and none before or after his comrade.'

The idea of a table was derived, most likely from a primitive Celtic source. Wace's additions evidently embody many popular traditions, which, as a West Countryman, he derived from Cymric sources.

In his poem *Roman de Rou*, Wace enumerates the Breton knights who were present with Duke William of Normandy when he landed at Hastings:-

> 'The duke had many men from many and various parts. Haimon, the viscount of Tours, a man of very great power who could bring much people. Alan Felgan came to the crossing and brought with him baronage from among the Bretons; and Fitz Bertram de Pelit and the Sire of Dinan came also; and Raol de Gael and many Bretons from many castles, and from about Brecheliant, concerning which the Bretons tell many fables.'

Wace tells in this poem how he is indebted to Breton 'conteurs' for many traditions about the forest of Brocéliande, about the prophet Merlin, and above all about King Arthur.

It is of interest that Wace also speaks in more detail than Geoffrey of Monmouth of the belief of Arthur's return and says that Arthur, 'was awaited of the Britons, for they say and deem he will return from whence he went and live again.' Furthermore, he remarked, 'Men have ever doubted, and - as I am persuaded - will always doubt whether he liveth or is dead.'

Then came Layamon, a priest of Worcestershire, living at the church of Emly, or Arley Regis, on the banks of the Severn, who at the close of the twelfth century produced the finest long poem written in the English language. He did not use Geoffrey's work directly, but wrote an amplified imitation of Wace's version of the Chronicle. Layamon's work contained just over double the number of lines in Wace's poem, the additions consisting chiefly of interpolated dramatic speeches. Anglo-Saxon and Celtic cultures are blended to make Arthur a national hero, who rallies his men against the Saxons.

With Artus (Arthur) the main figure and with courtly chivalry for the theme, these variations and expansions of the story exercised as powerful and enduring an influence upon the people of France and Germany as they had done, and continued to do, on the people of Britain.

Lifris,[12] who compiled the *Vita Cadoci* between 1073 and 1086, was the son of Bishop Herewald of Llandaff who died in 1104. This work preceded Geoffrey of Monmouth's *Historia* by two generations and it thus shows that Arthur was well known in south-east Wales as one of the prominent kings of his time.

This manuscript is of particular importance in the search for the identity of King Arthur for it mentions King Arthmael, who was ruling at exactly the same time as when Arthur is said to have been in power. The following extract from the *Vita Cadoci*[13] is of particular significance:

'The islands[14] became unsafe, owing to the pirates who infested the estuary of the Severn making upon them landing places, and Cadoc was obliged to look out for some other place of retreat. He found one on the banks of the River Neath, where on a certain day he found a white boar lying under a tree which his companion killed, secondly, bees entering a hollow tree; and thirdly a hawk's nest on top of the tree. He sent these gifts to King Arthmael, who thereupon made a grant of the spot (Cadoxton-juxta-Neath) to Cadoc.'

The very same *Life* records St Cadoc's dispute with King Arthur over the sanctuary granted to Arthur's enemy Ligessauc Lawhir. According to the genealogy of the kings of Morgannwg and Gwent contained in the *Book of Llandaff*, compiled between 1120 and 1140, the king reigning at this time was Athrwys ap Meurig ap Tewdrig. It therefore follows that Athrwys and Arthmael were one and the same person.

Apart from the Breton *Life of St Arthmael*, the only other *Life* of a Welsh saint to mention Arthmael is the *Vita Cadoci* (Life of St Cadoc) by Lifris. The version of this 'life,' which has survived in the Cotton Vespasian Axiv Ms., is a composite one with the additions of cartulary and administrative documents relating to the monastery of Llancarfan and it is significant that Lifris held the post of 'magister sancti Catoci de Lancarvan' (Master of St Cadoc's of Llancarfan). There is no doubt that Lifris had access to records of land grants and charters which no longer exist. In this way he knew of the existence of the grant of Cadoxton-juxta-Neath by King Arthmael to St Cadoc in about 530.

Caradoc of Llancarfan (fl.1135) was a son of Llefoed Wynebglawr (Llevoed with the flat face) and a domestic bard of Gruffydd ap Morgan ap Iestyn ap Gwrgan. He is best known from the reference to him at the end of Geoffrey's *Historia*, where he states that he leaves the task of dealing with the kings who ruled in Wales (after 689) 'to my contemporary Caradoc of Llancarfan.' Geoffrey at the same time gives leave to William of Malmesbury and Henry of Huntingdon to tell the story of the Saxon kings.

It is of interest that Caradoc wrote his *Vitae Gildas* (Life of St Gildas) at Llancarfan shortly before Geoffrey of Monmouth wrote his *Historia*, and thus gained his initial literary reputation. It seems doubtful that Caradoc ever did carry out the task suggested by Geoffrey. The suggestion that he did so in the earlier annals of *Brut y Twysogion* was not made until the 16th century and the evidence is strongly against such an assumption.

In one copy of Geoffrey's Historia he says 'The kings that were from that time forward in Wales, I shall commit to Caradog of Llancarfan, my fellow student, to write about...'

In a subsequent edition of the *Historia*, the commission given to Caradog is spoken of in the past tense: 'The princes who were afterwards ruling successively over Wales, I committed to Caradog of Llancarvan; he was my contemporary, and to him I left materials for writing that book.'

It would appear that Geoffrey first entrusted Caradog with the task of compiling the Chronicles of the Princes, before he had completed his work on the *Historia*. Caradog was now dead for Geoffrey states that he **was** my contemporary.[15]

Eleven

GERALD OF WALES

Gerald de Barri, otherwise known as Giraldus Cambrensis,[1] or Gerald of Wales, was one of the most colourful characters of medieval history. Born in 1147 at Manorbier Castle in West Wales, he had both Welsh and Norman blood in his veins. His mother, Angharad, was the grand-daughter of Rhys ap Tewdwr, and his father William de Barri was the son of Walter Fitz Other, Castellan of Windsor at the time of William the Conqueror.

As a youngster, Gerald de Barri[2] was sent to the Benedictine Abbey of St Peter in Gloucester, where his teacher was a monk called Haimo. He then returned to old Menevia (Dyfed) to receive further education under the direction of his uncle David Fitzgerald, the Bishop of St David's, with whom he remained until he was twenty years of age. He was then sent to complete his studies at the University of Paris, which at that time was the greatest centre of learning in Western Europe. Gerald was here from 1165 until 1174, during which time he worked hard, applying himself diligently to the study of canon and civil laws and the usual curriculum of a clerical education.

By this time, Gerald was twenty-seven years of age and he decided to return to Wales, for his main ambition was to follow in his uncle's footsteps and become Bishop of St David's. On 23 May 1176, the old man died and the Chapter elected Gerald to the vacant see, but the Archbishop of Canterbury and Henry II would not consent to his appointment. Peter de Leia, Prior of a Cluniac House at Wenlock in Shropshire, was chosen instead. This was the beginning of a bitter estrangement between Gerald and King Henry, and he never missed an opportunity of showing, within the limits of his discretion, his hatred for the English advisers.

Gerald then returned to Paris, where he lectured on Latin, logic and rhetoric until the summer of 1179, when he left for for England. He first visited Canterbury to complain to the Archbishop about the non-payment of tithes of wool and cheese in the diocese of St David's. He then travelled to St David's in West Wales, where, in the absence of the Bishop, he was appointed special commissioner for the diocese. When the Bishop, Peter de Leia, returned, Gerald resigned the position, but his good work did not go to waste, for having made a success of his role he was rewarded with the incumbency of three livings in Pembrokeshire and one in Herefordshire. He was also made Prebend of Mathry and a canon of St David's and Hereford.

Manorbier Castle stands on the edge of the sea in Pembrokeshire and is well known as the birthplace of Gerald of Wales in 1146, but he would have been born in an earlier castle on this site for the existing structure is the work of John de Barri, who commenced building it in 1275. Completed by his descendants fifty years later, it remained in the de Barri family down to the reign of Edward III. A baby girl born within its walls in 1928 was said to be the first baby born in the castle since Gerald and she was named Geraldine in his memory.

The tomb of John de Barri c.1324 can be seen
in the north transcept of Manorbier Church

It was about this time (1180) that Gerald turned his attention to the behaviour of the clergy, and on discovering that Jordan, the Archdeacon of Brecon, was keeping a concubine, he denounced him. Following Jordan's suspension, Gerald was appointed in his place. So by the age of 28 Gerald had obtained a good income and a position of some authority.

In 1183 Gerald visited his relations in Ireland and stayed there for about a year. On his return to England, he was asked to join the court of Henry II as one of his councillors. In particular, he acted as liaison officer between King Henry, Rhys ap Gruffydd and the other princes of Wales, many of whom were his relations. Gerald's next appointment came in 1185, when he was made Court Chaplain and adviser to Prince John, with whom he sailed that year to Ireland. It was during this journey that Gerald wrote his first two books: *Topographia Hibernia* (The Topography of Ireland) and *Expugnatio Hibernica* (The Conquest of Ireland). In the latter book Gerald provided a detailed description of Henry II, who was then in his fifties:-

'(He) had hair that was red in colour, grey eyes and a large round head. His eyes were bright, and in anger fierce and flecked with red. He had a fiery complexion, his voice was husky, his neck bent forward a little from his shoulders, and he had a broad chest and powerful arms. His body was fleshy, and he had a very large belly, naturally so, and not due to the effects of gluttony...In order that he might keep this defect of nature under control and mitigate its effects, and improve the shortcomings of his body by the sterling quality of his mind...he used to torment his body with an excessive amount of exercise.'

News arrived in 1187 of the capture of Jerusalem by Saladin and all of Western Europe was thrown into a state of great excitement. A crusade was declared to recover the Holy Land from the infidel Saladin, and Archbishop Baldwin[3] (appointed in 1184) was sent into Wales on a preaching tour. Gerald was chosen to accompany him for it was no doubt considered that, as the champion of the Welsh Church, his presence would be of considerable benefit in raising the profile of Baldwin in the eyes of the Welsh.

Ostensibly, Baldwin's main purpose was to recruit men for the recovery of Jerusalem, but at the same time he also wished to strengthen his superiority as Archbishop of Canterbury over the Welsh bishops by celebrating mass in each of the four cathedrals. They succeeded in obtaining three thousand volunteers and were well received wherever they went.

Llandew Church stands near the site of at Gerald's official residence as Archdeacon of Brecon

Part of the boundary walls of Llandew Palace and the remains of a Gothic arch can still be seen on the north side of the church. As Archdeacon of Brecon, this was the home of Gerald of Wales. Bishop Henry Gower of St David's rebuilt the palace in about 1340 and it was used by visiting bishops and other dignitaries of the diocese. By the time John Leland saw it in the 1530s, it was just an 'unseemly ruin'. A vicarage was built on the site of the palace in 1869, using stone from the old building.

Gerald was appointed by the Archbishop to be the official chronicler of the journey and his resultant book entitled *Itinerary through Wales* is a curious mixture of credulity and patient observation. As an ecclesiastic, he was able to appreciate the superstitions of the age, but as an author he endeavoured to place the bare truths before the reader for the benefit of future generations. As a result, the account of his party's long journey[4] around Wales is full of marvels, wonders and historical detail, providing a vivid picture of the principality in those times.

On Saturday 12 March, 1188, the party rode from Usk Castle to Caerleon-upon-Usk on their way to Newport, and Gerald, who was obviously familiar with the writings of Geoffrey of Monmouth, later wrote in his journal:

> 'Caerleon is beautifully situated on the banks of the River Usk. When the tide comes in, ships sail right up to the city. It is surrounded by woods and meadows. It was here that the Roman legates came to seek audience at the great Arthur's famous court. Here, too, Archbishop Dyfrig handed over his supreme function to David of Menevia, for the metropolitan see was moved from Caerleon in accordance with the prophecy of Merlin Ambrosius: 'Menevia shall be dressed in the pall of the City of the Legions.....'

Gerald's description of the splendours of Caerleon is very similar to that of Geoffrey of Monmouth: 'There are immense palaces, which, with the gilded gables of their roofs, once rivalled the magnificence of ancient Rome.' Fifty years earlier, Geoffrey had written: '...they had adorned the city with royal palaces, and by the gold-painted gables of its roofs it was a match for Rome.'

Gerald commented that little was known about Arthur's life for Gildas, the sixth-century British churchman, had thrown everything that he had written about Arthur into the sea.

During the tour, whilst at Nefyn on Llyn, in North Wales, Gerald found a manuscript which he claimed had been written by Myrddin Sylvester, who was also known as Myrddin Wyllt (Merlin the Wild) and said to be one of the Principal Bards of the Island of Britain.

In the spring of 1189, Gerald crossed to France with the Crusade, and on 10 May he was in Chinon, but shortly afterwards Henry II died and his successor, Richard I, was advised by Baldwin to send Gerald back to Wales to persuade the Welsh not to revolt. This was a task in which Gerald was eminently successful.

Queen Eleanor, the widow of Henry II, was ruling as Regent at this time and she used Gerald as her Welsh agent, which meant that for the next ten years he worked for the English court as a sort of Secretary of State for Wales, dealing with the administration of Welsh affairs.

In 1190, Gerald was elected to the vacant bishopric of Bangor, but he declined the position for his heart was set on St David's and he would accept no other diocese.[5] The following year the bishopric of Llandaff was also offered to Gerald on the death of William de Salso Marisco, but he declined that as well.

One of the most famous incidents in the life and writings of Giraldus Cambrensis was detailed in his two visits to Glastonbury in 1192 and 1193. Intrigued by the news that the grave and remains of King Arthur and Queen Guinevere had been discovered by the monks of Glastonbury Abbey, he could not resist making a visit to inspect the relics for himself. He seemed convinced that they were indeed genuine (see page 145) .

By 1194 Gerald had retired to Lincoln to live the life of a secluded scholar and he joined the theological school of William de Monte, but four years later he had another opportunity to become Bishop of St David's, on the death of Peter de Leia who had held the post since 1176. Among other hopeful candidates, Gerald was nominated as Bishop by the Chapter. They sent a deputation to London to consult the king and obtain his consent, but by this time Richard I was in Normandy and before the deputation arrived he was dead.

His successor, King John, accepted Gerald's nomination, but, as soon as he realised that the appointment was inconvenient, he refused officially to acknowledge and ratify the consent that he had given informally. Although Gerald was elected by the Chapter of St David's, his appointment was treated as void by Hubert Walter, the new Archbishop of Canterbury. He considered that to appoint a Welshman to the metropolitan see of Wales would be dangerous to the supremacy of the English. A church free from the control of an English primate would encourage opposition to the authority of an English king. It had thus become a fixed policy never to make a Welshman bishop.

Gerald was furious and he set off to Rome to make a personal appeal to Pope Innocent III. It was a long and tedious journey for a man of his age and he took with him what he considered to be his most valuable possessions - six of his own books as a present.[6] However, the Pope obviously did not take him very seriously and delayed giving him an audience. He no doubt admired Gerald's courage in standing against such powerful opponents, but he was too astute a pontiff to support his demands against the wishes of the powerful English king.

Gerald's statue in St David's Cathedral shows him with book and pen in hand, but with the longed-for mitre lying at his feet.

After a gap of four years, Geoffrey de Henelawe, the Norman prior of Llanthony, was appointed in 1203 to the see of St David's, and Gerald now finally gave up his fight, announcing: 'I have struggled enough. I have revived the claim of our Church, which lay buried so long.' Gerald uttered such wrathful and biting words that he was declared an enemy of the Crown and his lands were seized. However, he soon made his peace with the king and recovered his property.

During his life, Gerald had also fought hard for the independence of St David's and he acquired a well respected reputation for his determination in championing the rights of that see against Canterbury.[7] A similar contest was being fought by the canons of Bangor at this time.

On the death of Geoffrey de Henelaw in 1215, the see of St David's once more became vacant, but Gerald was now 69 years of age and tired of all the controversy. He retired from the fight, a beaten man. Iorwerth, the Welsh Abbot of Tally, near Llandeilo, was then consecrated Bishop of St David's on 21 June, 1215. The remaining years of Gerald's life were spent in Lincoln, where he devoted himself to his writing. He died in about 1223 at the age of 76 and was probably buried in St David's Cathedral.

Gerald is believed to be buried in St David's Cathedral which was built by his first rival, Bishop de Leia, but it is not certain that the tomb, shown to be Gerald's, is really his resting place. Situated under the easternmost arch of the south choir aisle, it is made of local stone and shows a full length recumbent effigy of a priest. The head of the effigy is supported by angels and the feet rest on a dog.

Twelve

THE MYSTERY OF THE GRAVE
AT GLASTONBURY

Glastonbury, in the heart of Somerset, has been called the 'most sacred spot in England,' and it is famous as the place where Joseph of Arimathea is said to have built his first Christian church, but it is also renowned as the place where King Arthur was supposedly buried with his wife, Queen Guinevere, by his side.

Through the passing centuries, visitors came here from far and wide to visit the site of the magnificent tomb, which once stood before the High Altar. A plaque set into the grass reads:-

> 'In the year 1191 the bodies of King Arthur and his Queen were said to have been found on the south side of the Lady Chapel. On 19th April 1278 their remains were removed in the presence of King Edward and Queen Eleanor to a black marble tomb on this site. The tomb survived until the Dissolution of the Abbey in 1539. '

The story of this famous 'discovery' is said to start in 1165 with King Henry II being entertained at Cilgerran Castle in Deheubarth by the Lord Rhys. Whilst he was there, Henry heard a bard sing of the mighty deeds of Arthur, his death in battle and his burial place. Unfortunately, the exact details of what Henry heard, or if indeed that this incident even took place, have not been recorded. We only have a passing reference to this supposed incident in the writings of Giraldus Cambrensis.

On the feast of St. Urban, 25 May 1184, a fire at Glastonbury Abbey consumed the greater part of the large Norman church of Abbot Herlewin, and also the old wattle church. A succinct account of this disaster is given by Adam of Domerham, a monk of Glastonbury, writing in about 1291:-

> '...the whole of the Monastery, except a chamber with a chapel constructed by Abbot Robert (1178-9) into which the monks afterwards betook themselves, and the Bell Tower, built by Bishop Henry, was consumed by fire.'

No reason is given, nor are there any particulars to be gathered from other writers of those times. It is only Adam of Domerham who very feelingly remarks:-

> 'The beautiful building, lately erected by Henry of Blois, and the Church, a place so venerated by all, and the shelter of so many saints, are reduced to a heap of ashes! What groans, what tears, what pains arose as they (the monks) saw what had happened, and thy pondered over the loss they had suffered. The confusion into which their relics were thrown, the loss of treasure, not only in gold and silver, but in stuffs and silks, in books and the rest of the ornaments of the church, must even provoke to tears, and justly so, those who far away do but hear of these things.'

At this time, the Abbey was under the ownership of Henry II, and he, after enforcing the condition that all the revenue of the Abbey, except that portion necessary for the maintenance of the monks, should be used for the re-building, made himself responsible for its re-erection.

Work started under the supervision of Randolph (a son of King Stephen and a chamberlain of Henry II), and good progress was made with the Lady Chapel, on the site of the old wooden church, being completed in 1189. This was the year in which Henry II is said to have instructed the monks to search for the grave of Arthur.

Henry would have had personal reasons for wanting the remains of Arthur to be discovered, for it would be a certain way of putting to an end the old Celtic prophecies that Arthur would one day return to lead his people. This second coming was eagerly awaited by the Celts of Wales, Cornwall and Brittany and the revelation that Arthur was really dead **and buried in England** would finally put an end to such superstitious beliefs.

However, for some reason the monks seemed reluctant to carry out the king's instructions and before the end of the year Henry had fallen sick and died. His son Richard became king and Glastonbury's financial problems immediately increased for Richard needed all the funds that he could lay his hands on for the Third Crusade. This meant that the monks had to find a new way of raising money to rebuild their abbey and it would seem that their solution to this problem was to create a popular 'tourist attraction'. Pilgrimages to the tombs of saints and kings were a fruitful source of income in the Middle Ages, and William of Malmesbury tells us that the monks of Glastonbury Abbey made a point of collecting as many relics of saints as they could.

Glastonbury Abbey in Somerset, where in 1191 the monks claimed to discover the grave of King Arthur and Queen Guinevere.

Adam of Domerham,[1] a monk of Glastonbury writing in the 13th century, comments:

> 'The King (Richard I)...elevated as Abbot Henry de Sully, Prior of Bermondsey, a man born of royal stock...He frequently urged to dispose more fittingly of the famous King Arthur for he had lain for 648 years near the Old Church, between two pyramids, once magnificently carved, one day surrounded the place with curtains and ordered that digging should be carried out...'

So in 1191 the monks finally decided to search for Arthur's reputed grave and hopefully reveal his last resting place to bring fame and fortune to the abbey. On digging a hole (behind closed curtains) seven feet down they found a stone slab and under it was a leaden cross bearing a Latin inscription

HIC JACET SEPULTUS INCLITUS REX ARTHURI
IN INSULA AVALONIA

Translated from the Latin this reads: 'Here lies buried the renowned King Arthur in the Isle of Avalon.'

The monks continued digging and at a depth of sixteen feet[2] they found a hollowed-out tree (an oak says Giraldus Cambrensis, but others say it was an alder), containing two skeletons which they declared to be the remains of King Arthur and Queen Guinevere.

A well documented description of the monks' excavation can be found in two works of Giraldus Cambrensis, who visited Glastonbury in 1192 and 1193. These two manuscripts are entitled *De Principes Instructione* (1194) and the later *Speculum Ecclesia* (1216).[3]

> 'Arthur, the famous British king, is still remembered, nor will this memory die out, for he is much praised in the history of the excellent monastery of Glastonbury, of which he himself was in his time a distinguished patron and a generous endower and supporter...His body, for which popular stories have invented a fantastic ending, saying that it had been carried to a remote place, and was not subject to death, was found in recent times at Glastonbury between two stone pyramids standing in the burial ground. It was deep in the

earth, enclosed in a hollow oak, and the discovery was accompanied by wonderful and almost miraculous signs. It was reverently transferred to the church and placed in a marble tomb.

And a leaden cross was found laid under a stone, not above, as is the custom today, but rather fastened on beneath it. We saw this, and traced the inscription which was showing, but turned in towards the stone: " Here lies buried the famous king Arthur with Guinevere his second wife in the isle of Avalon." In this there are several remarkable things: he had two wives, of which the last was buried at the same time as him, and indeed her bones were discovered with those of her husband; however, they were separate, since two parts of the coffin, at the head, were divided off, to contain the bones of a man, while the remaining third at the foot contained the bones of a woman set apart. There was also uncovered a golden tress of hair that had belonged to a beautiful woman, in its pristine condition and colour, when a certain monk eagerly snatched it up, suddenly dissolved into dust. Signs that the body had been buried here were found in the records of the place, in the letters inscribed on the pyramids, although these were obliterated by age, and in the visions and revelations seen by holy men and clerks; but chiefly through Henry II, King of England, who had heard from an aged British singer that his (Arthur's) body would be found at least sixteen-feet deep in the earth, not in a stone tomb, but in a hollow log. This Henry had told the monks; and the body was at the depth stated and almost concealed, lest in the event of the Saxons occupying the island, against whom he had fought with so much energy in his lifetime, it should be brought to light; and for that reason, the inscription on the cross which would have revealed the truth, was turned in-wards to the stone, to conceal at that time what the coffin contained, and yet inform other centuries. What is now called Glastonbury was in former times called the Isle of Avalon, for it is almost an island, being entirely surrounded by marshes, whence it is named in British Ynys Avallon, that is the apple-bearing islands, because apples (in British aval) used to abound in that place. Whence Morgan, a noblewoman who was ruler of that region and closely related to Arthur, after the Battle of Camlan carried him away to the island now called Glastonbury to be healed of his wounds. It used to be called in

British Ynys Gutrin, that is, the isle of glass; hence the Saxons called it Glastingeburi. For in their tongue glas means glass, and a camp or town is called buri. We know that the bones of Arthur's body that were discovered were so large that in this we might see the fulfilment of the poet's words:

"Gradisque effossis mirabitur ossa sepulchris."

The thigh bone, when placed next to the tallest man present, as the abbot showed us, and fastened to the ground by his foot, reached three inches above his knee. And the skull was of a great, indeed prodigious, capacity, to the extent that the space between the brows and between the eyes was a palm's breadth. But in the skull there were ten or more wounds, which had all healed into scars with the exception of one, which made a great cleft, and seemed to have been the sole cause of death.'

Gerald was not present at the excavation but seems convinced by the monks' story and elsewhere makes the comment that 'Many stories are told and many legends created around King Arthur and his mysterious end. The Britons in their stupidity maintain that he is still alive.'

He then adds, 'the credulous Britons and their bards thought up the story of Arthur's body being brought to the Isle of Avalon by a marvellous sorceress, Morgan, in order to heal him of his wounds. According to them, this strong and all-powerful king will return to resume his reign over the Britons.

All the essential ingredients have been put together in this famous Glastonbury discovery. We are provided with a cross bearing Arthur's name and that of the Isle of Avalon, and also a coffin containing two skeletons, a skull with a battle wound and for good measure a few strands of Guinevere's blonde hair. The result of these finds was that the English kings were able firmly to dismiss the belief that Arthur would one day return to save the Welsh from their enemies, for he was obviously dead and not immortal. Also, as he had been buried in England, he must have been an English king anyway! Such a myth still continues to this day.

It must be emphasised that Geoffrey of Monmouth did not state where Avalon was located. He merely stated that after the battle of Camlan, Arthur was taken to 'Insula Afallonis'. It is significant that all the Welsh versions of the manuscript render the name as 'Ynys Afallach' (the Island of Afallach).

William Camden's drawing of the 'Arthur Cross' was published in 1607

The Inscribed Cross

It is interesting to compare the different versions of the lettering on the cross which has been recorded by those who claimed to have inspected it.

'Hic iacet sepultus inclytus rex Arthurus cum Wenneveria
uxore sua secunda in insula Avallonia' (Giraldus Cambrensis)s

Trans: 'Here in the Isle of Avalon lies buried the renowned King Arthur with (Queen) Guinevere his second wife.

'Hic iacet sepultus inclytus rex Arthurius in insula Avallonia
cum uxore sua secunda Wenneveria' (Giraldus writing 25 years later in his *Speculum Ecclesiae* (Mirror of the Church).

'Hic iacet inclitus rex Arturius, in insula Avallonis sepultus' (Ralph Coggeshall *Anglican Chronicle*).

Trans: 'Here lies the tomb of the renowned King Arthur, buried in the Isle of Avalon.'

'Hic iacet sepultus inclitus rex Arturius in insula Avalonia'
(John Leland, chaplain to King Henry VIII and the king's antiquarian from 1533)

He saw the cross in 1542 and said that it was about one foot in height and commented that, 'I contemplated it with a curious eye.'

'Hic iacet sepultus inclitus rex Arturius in insula Avalonia' (Camden, thus agreeing with both Ralph Coggeshall and Leland)

The illustration of the cross which is now very familiar to any Arthurian enthusiast is taken from William Camden's *Britannia* (1610 edition). He was Queen Elizabeth I's historian (1551-1623)

Camden commented:-
'...which inscription or epitaph, as it was sometime exemplified and drawn out of the first copie in the Abbey of Glaston, I thought good for the antiquitie of the characters here to put downe. The letters being made after a barbarous manner, and resembling the Gothish character, bewray plainly the barbarism of that age...'

Camden's version of the inscription is different from that of Giraldus Cambrensis, but more likely to be the correct one. He recorded that it read-:

'Here lies the renowned King Arthur in the Isle of Avalon'.

Ralph de Coggeshall was writing at about the same time as Giraldus's first account, and under the year 1191 he records the finding of King Arthur's bones when a grave was being dug for a monk, who had specially desired to be buried between the two pyramids. He too gives the inscription on the leaden cross, but without mention of Queen Guinevere:

'1191: This year were found at Glastonbury the bones of the most renowned Arthur, formerly King of Britain, buried in a very ancient coffin, over which two stone pyramids had been built: on the sides were an inscription, illegible on account of the rudeness of the script and its worn condition. The bones were discovered as follows: as they were digging up the ground to bury a monk who had urgently desired in his lifetime to be interred there, they discovered a certain coffin, on which a leaden cross had been placed, bearing the inscription, 'Here lies the famous King Arthur, buried in the Isle of Avalon'.' For this place, which surrounded by marshes, was formerly called the Isle of Avalon, that is, the isle of apples.'

Giraldus Cambrensis seems to be the odd man out in his description of the leaden cross for in both his accounts he added the words:-

CUM WENNEVERIA UXORE SUA SECUNDA'

'with Guinevere his second wife.'

However, he does seem confused, for in his first account he puts these words before, and in the second account, after 'in insula Avallonia.' He expressly says that he read them himself.

There is no doubt that Gerald was doing his best to please his Norman masters and going along with the idea that now that Arthur had been found dead and buried there was no earthly possibility of his rising again.

The fact that the word 'inclitus' (renowned) appeared on all versions of the inscription is of particular significance for it was a word used by Geoffrey of Monmouth in his *Historia* which was published less than fifty years earlier. Also, it must be of significance that the reference to the Isle of

Avalon in the inscription was obviously intended to fit in with his account of the death of Arthur when he wrote: 'Arthur himself, our renowned king, was mortally wounded and was carried off to the Isle of Avalon.' A genuine 6th-century inscription on the cross would certainly not have mentioned that Arthur was 'buried on the Isle of Avalon', for if the place was Avalon, then there would have been no need to remind the reader of that fact. The reference to the Isle of Avalon in fact dates it as being inscribed in the second half of the 12th century, since all early 12th century writers call Glastonbury 'Inis Gutrin'.

The repeated use of Geoffrey of Monmouth's word 'inclitus' (renowned) which also appears on the cross, is particularly significant for it helps to confirm that the forger drew on Geoffrey's writings for the wording of the inscription.

There have been many learned observations on the style of the lettering and some historians have expressed the opinion that it belongs to the 10th century. One would expect a forgery at the time of the monks' excavation of 1191 to be either a realistic copy of sixth-century style lettering, or a not so clever example of the style of a later period. The forger perhaps tried to make the lettering look old and his only samples to hand were of the previous two centuries.

However, having said that, of particular interest is a tympanum above the north door of St. Mary's Church at Stoke-sub-Hamdon in Somersetshire, which bears a twelfth century carving and lettering which is identical to that shown on the Camden drawing of the cross.

· The last documented whereabouts of the cross is given in a seventeenth century manuscript (Bodleian Rawlinson B.416A. fol.10v) which states that 'the plate of lead in the underside of the cover of his (Arthur's) coffin at the dissolution of the Abbey happened to be preserved and was within this 100 years in the revestry of the parish church of St. John's in Glaston but is now lost.'

The only evidence for the identity of the persons buried in the grave is the cross and it was necessary for the monks to 'find' the cross in order to provide the proof that indeed this was the last resting place of King Arthur. We are completely reliant on the skill and integrity of Camden's engraver for the style of lettering on the cross. Perhaps Camden only gave him the actual wording and the shape of the cross and he made up the style of lettering by copying it from another example. Without the cross itself we will never really be sure and we can only hope that one day it will be found. In April 1982 a certain Derek Mahoney claimed that he had re-discovered the cross, but this was probably yet another hoax.

Tympanum at St Mary's Church, Stoke-sub-Hamdon, Somerset

Sign marking the site of the wattle church
said to have been erected by St Joseph of Arimathea

149

The Two Pyramids

The pyramids standing above the site of Arthur's supposed grave were presumably the tapering shafts of two square stone crosses which had lost their heads. William of Malmesbury saw them and deciphered fragments of the inscriptions, but, judging from his account, they would have had no connection with Arthur and Guinevere for they were of Saxon origin. They would have been headless shafts* of two Saxon Memorial crosses with inscriptions on their sides.

William of Malmesbury commented: -

> 'I would willingly explain, if I could get at the truth, what those pyramids mean which, placed a few feet from the Old Church, border the Monks' Cemetery.
> The taller, which is nearest the church, has five tablets and is twenty-six feet high. This, though very old and threatened with ruin, has not a few traces of antiquity, which can certainly be read though they cannot be fully understood. In the top tablet, i.e., there is an image made to represent a pontiff; in the second is an image representing royal dignity, and the letters Her, Sexi and Blisyer; in the third there are names, Wemcrest, Bantomp. Winethgn; in the fourth Hate, Wulfred, and Eanfled; in the fifth, which is also the bottom one, is an image and this writing: 'Logwor, Weslicas, and Bregden, Swelwes, Hwinganses Bern.' The other pyramid is eighteen feet high, and has four tablets in which this is to be read: 'Hedde bishop and Bregored, and Beorward.' What these mean I will not venture to define, but I conclude with some hesitation that in the hollow stones the bones are contained of those whose names are written outside. Certainly this much can be asserted of Logwor, from whom Logweres-beorh gets its name, which is now called Mons Acutus[4] (the pointed Mountain*); Bregden, from which comes Brentacnolle, now called Byentamerle. Beorwald was in any case an abbot after Hemgiselus, concerning whom, and all the rest who may come up, an orator will arise elsewhere in a freer field.'

(The Antiquities of Glastonbury)

* The shafts were still standing in position as late as 1777.

Joseph Ritson in his book *The Life of King Arthur* comments:-

'These names are clearly of Saxons interred in this cemetery, and certainly have no connection with Arthur. *Beorwald* is Beortwald, archbishop of Canterbury, who died 731 (*Saxon Chronicle*); *Bern;* Beorn, general burned in Silton, 780, or Beorn, earl, killed by Swain and buried at Winchester, 1046. *Eanfled* : Eanfled, daughter of King Edwin, born 626; *Hedde* bishop : Hedde, bishop of Winchester, died 703.'

The foundations of the pyramids were found by Dr. C.A. Raleigh Radford when he excavated the grave site in 1963, and proved that the monks had dug where they claimed and that the hole had been refilled. The site lies 15 metres from the south door of the Lady Chapel, but is unmarked.

The new tomb of Arthur and Guinevere

The bones were first placed in a new tomb near the south door of the greater Church, leading to the Treasury and a new epitaph was composed by Abbot Swansey:-

'Here lieth Arthur, flower of kings, of the kingdom the glory;
One whom probity, manners, commend to perennial praises.'

At Easter in 1278, King Edward I and Queen Eleanor honoured Glastonbury with a visit. They were accompanied by Robert Kilwardby, Archbishop of Canterbury, and the royal party was entertained by Abbot Adam of Sodbury. The main purpose of their visit was to witness the moving of the relics of Arthur and Guinevere and also the consecration of the High Altar.

Adam of Domerham provides a detailed account of the event:-

'The lord Edward...with his consort, the lady Eleanor, came to Glastonbury...to celebrate Easter...The following Tuesday...at dusk, the lord king had the tomb of the famous King Arthur opened. Wherein, in two caskets painted with their pictures and arms, were found separately the bones of the said king, which were of great size, and those of Queen Guinevere, which were of marvellous beauty. On the following day the lord king replaced the bones of the king and those of the queen, each in their own casket, having wrapped them in costly silks. When they had been sealed they ordered the tomb to be placed forthwith in front of the high altar, after the removal of the skulls for the veneration of the people.[5]

It would seem that the bones were replaced in the caskets, with the exception of the two skulls and the knee-joints which were kept outside 'for the people's devotion'. Edward I and his queen during their visit to Glastonbury in April, 1278 had the bones of Arthur and Guinevere transferred to a new tomb, which was placed before the high altar in the presbytery. Leland saw it in this position when he came to Glastonbury in about 1542. It was constructed of black marble and had two lions at each end. There was an image of King Arthur at the foot and an epitaph bearing the name of a certain Abbot Henry. Leland also saw the leaden cross, which at that time lay on top of the tomb for all to see and examine.

Edward and Eleanor placed within the sepulchre a solemn written record of what they had seen, together with the names of the principal witnesses:-

'These are the bones of the most noble King Arthur, which in the year of the incarnation of the lord 1278, in the 13th Kalends of May (19th April), by the lord Edward, the illustrious King of England, were here so placed: Eleanor, the most serene consort of the same king, and daughter of the lord Ferrand, king of Spain, master William de Middleton, then elect of Norwich, master Thomas de Becke, archdeacon of Dorset, and treasurer of the aforesaid king, the lord Henry de Lascy, earl of Lincoln, the lord Amade, earl of Savoy, and many great men of England, being present.'[6]

Edward subsequently asserted his authority as 'Arthur's true heir' and in 1283 was given an ancient circlet of metal which was claimed to be Arthur's crown. It was soon after his visit to Glastonbury that Edward proclaimed his son, the future Edward II, Prince of Wales, thereby killing all hopes of Welsh independence, and linking the throne of Wales to the English monarchy.

Edward III came to Glastonbury with Queen Philippa in 1331 and they were lavishly entertained by Abbot Adam of Sodbury. Edward subsequently decided to found the British Order, revive the Round Table assemblies, and make Windsor Castle the centre of European chivalry (see page 186).

Site of the supposed burial place of Arthur and Guinevere

The notice marks the spot where the new tomb of 'Arthur and Guinevere' was erected, before the high altar, following Edward 1's visit with Queen Eleanor to the abbey in 1278. The exact position was identified in 1931 when the base of the cavity with a lining of fine ashlar was revealed. The tomb itself had been destroyed during the Reformation and the bones either destroyed or dispersed.

Observations

The 12th century writer William of Malmesbury was a meticulous historian and he had searched the Glastonbury Abbey archives specifically for any mention of King Arthur. He actually stated in his writings that he failed to find any reference which connected Arthur with Glastonbury. Furthermore, in his *History of the Kings of England*, he states that 'the tomb of Arthur is nowhere to be seen, wherefore the ancient songs fable that he is yet to come!'

In 1189 the monks of Glastonbury were undoubtedly facing financial difficulties for Henry II had died and his successor Richard I was not prepared to assist them with their rebuilding programme. What were they to do?

Professor Treharne in his book *The Glastonbury Legends* (Cresset, 1967), puts forward the following hypothesis:-

> 'In this crisis some unknown monk must have come forward with a suggestion which marks him out as a genius who would have made his fortune in a modern advertising agency. By a brilliant stroke of imagination he proposed a superb advertising stunt - 'Find Arthur's tomb!' To an age which reads more avidly of King Arthur and his Queen, his Knights of the Round Table, and of their treacherous foes, than it read of the whole calendar of saints, the impact of such a discovery would be tremendous, the appeal irresistible. In the golden age of forgery here was the master-forgery of all! Perfectly timed and staged, on any grounds other than those of morality and religion it deserved to succeed, and succeed it did, and has gone on succeeding down to our day.'

It is significant that Adam of Domerham tells us that Abbot Henry de Soilli kept curtains around the excavation and it is reasonable to suppose that the monks were aware of some distinguished man and woman who had been buried centuries before in their grounds. Such examples being Edmund I (d.946), Edgar (d.975) and Edmund Ironside (d. 1016).

The monks no doubt did excavate a genuine ancient burial for if they had been intent on concocting a complete fake then they would have introduced a stone sarcophagus to suit the custom of the sixth century. Their discovery of bones in a hollowed out tree trunk is an indication that they must have revealed an ancient grave site dating back to pagan times.

Perhaps the bones were those of an Iron Age warrior and his wife that the monks had found buried in a dug-out canoe from the Glastonbury lake village, and they had found them by chance whilst digging another grave and placed them in the hole that they dug behind the closed curtains.

In our book *Journey to Avalon* we put forward the theory that the grave is more likely to be that of King Arviragus who was reigning in this part of Britain in the middle of the first century. In A.D. 63 he is said to have granted twelve hides of land, the site of the future monastery, to St Joseph of Arimathea to found a simple church here. Arviragus made use of the hill fort known as Cadbury Castle, where excavation during 1966-70 revealed evidence of a massacre carried out by the Romans. It is possible that Arviragus perished in this massacre and was buried with his wife, Gennissa (a similar sounding name to Guinevere!) at Glastonbury near the site of the church founded by St Joseph of Arimathea. It is significant that Arviragus also bore the Gaelic-Pictish name of Arc-wyr-auc meaning 'the Bear -folk chief' The Gaelic 'c' would become 't' in Pictish and in Welsh the name would become Arthwyr, meaning 'the Bear Exalted', which was in effect a title that was given to British leaders in times of crisis. It is thus conceivable that he became confused with Athrwys ap Meurig, the 'Arthwyr' of the sixth century, who is remembered as King Arthur.

A 17th century impression of the original wattle church
said to have been erected by Joseph of Arimathea

It is quite likely that the Glastonbury monks invented the story that the secret of Arthur's burial place had been told to Henry II by a bard in Wales, for such an account obviously gave credence to their discovery and it is also significant that they carried out the excavation after the death of Henry II.

Glastonbury had to be identified as the Isle of Avalon for, according to Geoffrey of Monmouth, such a place had been Arthur's last destination and, by finding the grave of Arthur at Glastonbury, that place would accordingly become known as Avalon.

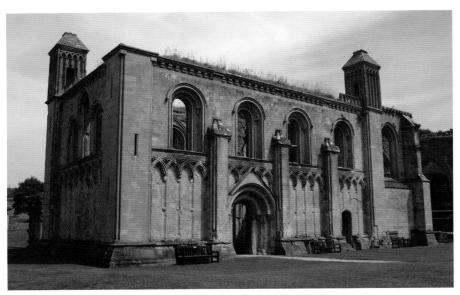

St Mary's Chapel, view from the south west

A 15th century illustration
of Arthur and Guinevere's tomb

This fragment of 13th century carving was found during excavation of the area around the High Altar. The archaeologist, Bligh Blond, speculated that it could be part of the tomb erected over the reputed remains of King Arthur and Guinevere when their tomb was relocated to that spot in 1278, in the presence of King Edward I and Quween Eleanor.

By 'discovering' the bones of Arthur at Glastonbury the monks firmly established the idea that Glastonbury was Avalon, and to this day such a belief is maintained by tourism literature and road signs. In this way, Arthur is firmly established in most people's eyes as an English hero rather than a Celtic one.

The Church was not slow to turn the interest in King Arthur and the resultant literature to its own purposes, transmuting and breathing into it a religious mysticism. The traditions which gathered around Glastonbury, the scenes enacted there, its repute as the supposed sanctuary of the Grail, which was the holiest of Christian relics, all point to the endeavour to exalt Glastonbury.

It was the 12th-century historian William of Malmesbury who provided one of the oldest recorded names for Glastonbury. He referred to the place as Ynys Witherin. Owing to the fact that the word witrin means glass and, taking into consideration Glastonbury's former marshy situation, the place name was misinterpreted as 'the Island of Glass' when in fact the name 'Witherin" stems from a Dark Age personality. He was St Gwytherin (Victorinus), a great great grandson of Cunedda Wledig, and he founded a community here which became known as Ynys Witherin.

The name Glastonbury has its origins in the seventh century and it means 'the fort of the descendants of Glast'. It would appear that Glast was also a descendant of Cunedda Wledig, being his great grandson and he was probably a cousin of Witherin. There is a tradition that he fought with Arthur at the battle of Bassas near Lichfield. After routing the heathen Middle Angles, Arthur perhaps instructed Glast to travel home to protect his family domain and the holy sanctuary founded by St Joseph of Arimathea. So Glast and his followers travelled south via the Icknield Way and the Fosse Way to Bath, from where they continued through Wells and on to the place we now call Glastonbury. Here Glast remained and ruled over his ancestral estates. His name was remembered a hundred years later, when the Saxons captured the Celtic settlement in 658 and called it Glaston.

Glastonbury is first named Avalon by Ralph Coggeshall and Giraldus Cambrensis. Ralph calls it Insula Avallonis and Giraldus uses the form Avallonia. It seems quite obvious that Ynis Witherin was the Celtic name for the place and that Avalon was the name given to it after 1191. Around 1200 the name for the place would have been something like Glaestingaburg. The word glass was perhaps thought to be recognised in this name and it later became known as Glass Island, which in turn related to Ynys Witrin. In assuming that Ynystwytryn meant the 'Isle of Glas,' Giraldus Cambrensis explained the term as referring to the surrounding water in which the island would be mirrored.

When Geoffrey of Monmouth referred to Insula Avallonis as the place to which Arthur was taken after the battle of Camlan for his wounds to be tended, he gave rise to the belief that Arthur was buried on the Isle of Avalon. So when the monks found 'his bones' at Glastonbury, they reinforced their claims by establishing the place as Avalon with the faked inscription on the leaden cross.

As one might imagine, for the pilgrims of the Middle Ages it was no small privilege to gaze on the very relics of King Arthur and his Queen. However, these artifacts paled into insignificance beside the other objects which were provided to satisfy the curiosity of the throngs of visitors who came to the Abbey. There was a piece of Mose's Rod; some of the gold offered by the Three Wise Men from the East; a thorn from the Crown of Thorns, some splinters of the True Cross, and portions of the Holy Sepulchre. Bones of John the Baptist, of St Peter and St Paul, set in silver or crystal, completed the list of corporeal relics. Most of these relics were said to have been procured and presented by three kings, Athelstan, Edmund and St Edgar, and other magnates.

It was also claimed that the bones of St David had been brought here from Vallis Rosina and they attracted crowds of Welsh pilgrims. Here also it was claimed lay the bodies of St Illtyd and of St Gildas

In 1536 Henry VIII dissolved the monasteries of England and Wales and all that they contained. We can only assume that the double tomb of 'Arthur and Guinevere' was smashed open and their bones destroyed or dispersed.

The historian Speed tells with obvious indignation of the doom that befell the Abbey in Henry VIII's time, when 'this noble monument, among the fatal overthrow of infinite more, was altogether razed by those whose over-hasty actions and too forward zeal in these behalfs hath left us the want of many truths, and cause to wish that some of their employments had been better spent.'

Whatever the old monks of Glastonbury said about their discovery of King Arthur's grave they certainly failed to convince the peasants of South Cadbury, a dozen miles away, that Arthur and his knights were not sleeping under the hill of Cadbury Castle for Leland found this belief current in about 1540.

'At South Cadbyri standith Camallate, sumtyme a famose toun or castyelle. The people can tell nothing thar but that they have hard say that Artuire much resotid to Camalat.'

John Leland 1542

Thirteen

THE LORDS OF AFAN

Surprisingly, the Normans allowed Iestyn ap Gwrgan's son Caradoc to retain all the territory between the rivers Neath and Afan. This territory became known as the lordship of Walia, and it reached to the north almost as far as the boundaries of Rhigos and Ystradfodwg.

Caradoc became the first lord of Afan and at Aberafan[1] he constructed a castle and a church, which apart from Margam Abbey was the most important place of worship in the locality. He married Gwladus, the daughter of Gruffydd ap Rhys ap Tewdwr, and thus formed an alliance with the House of Dinefwr, which was maintained until the supremacy in Welsh affairs eventually passed to Gwynedd and allegiance was transferred to the princes of that province.

It is obvious that Caradoc and his family were a constant menace to the Normans for it is recorded that they made numerous attacks on the neighbouring borough of Kenfig. There are accounts of the castle being burnt on no less than five occasions up until 1295, giving rise to a chronicler recording, with obvious sarcasm, that 'Kenfig had not been burned for a year or more.'

When Caradoc ap Iestyn was killed in battle in c.1148, his lands were divided between his five sons, Morgan,[2] the eldest, inherited Afan, Cadwallon received Glynrhondda, Mareddudd took Meisgyn Rhys, the locality now known as Resolven, whilst the fifth son Owain possibly inherited Llangynwydd. According to Giraldus Cambrensis, Cadwallon murdered his brother Owain, but 'the wrath of God caught up with him. He was leading an assault on a certain castle when a wall collapsed on top of him and he was crushed to pieces and killed.'

Morgan ap Caradoc, the next lord of Afan, built a fortress on the highest point of Mynydd Dinas overlooking the river Afan. Its site is marked by the surviving motte, which has a diameter of 40 metres and is surrounded by a ditch 7 metres broad and about 2 metres deep.

Giraldus Cambrensis mentions Morgan ap Caradoc as the guide who escorted him and his party along the sea shore towards the Neath river in 1188, whilst on the way to Swansea. They had problems approaching the river:

> '...because of its dangerous quicksands, which suddenly suck
> everything placed upon them. One of our packhorses (the only
> one possessed by the writer of these lines) was trotting along

the lower road near the sea, and although it was in the middle of a group of others, it alone was nearly plunged into the abyss. Eventually, it was pulled out, with great difficulty ,and after much hard and dangerous work by the horse-boys, though not without danger to my books and belongings. Although we had Morgan, the leading man of those parts, as our guide, we only reached the river after suffering many perils and even more falls. Of course, fear of the unknown made us hurry through these quicksands, despite the warnings of our guide.'

Not surprisingly, they decided to cross the river by boat instead of wading and probably crossed at the place now known as Briton Ferry.

Morgan ap Caradoc presented large tracts of land[3] to Margam Abbey and he was not the only descendant of Iestyn ap Gwrgan to part with his estates for the benefit of the White Friars, for his example seems to have been followed by every scion of the family.

Seal of Morgan ap Caradoc

By 1208, Morgan ap Caradoc was dead and he was succeeded by his eldest son Lleision, who seems to have been of the same vacillating nature as his father. He had many disputes with the Abbot of Margam concerning the lands of his ancestors, but he invariably gave way, by swearing 'on a portion of the True Cross, and the relics of saints' to forego his claims. On his death in 1217, the lordship of Afan went to his brother, Morgan Gam (Morgan 'the crooked eyed').[4] He was made of sterner stuff, and gave the Norman nobles and abbots a worrying time.

In 1226 he attacked the villages of St Nicholas, Laleston and Newcastle, which at that time was in the ownership of Gilbert de Turberville, Lord of Coity, son-in-law of Morgan Gam. The following year he attacked and burned Penhydd Grange, killing many animals. Resolven Grange was also destroyed and one of the abbey labourers killed. In 1231, he joined Llywelyn the Great in the storming of Neath. They jointly attacked the town and razed the castle to the ground, exterminating all the Normans residing there. The monks of Margam had to pay a ransom of sixty silver marks to Llywelyn to save their abbey from destruction. Morgan, the following year, attacked Cynffig and succeeded in entering the town, but failed to take the castle. He showed restraint in sparing the town's church and the lives of those sheltering inside. Even in his peaceful periods, he feared the ban of the Church, for we later find him admitting to the considerable damage which he had inflicted upon the horses and cattle belonging to Margam Abbey. He accordingly agreed to reduce the rent of twenty shillings due by the Abbey to him 'for Hauothalock to two shillings with penalty of excommunication or interdiction by the Bishop of Llandaff in case of his breaking the agreement.'

In another charter we find further reference to his evil deeds, when he promises the monks of Margam, 'that he will not molest them in the Avene waters, nor drive away their sheep , nor trouble them in the cultivated lands,' all of which he had evidently done previously. He was a firebrand, who had no doubt inherited the character of his maternal grandfather, Ifor Bach of Senghenydd, and he certainly left his mark on the pages of Glamorgan's history. As Lord of Afan he managed to unite the Welsh to arms on a number of occasions and even did considerable damage to Margam Abbey. Aided by his relations, Morgan ap Owain and Hywel ap Maredydd, Lord of Miskin, he was continually at war with Gilbert de Clare, who held the lordship of Glamorgan from 1218 to 1230.

Morgan Gam was seized in 1228 by Gilbert de Clare and sent, with his feet bound in irons, into England, so that peace could be maintained. At this time the local Welsh lords were also quarrelling amongst themselves. Hywel ap Maredydd seized his cousin Morgan ap Cadwaladr, put out both of his eyes and inflicted other nasty mutilations. He also burned the churches of St. Hilary and St. Nicholas.

In 1229 Morgan Gam was released on giving hostages as a guarantee for good conduct, but within two years he was causing trouble for the Normans again.

Following the death of Gilbert de Clare on 25 October, 1230, the Welsh once again started to rebel against the Normans. Morgan Gam, not bothered about the hostages which he had given, joined forces with Llywelyn ap

Iorwerth, Prince of North Wales, who had been active in Breconshire and east of the Usk. In June 1231 they laid siege to Neath, which, after its surrender, they burned, razing the castle to the ground. They then went on to Margam Abbey where they extorted 60 marks from the abbot. The following year Llywelyn again came into Glamorgan with Cynffig as his objective. The defenders of the castle had removed all the cattle and even burned part of the town around the castle to make defence easier. At this time the castle was only encircled by a ditch and earth rampart; Morgan Gam tried to storm the keep but the defences were too strong and he and his men were finally driven off. According to the *Annals of Margam,* Morgan Gam died in February 1240 and was buried at Margam Abbey[5]

Seal of Morgan Gam

He was succeeded by his eldest son Lleision,[6] who died without heirs and the lordship then went to the second son, Morgan Vychan ('the Younger'). In 1276 he married Maud, heiress of Walter de Sully and they had two sons, Lleision and Rhys. Morgan Fychan died on 6, August, 1288.

Lleision ap Morgan was the next to hold the title of Lord of Afan Wallia and his tenure of power is memorable in the annals due to the granting of a Charter to the citizens of Afan ('Carte,' III, 922). This is the oldest extant Charter of the Borough. Lleision was the third of that name in the Caradoc dynasty and he appears to have become thoroughly Normanised, probably owing to maternal influence. He even adopted a Norman name by taking the prefix 'de' to become De Afan or De Avene. On receiving a knighthood, he adopted a coat of arms in Norman style, and even gave his sons English names - Thomas and John.

In 1315, at the time of the insurrection of Llywelyn Bren, when the greater part of Glamorgan rose in support of the oppressed chief of Senghenydd, Sir Lleision de Avene stood for the king and no doubt hoped to receive favour in return for his loyalty. He assisted in the defence of Cynffig against Llywelyn Bren and claimed forty marks for his expenses, but he was ignored by the king in his pretensions and also had to bear the expense of his share of the campaign.

Following the death of Sir Lleision de Avene, his eldest son John inherited and he married Isabella who gave him two sons, whom they named Thomas and William. John de Avene was the last member of the family in the direct line to figure in history. On 26 April 1350, he gave a charter to the citizens of Avene and this is one of the most precious legacies of that period. His name appears as a witness to a Margam deed in the same year.

Thomas was the last member of the family to hold the lordship, for, having no male issue, the property on his death fell to his daughter Jane de Avene. She, on marrying Sir William Blunt, an English knight, exchanged her Welsh property for English lands in the North, either with Despenser or De Clare. The date of this exchange is not known, but it certainly took place before 1373, in which year Edward de Despenser granted a charter to the Borough.

By 1240 the inhabitants of Aberafan were called 'Kinges burgesys,' which confirms that some time before that date the lordship of Afan had fallen to the Crown.

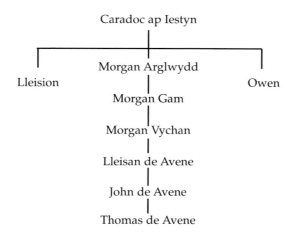

Caradoc ap Iestyn

Lleision — Morgan Arglwydd — Owen

Morgan Gam

Morgan Vychan

Lleisan de Avene

John de Avene

Thomas de Avene

Margam Abbey

The *Iolo MSS* and Sir Edward Mansel's *Account of the Conquest of Glamorgan* both state that Morgan Mwynfawr erected a court or palace at Margam, and that he raised the place to a bishopric, which was served by five bishops before it was united with Llandaff. Such records, although treated by historians with strong suspicion, support the tradition that a religious house of Celtic foundation existed at Margam, but all traces of it were no doubt destroyed when the Norman abbey was built.

During the last year of his life, in 1147, Robert, Earl of Gloucester, founded an abbey on the site of the old Celtic monastery. The foundation charter is not extant, but its text has been preserved in a charter of Hugh de Despenser, son and heir of Hugh de Despenser.

Fourteen crosses ascribed to the 9th, 10th and 14th centuries have been found within the former parish of Margam. Seven were found near the abbey, four at or near the now destroyed farms of Cwrt Ucha and Cwrt Isaf, one at Eglwys Nunydd, and the others at Penhydd Fawr and Penhydd Waelod. The finest of these ancient monuments is the Great Wheel Cross of Conbelin which can be seen in the Margam Abbey stones museum.

Almost from its foundation, Margam Abbey flourished considerably and became famous for its hospitality and social and political influences. It quickly acquired extensive lands and gained liberal grants, which extended as far as Bristol and Tewkesbury, from the lords of Glamorgan, Welsh princes, and the powerful tenants-in-chief such as the Turbervilles.

It was to become one of the greatest Cistercian monasteries in Wales and the Abbey library contained many valuable manuscripts, including a copy of the *Historia Regum Britanniae* of Geoffrey of Monmouth. This was hardly surprising, for the the founder of the abbey, Robert, Earl of Gloucester, was of course Geoffrey's sponsor.

Earl Robert had granted the Cistercian monks all the land between the Afan and the Cynffig, from the summit of the hills to the coast, and in 1180 Morgan ap Caradoc, the grandson of Iestyn ap Gwrgan, made further additions to the Abbey's lands. He granted the monks common pasture in the mountains between the rivers Taff and Neath, a territory which included not only Afan, the land which later came to his own son Morgan Gam, but also Meisgyn and Glynrhondda. This grant was confirmed by King John.

A later grant by Morgan ap Caradoc in 1205 refers to land between Witherell and Ellenepulle Lake and fifty acres of Roflesland near to Clackeston. This he granted (for Masses and Prayers) for the souls of his father and mother, and all of his ancestors, and for his own soul's sake, with the stipulation that when he died he was to be buried within the Abbey.

The now roofless Chapter House at Margam Abbey is a beautiful example of the Early English style of Gothic architecture

Remains of the cloisters of Margam Abbey

The Abbey Church at Margam has survived and is a rare example of a Cistercian nave being used after the Dissolution as a parochial nave

On 29 October 1187, the altar of the Holy Trinity was solemnly consecrated at Margam by William, Bishop of Llandaff. This event was a particularly important one in the history of the Abbey, for it evidently marked the completion of the monastic church. It was just a few months later, in the spring of 1188, that Baldwin, Archbishop of Canterbury, during his journey through Wales, preaching the Crusade, visited the Abbey in the company of Giraldus Cambrensis.

Planned on typical Cistercian lines, the conventional buildings of the abbey ranged around the cloister garth on the south side of the church, as at Neath. Sadly, little remains of this once grand abbey today, apart from the remains of cloisters and the very fine Chapter House, which when complete was a beautiful example of the Early English style of Gothic architecture. It had twelve beautifully proportioned lancet windows and was covered by a very fine vaulted roof, supported in the centre by a pillar which splayed out at the top to form supporting ribs. The roof was intact when Wyndham visited Margam during his tour of Wales in 1777. Neglect and the removal of lead from the roof caused it to collapse after heavy rain in 1799.

The Chapter House had twelve sides and was thus a copy of the Gorsedd circle which was composed of twelve stones. The segments of 30 degrees each of the Chapter House correspond to the similar divisions of the Gorsedd circle, and an opening in the east wall is exactly placed to observe sunrise; as were the avenues of stone to the east of the ancient circles. It is relevant that the bardic chair of Tir Iarll was endowed and encouraged by the founder, Robert, Earl of Gloucester, for the bards and the monks at this time had much in common.

Immediately above the south window of the Chapter House was the scriptorium, the room where the Margam monks undertook their literary tasks. In this chamber for three and a half centuries were carefully recorded the deeds and charters known as the *Annals of Margam*, the important events, gifts, legacies and business transactions of the Abbey. It traces the abbey's history from 1066 to 1232 and is a valuable source for the history of Glamorgan after 1185.

An impressive library here held many charters of great historic interest. Notable possessions included a twelfth century copy of the *Domesday Book*, the *Gesta Regum*, and *Novella Historia*' of William of Malmesbury, and the *Historia Regum Britanniae* of Geoffrey of Monmouth. Undoubtedly, this abbey gained a considerable reputation as a centre of learning. It is of interest that the *Annals of Margam* is the only contemporary authority to accuse King John of the murder of his nephew Arthur of Brittany.

Following the Dissolution, the last Abbot of Margam, Lewis Thomas, on 28 February 1537 relinquished the abbey and its possessions and for the remainder of his life received an annual pension of twenty pounds. The Abbey and its lands were then sold by the Crown to Sir Rice Mansel, the king's 'faithful friend and councillor', for £678 From his descendants the lands passed into the possession of the Talbot family, who were later to give their name to Port Talbot.

The Abbey Church is well preserved because it was the parochial portion of the original Abbey, and was fortunately protected from spoilation at the Reformation. It occupies the six westernmost bays of the old monastic church, the present east wall being near the site of the pulpitum screen. In the eastern section of the south aisle can be seen some interesting altar tombs erected to the memory of the four members of the Mansel family, who successively held the Margam Estate during the century which followed the Dissolution. Set within the angle of the south and east walls is the tomb of Sir Rice Mansel,[7] the first of the Margam Mansels. It bears his effigy and that of his third wife, Cecile Dabridgecourt. The adjacent tomb is that of Sir Rice's son and heir, Sir Edward Mansel. It bears his effigy and that of his wife, Lady Jane Somerset. Next to it is the tomb of Sir Edward's son, Sir Thomas Mansel, who is depicted sleeping between his two wives. The fourth tomb contains Sir Lewis Mansel, fourth of the Morgan line.

Tomb of Sir Rice Mansel and his wife

In 1839 Christopher Rice Mansel Talbot, who owned a vast estate at Penrice in Gower, demolished the old mansion of his ancestors and built Margam Castle. This castellated Gothic mansion was designed by Thomas Hopper of Essex (1776-1856) and was later occupied by Lady Emily Charlotte Talbot (1840-1919). It was then used by Captain Andrew Mansel Talbot Fletcher. The building was extensively damaged by fire in 1970 but has now been fully restored by the local council, who have established a Country Park in the extensive grounds.

Fourteen

THE LORDS OF CAERLEON

Caerleon upon Usk is a favoured location for one of Arthur's courts in Geoffrey of Monmouth's *Historia*. In addition, he makes it the seat of the Archbishop of Wales and also the scene of Arthur's magnificent coronation. Confusingly, Geoffrey states that Caerleon was in the principality of Glamorgan, while in the present day we think of it as in the ancient kingdom of Gwent, but it should be remembered that during the 1130s, when Geoffrey was writing his book, the Lord of Glamorgan (Robert, Earl of Gloucester) was Geoffrey's patron, so no doubt there were underlying political reasons for such a statement.[1]

Situated on the banks of the river Usk, four miles from Newport, Caerleon has been a place of importance since it became the headquarters of the Second Augustan Legion. This remarkable fighting force was brought from Germany in the year 43 by the Emperor Claudius to deal with the Silures, who were proving very difficult to subdue. The fort they established here became known as Isca Silurum.

After the departure of the Romans in 403, Caerleon remained firmly in the control of its native princes and it was still regarded as a place of strategic importance, being situated at the junction of land routes into Wales, at a point where the Usk was easily bridged. It was also at the head of a tidal estuary which was convenient for sea-going ships.

The Book of Llandaff records that when William I conquered England in 1066 a certain King Caradoc reigned in Gwent-uth-coed (Gwent above the wood), Ystradyw (a small part of south-east Powys) and Gwynllywg (Wentlooge). His second son Rhydderch reigned in Ewyas and Gwent-is-coed (Gwent below the wood). At this time there were three independent provinces in South Wales with river boundaries: Gwent between the Wye and the Usk, Gwynllwg, between the Usk and the Rhymney; and Morgannwg, west of the Rhymney. These areas were probably held as vassal states of Rhys ap Tewdwr, who was styled Prince of South Wales.

Caradog ap Gruffydd is particularly remembered for his opposition to Harold Godwinson, whose first campaign into Wales was in 1055. Harold decided to make the area between the Wye and the Usk a hunting ground for King Edward, who held one of the great Courts of the Witangemot annually at Gloucester, which was within easy reach of the extensive forest of Wentwood, where game was plentiful, but King Caradog refused to grant this territory to Harold, even though he was promised the sovereignty of South Wales if he would consent to the arrangement. Consequently, Harold took possession of the area by force. He then commenced building a substantial hunting lodge at a location now known as Portskewett, which has been named after the one-time harbour of Porth-is-coed (Port below the wood) on the Severn Estuary.

The Saxon Chronicle records that in 1064, when King Edward was at Winchester, Harold's brother, Tostig, being jealous of the favour shown by the king to his brother, seized Harold by the hair and threw him to the ground. As a result, Tostig was banished from the Court and he decided to take revenge. He made his way to Harold's new establishment at Portskewett and butchered all the servants. We are told that he cut off the legs and arms of some and decapitated the others. The heads were placed in the vessels containing choice wines, mead, ale and cider, which had been stored in readiness for the king's proposed visit. He then sent a message to Harold, saying that he need bring with him no other provisions for the king, as he would find ample quantities of preserved meats and sauces already provided by his loyal servants.

It is uncertain whether King Edward did in fact visit Portskewett, but the following year Harold's grand hunting lodge was destroyed in a raid carried out by Caradog ap Gruffydd. On the 5th January 1066, King Edward the Confessor died and the Witon or Great Council chose Harold as his successor. But the new king's reign was brief for on 14 October 1066 he was defeated and killed at the battle of Hastings by William, Duke of Normandy.

Though the death of Harold terminated Saxon rule in England, it made no perceptible difference in the regime of the Welsh princes. Gruffydd ap Llywelyn had been succeeded in North Wales by Bleddyn and Rhiwallon - the one becoming king of Gwynedd and the other king of Powys. Cadwgan ap Meurig was King in Morgannwg, Caradog ap Gruffydd of Caerleon was King of Ystradyw, Gwent-uth-coed and Gwentllwg, while Rhydderch, his son, was King in Ewyas and Gwent-is-coed.

In 1067 William FitzOsbern established a base at Chepstow and penetrated Gwent. A large portion of King Caradoc's territory fell into his hands, but it would appear that FitzOsbern halted his advance at the banks of the Usk and allowed Caradoc to retain Gwynllwg (Wentlooge) and the hill commote of Machen, subject to his overlordship. Caradog in 1072 defeated and slew Prince Maredudd ab Owen ab Edwin in a battle on the River Rhymney and six years later slew his successor, Rhys ab Owen.

Caradog ap Gruffydd met his own death in 1081, during the battle of Mynydd Carn in West Wales, whilst assisting his cousin Trahairn in his campaign against Rhys ap Tewdwr (see page 54).

Caerleon upon Usk is a favoured location for one of Arthur's courts in Geoffrey of Monmouth's 'Historia' and he makes it the seat of the Archbishop of Wales and the scene of Arthur's magnificent coronation. It is significant that during the time that Geoffrey was writing his 'Historia', Caerleon was the centre of the principality of Glamorgan. Following the success of the Welsh in 1136, when Morgan ap Owain ap Caradog killed Richard Fitz Gilbert de Clare and was reinstated in the dignities of his grandfather, taking the title of King in the principality, Caerleon was of some political significance.

Just outside the eastern corner of the Roman fortress wall, the Normans constructed a high earthen motte and a pentagon shaped bailey of about 3 acres in area. The mound has a circumference of about 220 metres and its original height would have been about 10 metres. The original keep erected on this mound in the twelfth century was constructed of timber and was destroyed by Morgan ap Hywel in 1238.

Caradog was succeeded by his son Owen Wan ('the Weak'), who is supposed to have surrendered his lands to FitzOsbern in that year, or perhaps, being under age, he became a ward of the Conqueror. This is thought to explain the appearance in his lordship of two Norman knights. However, Owen appears to have continued his allegiance to the crown of England, and in 1113 he was entrusted with the defence of Carmarthen Castle, then in the hands of the Normans, against Griffith ap Rhys, prince of South Wales.

The lordship of Caerleon was placed in the hands of the Norman knight Robert de Chandos, whose father had accompanied King William in the conquest of England. Robert founded the Benedictine Priory of Goldcliff,[2] which in 1113 he granted to the Abbey of Bec in Normandy. In the gift he included the chapel of Nash, the church of the Holy Trinity (Christchurch), near Caerleon, and the churches of Julius and Aaron.

At this time the west side of the Usk was held by Winebald de Balun, who founded a Cluniac cell at Malpas for the priory of Montacute sometime before 1124. Robert de Chandos died in 1120 and is said to have been buried at Goldcliff Priory. Once these two Normans disappeared from the scene the hereditary rights of the two Welsh owners were restored either by the king or the lord of Striguil, apparently after strong representations had been made by Rhys ap Gruffydd, Prince of Deheubarth, and we find Owen Wan once again in possession of the old Welsh lordship.

When Owen ap Caradoc died he left three sons, Owen, Morgan and Iorwerth. It appears that Owen was incapable of assuming his responsibilities due to ill health and his brother Morgan became Lord of Caerleon in the reign of Henry I.

The Welsh Chronicle records that on the 15 April, 1136, 'Morgan ap Owen, a man of considerable quality and estate in Wales, remembering the wrong and injury he had received at the hands of Richard Fitz-Gilbert, slew him together with his son Gilbert.'

Having been entertained at Abergavenny Castle by Brian Fitzcourt (also known as Brian de Wallingford), who was then lord of this area, Richard FitzGilbert had been making his way to the coasts of Ceredigion, where he had built and garrisoned the castle of Llanbadarn Fawr and Cardigan. He had his main seat at Tunbridge and was also known as Richard de Clare(after the manor of Clare in Suffolk). FitzGilbert was certainly a man of property for he was Lord of Usk and, in addition to his castles in Cardiganshire, he had property at Talgarth and Builth.

A lonely track took the Norman lord and his small party into the Black Mountains, north of Abergavenny, and led them over a pass which had already acquired a sinister reputation, for it was often referred to as 'Mal pas de Grono' - the bad pass of the Grwyne.

Brian de Wallingford, lord of Abergavenny, had accompanied Richard FitzGilbert with a strong guard as far as the start of the pass, but at his guest's insistence had reluctantly left him to continue his journey, accompanied only by his son and a handful of attendants.

The track ascended through a dense wood towards the summit of the pass and Richard FitzGilbert rode on careless of any danger that might await him. Two musicians walked on ahead of him, one singing and the other playing an accompaniment on a fiddle. Little did they know that Morgan ap Owen, the Welsh Lord of Caerleon, lay waiting with his companions to ambush the Norman party. He was still smarting from a past injury and injustice dealt to him by FitzGilbert and had vowed vengeance.

The place where this party of Normans was slain is known as Coed y Dias - the wood of din or clamour and the spot where the attack took place is marked by a stone, which has become known as Dial Garreg - the Revenge Stone.

Dial Garreg - 'The Stone of Revenge' marks the site of the ambush of Richard FitzGilbert at Coed y Dias in the Black Mountains

Morgan and his brother Iorwerth then seized the castles of Usk and Caerleon, which they held until 1158, and by the end of the year Morgan virtually controlled all the lands which had once belonged to his grandfather, Caradog ap Gruffydd. In a charter issued at some time between 1143 and 1154, we find Morgan being accorded with the title king in one of the charters of the earldom of Hereford. Morgan had evidently taken up the kingship which is supposed to have died with his grandfather, Caradog, and he even persuaded his neighbour Earl Roger of Hereford to acknowledge it.

It is significant that Morgan had probably adopted the title of 'king' during the period when Geoffrey of Monmouth was writing the final part of his *Historia,* and just as in King Arthur's time there was now once again a British king residing at Caerleon-upon-Usk.

In 1158 Morgan of Caerleon and his bard Gwrgan ap Rhys (a notable poet of that time) were ambushed and murdered by Ifor Meurig, Lord of Senghenydd (Ifor Bach - famous for his assault on Cardiff Castle in the same year).

Iorwerth succeeded to the title of Lord of Caerleon and was now the rightful heir to the old throne of Gwent. He married Angharad, the daughter of Uchtryd, Bishop of Llandaff, and she bore him two sons, Owen and Hywel.

In 1171, Henry II, on his way to Ireland, seized the town of Caerleon and placed a garrison there. Iowerth mustered his forces, and, with the assistance of his sons Owen and Howel, and his relation Sitsyllt ap Dyfnwal, attacked and retook the town, but was unable to regain possession of the castle.

Henry, then, in an effort to restore peace in the marches, invited Iorwerth to meet him on the borders to discuss a peace treaty and grant him safe conduct. Iorwerth sent his son Owen to meet the king, but young Owen was waylaid by the Earl of Gloucester's garrison at Newport and murdered.

It is possible that the soldiers were ignorant to the fact that the Welshman was under the protection of the king, but when news of this outrage reached Iorwerth he believed it to be a deliberate act of treachery by Henry II. He returned immediately, and, vowing vengeance against the king, he raised all the forces he could and ravaged the estates of the Normans to the gates of Gloucester and Hereford. The following year he retook Caerleon Castle.

Through the mediation of Rhys ap Gruffydd, Prince of South Wales, Iorwerth was reconciled to the king and, with several other Welsh noblemen, did homage to him at Gloucester on 25 July 1175, and had his estates restored to him.

In December of that year, Sitsyllt Dyfnwal[3] and many other Welsh noblemen received an invitation from William de Braose, the new Lord of Abergavenny, to gather at his castle for a Christmas day banquet in celebration of the re-conciliation. On arrival at the castle, the Welshmen were politely asked to leave their weapons in the gatehouse and they duly complied.

Inside the Great Hall the guests sat down to a long table loaded with food and William de Braose rose to his feet and welcomed them all to Abergavenny Castle, but after the goblets of mead had been passed around, he changed the tone of his voice and announced that henceforth all the Welsh of his domain would be deprived of their right to carry arms, and that all who were present should swear to agree to his demands.

His guests were deeply shocked by his words and stared at him in astonishment, for they had come to his castle that night in good faith and had not expected such a demand.

De Braose gave a pre-arranged signal and soldiers, led by Ranolph Poer, the Sheriff of Hereford, rushed into the hall with gleaming swords in their hands. The Welshmen now rose to their feet in horror. Without weapons they were unable to defend themselves and they were savagely cut to pieces. One by one they fell to the floor until the massacre was complete. It is reputed, however, that Prince Iorwerth[4] of Caerleon managed to escape by procuring a Norman sword and, hewing his way to the door, he fled from the castle.

Not satisfied with this bloodshed, the following morning, William de Braose ordered his men to ride down to Sitsyllt's home at Castell Arnallt, further down the Usk Valley. The Welshman's widow, Gwladys, was forced to stand helpless as her infant son Cadwaladr was slain before her very eyes. She was then taken back to Abergavenny Castle where she no doubt died in the castle dungeon.

In 1182, Iorwerth and other kinsmen of the murdered Welshmen attacked Abergavenny Castle and killed or took prisoner the entire garrison. They partially destroyed the castle but no doubt to their disappointment William de Braose and his wife, Maud, were not in residence at the time.

Giraldus Cambrensis visited Abergavenny in 1188 during his travels with Archbishop Baldwin, and he stated in his *Itinerary* that here was 'a castle dishonoured by treachery more often than any other in Wales.'

On the death of Iorwerth, who was buried in Goldcliff Priory, his son Hywel then inherited the lordship. He is generally referred to as Hywel of Caerleon and is best remembered for his endowment of the Cistercian Abbey of Llantarnam. This occurred during the lifetime of his father for the grant specifically states that it was made with the consent of Iorwerth ap Owen, and it also confirms the gift of Morgan ap Owen. Hywel also gave land to the monks of Bassaleg Priory and renounced all family claims to the throne of Gwent (for which his family had been clamouring since the Conquest) in return for a knighthood. Thus honoured, he was also allowed by Henry II to retain the lordship of Caerleon.

Giraldus Cambrensis tells us that Hywel was wounded in an attack by the Normans at Usk and he died soon afterwards in about 1178. He was succeeded by his son Morgan, who must have been just a child when his father died for he survived him by seventy years.

According to the Welsh Chronicles, William Marshall the Elder, Lord of Striguil, gained possession of Caerleon Castle, seemingly through a grant from Morgan in the following terms:-

'Know all men present and to come, that I, Morgan, son of Howel, have given and granted and by this my present charter confirmed to William Marshall, Earl of Pembroke, and his heirs, the castle of Caerleon, with its appurtenances, to be holden of the Lord the King, and his heirs, in capite, as Howel my father was accustomed to hold the said castle, with its appurtenances, justly and freely, and as I justly and freely do hold the said castle and its appurtenances, as of the gift of the King. Witnessed by Hubert de Burg, then Justiciary of England; Gilbert de Clare, Earl of Gloucester, and Hereford; ....Ralph Fitz Nicholas, William de Gamage, and others.'

It is unlikely that this grant of his property by Morgan was a voluntary act and he probably had no choice in the matter. He seems to have fled to Llywelyn, Prince of Wales, and to have put himself under his protection.

William Marshall rebuilt the castle, no doubt destroying the large Roman baths, which were still mainly intact, to provide building stone.

In 1231 Llywelyn attacked Caerleon Castle and town, and, having captured them after an obstinate resistance, killed all the garrison and burnt the castle to the ground. It was never rebuilt. William Marshall the Younger died the same year and was succeeded by his brother, Richard, who made peace with Llywelyn, and joined him against the king. The same year commissioners were appointed to meet at Montgomery to settle disputes between the king and Llywelyn, 'as to the castle of Caerleon.' The articles agreed upon contain an express stipulation that all the lands and goods that Gilbert Marshall held belonging to Morgan should be restored to him. This does not appear to have been carried out in full and, following the death of

Morgan, an inquisition held in 1249 reveals that he died possessed of the commotes of Edlogan and Lebenth only. His daughter Gwerfil was his sole heir. She had married Maredydd Gethin (d.1201), son of the Lord Rhys, and their son Gruffydd, who died before 1248, was succeeded by his son Maredydd ap Gruffydd. One of the sons of Maredydd was Morgan (Sir Morgan ap Maredydd) who married his daughter Angharad to Llywelyn ap Ifor, and from them sprang the line of the Morgans of Tredegar.

Maredydd was dispossessed in 1266 and was killed twelve years later by Gilbert de Clare. He was buried at the monastery of Strata Florida in Mid Wales.

Castell Meredydd, near Machen in Gwent, was built by Meredydd Gethin (Meredydd the Terrible) the great grandson of Rhys ap Tewdwr. After he died in 1201, the property continued in the family and passed with his great granddaughter Angharad to her husband Llywelyn ap Ifor. The great great grandson of this marriage was Sir John Morgan of Tredegar, Knight of the Sepulchre, whose tomb is in St Woolos Church at the west end. He died in 1493 and is often called 'Y Marchog Tew' (the stout knight).

During the thirteenth century, when the de Clare family were Lords of Caerleon, wandering minstrels visiting castles around Wales sang about the life and deeds of King Arthur. Gilbert de Clare, Lord of Caerleon, no doubt imagined himself as the new King Arthur; yet as the centuries passed Arthur as a popular hero faded into obscurity until Alfred Lord Tennyson visited Caerleon in 1856 and revived interest in the matter.

The Morgans of Tredegar House
and the Guinevere Connection

The home of Sir Morgan ap Meredydd[5] was at Machen, on the side of Machen mountain, where there are still to be seen the remains of Castell Meredydd. His daughter, Angharad, married Llywelyn ap Ifor of St Clears and Gwynfe in Carmarthenshire, a descendant of Cadifor Fawr, the lord of Cilsant (d.1089), and from them sprang the whole line of the Morgans of Tredegar.

Sir Morgan Meredydd's other residence, built within what is now Tredegar Park, was probably a Hafod or summer residence, where no doubt he came from his castle at Machen during the hay and corn harvest. It was probably a stone built house with a keep tower for defence standing within a moat. Until the close of the fifteenth century this house would have served as the residence of Llewelyn ap Ifor and Angharad and their descendants. Then Sir John Morgan, the first of the family to adopt that surname, built a stone mansion referred to by Leland in his *Itinerary* as 'The Faire Place'.

The only parts of this Tudor mansion which now remain are the west wing, known as the Servant's Hall, and a room on the adjoining corner, which became the Housekeeper's Room. The square leaded windows of this part of the building have projecting drip stones and are typical of the reign of Henry VII.

Over the years, many explanations and derivations of the name Tredegar have been suggested. One idea is that it is a contraction of the Welsh words *Troed-y-gaer*, 'the foot of the camp,' for there is an ancient earthwork on a hill in the park opposite the house, known as 'the Gaer'.

However, it is also possible that Tredegar took its name from the first founder or owner of the estate and that the name, in a corrupted form, has continued to this day.

A poem written by Gwilym Tew (William the Fat), who lived in the fifteenth century, provides the earliest written mention of a name for this location. Gwilym Tew flourished between 1430 and 1470 and presided at a Gorsedd in Glamorgan in 1460. About this time he wrote a complimentary poem in praise of Sir John Morgan of Tredegar, Knight of the Holy Sepulchre, whom in the title he styles Sir Sion ap Morgan of Dre-Degyr ; and again in the poem he writes the name Tre-Degyr.

There is a tradition that Deigr ap Dyfnwal Hen was Lord of Tref-y-Deigr (Tredegar), Caerleon and Gwynllywg (Wentloog) and it is of particular interest that one of his descendants was Gwythyr, the father of Gwenhwyfar who married Arthur.

Tredegar House, on the edge of Newport, was the home of the Morgan family for about four hundred years and is now a very popular tourist attraction.

The tomb of Sir John Morgan of Tredegar can be seen in the west end of St Woolos Church, Newport. He was knighted in 1448 and was known as the Knight of the Sepulchre because he had visited the holy places over which the Crusades had been fought.

Peniarth Manuscript No.127	**'De Situ Brecheniauc' No. 10**
Macsen Wledig	Macsen Wledig
Anhun Dunawd	Anhun Dunawd
Ednyfed	Tathal
Dyfnwal Hen	Teithrin
Deigr	Teithfallt
Enfael Adran	Tewdrig Fendigaid
Greidiol Galofydd	Meurig
Gwythyr (Uthyr)	Athrwys
Gwenhwyfar = Arthur	

The above pedigrees prove that Athrwys ap Meurig and Gwenhwyfar ferch Gwythyr were contemporaries. Admittedly, Athrwys would have been old enough to be Gwenhwyfar's father, but it was not uncommon in those days for a king in his middle age to have a teenage bride.

Thus, it may be said that 'Tredegar' was Gwenhwyfar's ancestral home. It may well be that, upon the death of his father-in-law, Gwythyr (Uthyr), Arthur, through his marriage to Gwenhwyfar, came into possession of Y Gaer, an Iron Age hill-fort in Tredegar park.

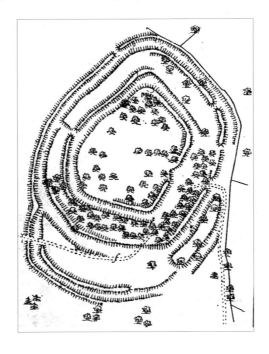

Ifor Hael, Lord of Maesaleg

The second son of Llywelyn ab Ifor (fifth descendant of Cadivor the Great) and Angharad, the daughter and heiress of Sir Morgan ap Maredydd, was Ifor ap Llywelyn ,who was known as Ifor Hael (the Generous) and was head of the branch of the family living at Gwern-y-cleppa, near Bassaleg. He became lord of Maesaleg, the Wenallt and Gwern-y-cleppa, and could trace his descent back to the lords of Caerleon and through them to the kings of Gwent, but most of all he was celebrated for his patronage of the arts of poetry and music. Under his patronage, an eisteddfod was held at Gwern-y -cleppa with the chair being won by his famous nephew, the great poet Dafydd ap Gwilym. Ifor Hael died at Bishton and a stone coffin found there in 1949 was believed to contain his remains.

This famous Lord of Maesaleg died without issue, and his estate came to his nephew Llywelyn, the son of Morgan ab Llywelyn, Lord of Tredegar, and from him in a direct line are descended the Morgans of Tredegar.[6] It is also relevant that the Morgans of Tredegar are descended from Iestyn ap Gwrgan via the Llewellyn Williams family of Dyffryn Clydach in the parish of Cadoxton-juxta-Neath.

The Pencoed branch of the family (east of Newport) traced its ancestry to Morgan ap Llywelyn, elder brother of Ifor Hael. From this branch were directly descended the Morgans of Llanfihangel Llantarnam. William Morgan purchased this Cistercian Abbey in 1561. He was married to Elizabeth, daughter of Sir Rice Mansel of Margam. William Morgan was buried in the Morgan Chapel of Llantarnam Church, where the framework of the remains of his alabaster monument bears the date 1590 and immediately beneath it is a shield displaying the Morgan arms.

Tredegar House was completed in 1674, and consists of two wings at right angles to one another forming a square. It is on the site of an ancient building, of which the hall in the south wing, with 15th century windows, is the only part remaining.

This fine brick mansion was the chief home of the Morgan family up to 1951, in which year the final Lord Tredegar moved to Monte Carlo. The building then became a girls' school run by nuns until 1974, when along with 90 acres of parkland, it was bought by Newport Borough Council. An extensive restoration programme was started in 1976, financed by such bodies as Cadw and the European Regional Development Fund. Tredegar House is now a major tourist attraction with its parklands and gardens providing a fine area for pleasant and peaceful enjoyment on the edge of Newport.

Y Gaer was at one time situated within Tredegar Park

The Tredegar Chapel in Bassaleg Church, near Newport, contains the mural monuments of the Morgan family. There are six hatchments of this family in the building.

The magnificent stone reredos illustrating the Adoration of the Child has one of the surrounding figures depicted in the uniform of a bewhiskered army officer complete with sword, gilt epaulettes, and dressed as for the Crimean War. It represents the young ensign, Godfrey Charles Morgan (later 1st Viscount Tredegar), who participated in the famous 'Charge of the Light Brigade'. He died in 1913.

Fifteen

THE ROLL OF THE ROUND TABLE

In 1155, Robert Wace, a Jersey man, wrote his *Roman de Brut* for Queen Eleanor of Aquitaine, basing his work on Geoffrey of Monmouth's *Historia Regum Britanniae*, and he became the first writer to bring the Round Table and its knights into the story of King Arthur.

Research shows that the idea of a 'Round Table' was not peculiar to the reign of King Arthur, but in fact common to all the ages of chivalry. Aethenaeus, a writer of the second century, tells us that the Gauls feasted at 'Round Tables,' their shield bearers standing behind them with their shields, and here we perhaps gain the first glimpse of what was to become a remarkable tradition. Apart from seeing the 'Round Table' as a solid object, it should also be understood that it once represented an ancient bardic tradition.

When Rhys ap Tewdwr, Prince of Deheubarth, returned from his long exile in Brittany to reclaim his kingdom in 1077, he is said to have brought with him the old bardic system of the Round Table, which by then had become quite forgotten in Wales. A bard named Iorwerth Fynglwyd, living about 1450, alludes to the bardic roll of Rhys ap Tewdwr in the following words:-

> 'The regulations are faultless
> Of Rhys ap Tewdwr, a good man who lived formerly,
> And the much respected Roll of Arthur,
> Which is also good and spirited.'.[1]

Thomas Stephens in his book *The Literature of the Kymry* , published in 1876, continues the story and relates how the system of the Round Table:-

> '...was placed under the protection of the Church of St Catwg in the Vale of Neath, in Morgannwg, which was from the time of St Teilo possessed of the privilege, ecclesiastically confirmed, that neither war nor weapons of slaughter should be brought into the parish of St Catwg, neither by the people of the adjacent country or any other whatever, under bond and pledged throughout all districts of the Island of Britain. And then, after placing the system under the protection of the Church, an honourable Eisteddfod was held by proclamation of a year and a day, to which an invitation was given, under

the protection of the State, to all bards to assemble in the hall of the church, where, according to the royal institution of the Round Table, degrees were conferred on the chiefs of song, and gifts and presents made to them, as in the time of the Emperor Arthur. And after being there forty days, all returned to their houses. And Iestyn, the son of Gwrgan, Prince of Glamorgan, took the Roll of the Round Table with him to his new castle in Cardiff, under the claim that he was prince of the territory, viz. that of the church and parish of Catwg, in his dominion, and that the custody of the Roll of the Round Table belonged to him. And because the court of Caerleon upon Usk, which was the court of King Arthur, was within his dominion, he asserted that his court was that of Arthur continued down to his time; and so he took the Roll of the Round Table by force to Cardiff Castle; and he suffered for that; for Rhys ap Tewdwr made a hostile expedition against Iestyn ap Gwrgan, and defeated him in the battle of Cadlas. Upon which Iestyn ap Gwrgan sent to Robert Fitzhamon and the Normans for assistance against Rhys ap Tewdwr and slew him in the battle of Cynllwyn Ddu ('the Black Treachery'); but the foreigners, having heard what Iestyn had done of violence and devastation, took from him his castle and his territory and expelled him. After that, Robert, Earl of Gloucester, the son of Henry I, married Mabli, the daughter of Robert Fitzhamon, and received the lordship of Glamorgan in right of his wife. He gave presents to the bards in Tir Iarll; and in a hall of his there he placed the Roll of the Round Table, in the custody of the bards of the Island of Britain; and from that time the two systems were united, viz. that of the White Stones and that of the Round Table, as they exist there at present; so that with the bards of the chair of Tir Iarll, more especially than any of the poets of Wales, are the principal systems preserved in their completeness to this day.'.[2]

Obviously, the 'Roll of the Round Table' had nothing to do with chivalry; but it certainly had something to do with King Arthur. It contained the ordinances concerning bardic festivals (known today as Eisteddfodau), at which the bards gathered and degrees and gifts were conferred on the winners of poetry and song competitions.

During the Middle Ages, the 'Round Table' developed into a tournament, in which feats of arms and skill in battle were demonstrated and put to the test. Jousting matches were fought on horseback with blunted lances and in the presence of noble ladies. Such events are recorded as taking place at Wallingford in 1252, Kenilworth in 1279, and at Nevin in Caernarvonshire in 1284. These tournaments became so prevalent throughout Europe in the twelfth century that Pope Alexander III found it desirable to restrain them by an Edict, which denounced such events as unlawful. Those who were slain in such encounters were thus excommunicated and deprived of Christian burial.

Jousting competitions were held during the 12th/13th centuries and were known as 'Round Table' Tournaments

The tournaments of the twelfth and thirteenth centuries were often rough and disorderly and frequently degenerated into real battles or free fights in which many of the combatants were seriously injured or killed.

At the meeting held at Neuss, near Cologne, in 1240, sixty of the combatants are stated to have been killed. In England an Earl of Salisbury died from his injuries; his grandson, Sir William Montague, was killed when jousting with his own father, and many prominent knights and nobles were so injured in the tournaments that they never regained their health. It was not until the reign of King Edward I that they were brought under any regular disciplined system of control.

King Henry II discouraged jousting tournaments and issued edicts against them, and we are told by William of Newbury that many young noblemen travelled from England to enjoy their favourite pastime in other lands, especially France. Tournaments were revived in England, after the return of the heroic Richard I from the Holy Land. He granted licenses for holding them and from this time unlicensed tournaments were treated as an offence against the Crown.

A 'Round Table' was held by Roger de Mortimer, Earl of March, at Kenilworth Castle in 1280, for the encouragement of military pastimes. Five years later Edward I also held one at that castle and during the proceedings he created no less than forty-four knights. In 1284, Edward I, having completed the conquest of Wales, held a Round Table tournament at Nefyn on the Lleyn Peninsula.

To hold a 'Round Table,' where knights and nobles assembled to take their repast together at a round table, 'without rank or precedence,' or to hold a 'Round Table' tournament, were synonymous expressions which were often used without discrimination by early writers. Matthew Paris, writing in the thirteenth century, referred to jousts and tournaments as, 'Hastiludia mensae rotundae'.

Edward III and his young Queen Philippa in 1331 made a pilgrimage to Arthur's supposed tomb at Glastonbury and subsequently decided to reform the British Order, revive the Round Table Assemblies and make Windsor Castle the centre of European chivalry.

In 1334 Edward invited the chivalry of all countries to assemble at Windsor Castle for the purpose of holding a medieval tournament to celebrate two resounding victories against England's traditional enemies, France and Scotland. After three days of jousting and feasting, the king ordered all his guests to assemble, and, dressed in his velvet robes and wearing his crown, he placed the Bible on his hand and took a solemn oath that he would begin a Round Table in the same manner as King Arthur and that he would cherish it and maintain it according to his power.

Edward then instructed his young secretary, William of Wykeham, to enclose the ancient motte - a circular, conical mound 33 metres in diameter - with a round tower to house his meetings of the 'Round Table,' but the building was never finished and just one feast was held in it in 1345.

Philip de Valois, King of France, established a similar event in his dominions; and several other instances may be cited of royalty holding 'Round Tables' at this period, supposedly in imitation of King Arthur and his followers.

It is said that a circular table, made of wood, was constructed at Windsor sometime before 1356; and that the Prior of Merton was paid £26 13s 4d for fifty two oaks, taken from his woods near Reading for the material.[1]

In 1348 Edward III founded St George's Chapel at Windsor, and Thomas of Walsingham tells us that during the following year the king was besieging Calais when he was moved by a sudden impulse. He drew his sword and exclaimed 'Ha! Saint Edward! Ha! Saint George!' The words and action communicated spirit to his soldiers: they fell with vigour on the French, and routed them with a slaughter of two hundred soldiers.'

Hanging on a wall inside the Guild Hall at Winchester is a massive oak table which was made for Edward III, who in 1344 swore an oath in the Chapel of St George at Windsor that he would, like King Arthur, create a Round Table for his knights. The surface of the table is divided into twenty-four segments which are painted green and white and indicate the named places of the knights who are supposed to have sat around its rim. Arthur's place is at the top.

King Edward III (1327-1377) honoured the Arthurian concept of chivalry by founding the Order of the Garter in 1348. He is shown here in an impression on his great seal, used to ratify state documents.

From that time, St. George replaced Edward the Confessor as Patron Saint of England, and in 1351 the celebrated order was instituted. Thus, the English order of knighthood was an Order of the Garter and not the Round Table, with St George instead of King Arthur as its patron.

Besides King Edward and his youthful son, the Prince of Wales (later to be called the Black Prince), two dozen other knights were admitted to the Order. In the beginning, the number of knights at any one time was restricted to twenty-six, i.e. the Sovereign and twenty-five companions, but in later years the number was increased by the creation of certain categories of knights.

Within the unroofed round enclosure at Windsor Castle, the knights of the Order of St. George and the Garter assembled, from the day of inauguration on St. George's day, 23, April, 1351, to the time of Charles II, and celebrated the annual festival of the Order, which for antiquity and dignity takes precedence over all others of its kind in Europe.

A little chapel, which stood just east of the present St George's Chapel, was built by Henry III, who dedicated it to St Edmund, King and Confessor, and it became known as the Garter Chapel when, in about 1350, Edward III had it rededicated to St George the soldier. St George's Chapel served the Garter Knights as the shrine of their order for at least the next one hundred and fifty years. By the middle of the fifteenth century, it had fallen into disrepair and Edward IV decided to build a new St George's Chapel. It took thirty years to build and a further twenty to complete.

In 1415, by the Constitution of Archbishop Chichley, St George's day was made a double feast and ordered to be observed the same as Christmas Day, all labour being ceased and St George received the title of spiritual patron of the English soldiery.

'It is from Froissart, the Court Chronicler, that we learn it was a romantic pilgrimage Edward III and his young Queen Philippa made to Arthur's tomb at Glastonbury which determined the Plantagenet monarch to refound the British Order, revive the Round Table Assemblies, and make Windsor the centre of European chivalry.'

E. O. Gordon
Prehistoric London
1914

The Bards of Tir Iarll
And the Chair of King Arthur's Round Table

The country between the rivers Garw and Afan in north west Glamorgan was included by Robert Fitzhamon in his lands as Lord of Glamorgan, on account of its reputation as a hunting ground. He was succeeded, in 1107 by his son-in-law, Robert, Earl of Gloucester, and that part of his possessions (called Maes Mawr) accordingly became known as Tir Iarll (The Earl's Land).

It is an area of approximately 90 square miles, bounded on the north and north-east by the River Afan and on the east by the Garw from its source to Brynmenyn. The southern boundary is partly marked by the sea coast between the mouth of the Afan and to Kenfig and by an irregular line joining Brynmenyn and Sker.

In 1147, the extent of this territory was reduced by Robert, Earl of Gloucester, when he made from it extensive grants of land (between the mouths of the rivers Afan and Cynffig) to the abbey which he founded at Margam. He also gave support to the ancient bardic institution in his lordship, and it would seem that in later years the Chapter House at Margam Abbey was used as a meeting place for the Gorsedd as there is evidence in the design that it was adapted for this purpose.

The literary traditions of the bards of Glamorgan can be traced over seven centuries, and it should not be ignored that Iolo Morgannwg (Edward Williams, 1747-1826) asserted that the Cadair Tir Iarll (Chair of the Earl's Land) was the Chair of King Arthur's Round Table, which was brought to Llangynwyd from Caerleon-upon-Usk. Furthermore, there is a possible connection between Cadair Tir Iarll and the Roll of the Round Table, which was kept at Llan Catwg (Cadoxton-juxta-Neath) and recovered by Iestyn ap Gwrgan, the direct descendant of King Arthur.

The Chair of Tir Iarll was affiliated to that of Glamorgan as established by Geraint the Blue Bard in the tenth century. The Chair of Glamorgan again was subject to the authority of the National Gorsedd of Wales - Gorsedd Beirdd Ynys Prydain; so the Chair of Tir Iarll was no mere local assembly, but a branch of the national institution and subject to its laws. Later, the Chair of Tir Iarll became incorporated with the Chair of Glamorgan, and was well protected as long as the lords of the county retained sovereign authority over Glamorgan, and the rights and privileges of the bards were renewed by them from time to time.

Much was done by the bards of Wales to encourage the efforts of Llywelyn the Last to retain the independence of Wales, so, after the rebellion of 1282, Edward I discouraged as much as possible the practices of bardism, which tended to keep aflame the spirit of Welsh patriotism. Thus, no gorsedd meetings were allowed and the bards of Tir Iarll were dispossessed of their ancient privileges and endowments. However, this did not prevent them holding meetings in secret until the Tudor period, when Welsh nationalism was re-awakened and the meetings of the Chair of Glamorgan came to be patronised once more by members of the Welsh aristocracy.

Several Gorsedds were held during the fifteenth century under the patronage of such men as Sir Richard Neville and others. One meeting was held for this purpose in 1570 under the auspices of William Herbert, Earl of Pembroke, a great patron of Welsh literature and the founder of the celebrated library of Welsh manuscripts at Raglan Castle, which was later destroyed during the Civil War.

Iorwerth Fynglwyd (fl. 1485-1527) is the bard most associated with Aberpergwm. He composed an elegy for Rhys ap Sion of Glyn Nedd, whose grandson was Lewys Morgannwg. The grandfather of Rhys ap Sion was Rhys ap Siankyn (fl. 1430-50), who lived at a mansion in Aberpergwm and owned a vast collection of Welsh chronicles, triads, genealogies of the princes, lists of saints and elegaic odes. It is more than likely that he assisted in the compilation of the Register of Neath in the fifteenth century.

It is possible that these treasures of the lords of Glyn Nedd at Aberpergwm may have passed into the family library at Ynys Arwed, which is a mansion in the parish of Lower Neath. This was the home of a family which patronised poets for at least four generations. The first known patron was Tomas ap Siankyn and he was followed by his son Richard and his grandsons Rhys and Thomas. The tradition was maintained for another generation by Thomas, son of Rhys.

'Claiming descent from the Welsh Princes and Lords of Glamorgan, the Williams family of Aberpergwm is of ancient lineage. Bardic references to an Aberpergwm of medieval days, written probably centuries later, conjure an idyllic vision of a simple life of music and poetry within the *neuadd* or hall.'

Elizabeth Belcham
About Aberpergwm

The Bards who presided over the Chair of Glamorgan

Meilyr	1120-1160
Gwalchmai	1150-1190
Cynddelw	1150-1200
Gwynvardd Brycheiniawg	1160-1220
Llywelyn Fardd	1230-1280
Bleddyn Fardd	1250-1290
Medawg ab Gwallter	1250-1300
Trahaearn Brydydd Mawr	1300-1330
Hywel Bwr Bach	1330-1360
Dafydd ab Gwilym	1360-1370
Ieuan Hen	1370-1420
Ieuan Tew Hen	1420-1430
Ieuan Gethin ab Lleision 1430-1460	
Gwilym Tew	1460-1470
Meredydd ab Rhosser	1470-1480
Ieuan Deulwyn	1480-1500
Iorwerth Fynglwyd	1500-1520
Lewys Morgannwg	1520-1560
Meiryg Dafydd	1560
Dafydd Benwyn	1560-1580
Llywelyn Sion	1580-1620
Watcyn Pywel	1620-1660
Edward Dafydd	1660-1680
Dafydd or Nant	1680 -1700
Samuel Jones, Ofeiriad	1700-1730
Dafydd Hopkin, or Coetty	1730-1760
Sion Bradford	1760-1785
Iolo Morganwg	1785-1826
Taliesin ab Iolo	1826-1847
Myfyr Morganwg	1847-1888

Some Noteworthy Glamorgan Bards

Ieuan Gethin (1430-1460) was a gentleman poet of Baglan and a descendant of Caradog ap Iestyn ap Gwrgant. He married the daughter of Tomas ab Ifor Hael. Bards from North and South Wales were frequently entertained at his grand house at Baglan.

Gwilym Tew lived in Llangynwyd and was a member of the the the most renowned family of Glamorgan bards being of the line of Rhys Fychan of Tir Iarll. He wrote his name in the *Llyfr Aneirin* (The Book of Aneirin) and states that he owned the manuscript. He is also the first Glamorgan bard who can be proved to be the copyist of manuscripts.

Iorwerth Fynglwyd (fl. 1485-1526) was born in St Bride's Major, Glamorgan, and his bardic teacher was Rhisiart ap Rhys Brydydd and his chief patron was Rhys ap Sion of Aberpergwm. He also made compositions for the gentlemen of his locality; members of the families of Games, Stradling, Bowdrip and Mansel. One of his poems, dated 1466, was addressed to Rhys ap Sion, Lord of Glyn Nedd, in which he writes in anticipation of his arrest, and of the confiscation of his lands. It is of interest that Iorwerth Fynglwyd likens Rhys ap Sion, in his zeal for Glyn Nedd, to King Arthur, who also lost his land.

Lewys Morgannwg (fl.1520-65) came originally from Llanharan but later lived at Llantwit Major. He was the chosen bard of Jasper, Earl of Richmond, at one time, while at another, or even at the same time, he appears to have been steward to Sir William Herbert of Raglan Castle. He was elected president of the chair of Tir Iarll in 1520 and was one of the greatest poets of his time.

Lewys wrote a poem about St Illtyd, the patron saint of his native district, in which he names King Arthur as ruling over the Land of Morgan. He also wrote an eloquent elegy on the death of Rhys ap Sion, Lord of Glyn Nedd, in which he describes his grandfather as a wise man and a gallant fighter. In his youth Lewys Morgannwg had a close cultural relationship with Lleision Tomas, the last abbot of Neath Abbey (1513-39), and he addressed to him an 'awdl', which gave a vivid portrait of monastic life as it existed in his day. He had been instructed in the craft of poetry by his father Rhisiart ap Rhys, and by Iorwerth Fynglwyd. He must have had access to the library of his grandfather Rhys ap Sion at Aberpergwm, the library at Neath Abbey,and the library of the Ynys Arwed family. His access to the latter two libraries must have been helped by his close cultural relationship to Lleision Tomas, who was the son of Rhisiart ap Tomas ap Gruffydd Goch of Ynys Arwed.

The patron of Lewys Morgannwg was Sir Edward Stradling of St. Donat's Castle, in whose library the *Register of Neath* was kept. There is no doubt that both the bards Lewys Morgannwg and Llywelyn Sion had access to the Register of Neath Abbey and were therefore aware of King Arthur's true identity. This knowledge was passed down to the succeeding bards, but in 1725 the *Register of Neath* disappeared from the library at St Donat's Castle and with it went the vital evidence confirming the identity of King Arthur. It is surely more than a coincidence that Sion Rhydderch (John Roderick) was in Glamorgan in about 1725 and that he borrowed many manuscripts which he never returned.

Twm Ifan Prys on offending his landlord in some way was imprisoned in Kenfig Castle by Sir Matthew Cradoc. After his release, he tramped around the area singing ballads and prophesying future events. For this reason he came to be known as 'Twm Celwydd Teg' (Twm of the Fair Lies). Like Lewis Morgannwg, he composed an ode to the Crucifix at Llangynwydd Church. His tombstone can still be seen at Margam Abbey, with the initials T.I.P and the date 1574 cut clearly upon it.

Dafydd Benwyn, or David of the White Head, was a native of Llangeinor in Tir Iarll and he was of the royal line in bardic succession, for he was one of the disciples of Lewys Morgannwg, who in his turn had been taught by Ieuan Deulwyn. Born at the close of the reign of Henry VII, Dafydd became president of the chair of Tir Iarll in 1560 at an early age. He settled at Tredegar House in 1570 and lived in Monmouthshire for many years, possibly till his death in the reign of James I. He was mainly a domestic poet, and thus became personally acquainted with most of the leading families of Gwent and Morgannwg. He was the most prolific of the Glamorgan bards and in particular sang the praises of most of the landed families of Glamorgan and Monmouthshire. His work contains the genealogies of many of the families of these two counties and they also provide us with the Welsh forms of place names in those areas. He wrote about two hundred poems in all and compiled genealogies relating to the families with whom he served as a domestic poet.

Llywelyn Sion (1540-1615) was born at Llangewydd in Laleston, near Bridgend. He is regarded as the greatest professional copyist of his time and there are thirteen of his manuscripts still in existence. It is due to his industry that many of the works of the minor poets of Glamorgan in the second half of the 16th century have been preserved. He had access to the substantial library in Raglan Castle, which held documents of the bards of Tir Iarll, but was unfortunately destroyed during the Civil War. Llywelyn Sion was noted as the most industrious scribe of his age, and valuable manuscripts in his handwriting are treasured in the British Museum, the Bodleian and the National Library of Wales.

Iolo Morganwg (1747-1826), whose real name was Edward Williams, was born at Penon, in the parish of Llancarfan in the Vale of Glamorgan. The family soon afterwards moved to Flemingston, where Iolo was to spend a great part of his life. His father had been a stonemason and Iolo was brought up to the same trade.

When he was 22, he had a row with his father and left home to work in London, dressing stones for Blackfriars Bridge. He returned to Glamorgan in 1770 and married a local farmer's daughter in 1781.

When his sons were old enough to work and run the stonemason's shop he had set up in Cowbridge, he resumed his literary interests and travelled around Wales collecting historical traditions and copying manuscripts. Iolo was a self-educated man who was deeply influenced by the cultural and antiquarian revival in Wales during the eighteenth century. He became a poet in both Welsh and English, a knowledgeable collector of manuscripts, and an antiquary of renown.

There has been much academic argument about Iolo's work and, as a result, much of it is treated with suspicion, for it has been claimed that he was a fabricator and a forger.

However, while some of the MSS in the *Myvyrian Archaiology of Wales*, in which he collaborated with Owen Jones and William Owen Pughe, were undoubtedly examples of his literary forgeries, many more were genuine texts made available to the general public for the first time. He was thus responsible for preserving many manuscripts which might otherwise have been lost.

He elaborated a ritual which he claimed to be that of the druids, and on June 21 1792, he held the first 'gorsedd' on Primrose Hill, in London. At Carmarthen in 1819, the gorsedd became an integral and colourful part of the eisteddfod.

Iolo Morganwg died in 1826 at the age of 79 and was buried in the churchyard at Flemingston. Inside the church is a memorial to Iolo and his son Taliesin. It was Taliesin, who, after his father's death, compiled a collection of his works, which were published under the title of the *Iolo Manuscripts* by the Welsh Manuscripts Society in 1848.

Taliesin ab Iolo (1787-1847) was the son of Edward Williams (Iolo Morganwg) and was said to be born in Cardiff prison on 9 July 1787. He was educated at a school in Cowbridge and then worked as a stonemason with his father. He then kept schools at Gileston and Neath. In 1816 he opened a school in Merthyr Tydfil, where he remained until his death on 16 February 1847.

He assisted his father in publishing *Cyfrinach Beirdd Ynys Prydain*, which appeared in 1829. When his father died, he spent many years putting his father's manuscripts into order and binding them into volumes. A selection from their contents was published by the Welsh MSS Society in 1848 under the title of Iolo Manuscripts.

Taliesin also wrote Welsh poems and won the chair in the Cardiff eisteddfod of 1834 and a prize at the Abergavenny Eisteddfod of 1838 for an essay on *Coelbren y Beirdd*.

**Chronology of events concerning
the Roll of the Round Table**

1077 Rhys ap Tewdwr returns from Brittany to South Wales to claim the throne of Deheubarth, and brings with him 'The History of King Arthur and the Round Table'. He places it under the protection of the Church of St Catwg in the Vale of Neath.

1092 Iestyn ap Gwrgan, the last independent prince of Morgannwg, seizes the Roll of the Round Table under the claim that the church and the parish of St Catwg lies in his dominion, and his court is that of King Arthur at Caerleon-upon-Usk. He takes the Roll of the Round Table with him by force to his castle at Cardiff.

1093 Following the expulsion of Iestyn ap Gwrgan and the death of Robert Fitzhamon, Robert of Gloucester receives the Lordship of Glamorgan. He places the Roll of the Round Table in the custody of the bards in Tir Iarll.

1106 Bleddri ap Kadifor ap Gollwyn, alias Bledri Latimer ('the Interpreter'), writes *Y Seint Greal - the Exploits of King Arthur and his Warriors*.

1120-9 The *Book of Llandaff* is drafted. Geoffrey of Monmouth is in residence at Llandaff Cathedral and is connected with the writers of the ancient charters.[2]

1129 Neath Abbey is founded by Richard de Granville.

1136 Geoffrey of Monmouth writes his *Historia Regum Britanniae*.

1140 *Book of Llandaff* is completed.[3]

1147 Neath Abbey affiliates to the Cistercian Order.

15th c. - Dafydd Ddu ('Black David') of Neath Abbey translates from Latin into Welsh *Y Seint Greal* - the Book of the Order of the Round Table'. He has a first-hand knowledge of the *Book of Llandaff* as he quotes *Llyfr Teilo* and gives a Welsh translation of one of its charters as evidence for the ancient boundaries of the kingdom of Morgannwg. It is also evident that a copy of *Y Seint Greal*, the romance so highly esteemed in Morgannwg at the time, is at the disposal of Dafydd Ddu, the scribe of *Y Cwta Cyfarwydd o Morgannwg* ('The Short Guide to Glamorgan'), which contains a pedigree of King Arthur. The Register of Neath is also compiled in the Scriptorium of Neath Abbey..[4]

It is also claimed that the *White Book of Hergest* and the *Red Book of Hergest* were copied in the Scriptorium at Neath Abbey during the fifteenth century.

Sixteen

THE LOST REGISTER OF NEATH ABBEY

The foundation of Neath Abbey is attributed to Richard de Granville, who is said to have assisted his elder brother Robert Fitzhamon in the conquest of Glamorgan. In return for his services, De Granville received the lordship of Neath, and he built a castle on the west bank of the Afon Nedd, near the Roman fort of Nidium, which was an important station on the Via Julia Maritima.

There is a tradition that, following a disturbing dream, Richard de Granville and his wife Constance needed to calm their consciences by granting land to the Church. In 1129 they made the decision to donate the chapel in their castle at Neath, with the tithes belonging to it, and also a large tract of land, to the abbot and convent of Savigny, near Lyons in France. The condition was that the Abbot should build and maintain a monastic establishment on the land which was an area of marsh to the west of Neath Castle.

The only surviving remains of Richard de Granvill's fortress are the main portcullis gateway, which is flanked by massive round towers on either side. It stands in the middle of the present-day town of Neath, and was built here to guard the area against marauders from the sea and the Welsh who regularly gave trouble from the north and west.

The task of designing the abbey was given to Lalys, a native of Palestine, who was brought to Wales by Richard de Granville[1] after a visit to the Holy Land. It is reputed that his employer later rewarded him with the gift of the manor of Laleston,[2] which bears his name, but this is just a myth for the name was derived from the Norman landowners whose name appeared in early records variously as Lageles, Laheles, etc; the place appearing as Lagelston and Lachelston.

Initially, Neath Abbey was dedicated to the Holy Trinity and its mother-church was at Savigny in France, but, when that church merged with the fraternity of Citeaux, its dedication changed to that of St Mary, in common with the houses of that Order. Neath Abbey was probably the first Cistercian Abbey in Wales, but unfortunately few of its charters or documents, or even transcripts of them, survive today.

Remains of the Abbey Church, Neath

In 1224, Neath Abbey was attacked and partially destroyed by Morgan ap Owen. He set fire to it, killed four of the servants, severely wounded another, and for good measure also destroyed four hundred sheep. Undoubtedly, this was an act of vengeance, carried out because the locality of Neath, now under Norman control, had for centuries been one of the chief residences of the princes of Morgannwg, who had frequently held court there.

It is believed, for example, that Gwrgan ab Ithel had a residence here which in turn was frequented by his son Iestyn. There is also a tradition that Iestyn ap Gwrgan held an eisteddfod at Neath in the eleventh century, to which he invited Rhys ap Tewdwr.

At the close of the fifteenth century the abbey was in very fine condition and its beauty was described in a poem by Lewis Morgannwg, addressed to Lleision Tomas, Abbot of Neath.[3] in about 1530:-

'Like the sky of the Vale of Ebron is the covering of this monastery...the dark blue canopy of the dwellings of the godly. Every colour is seen in the crystal windows, every fair and high-wrought form beams forth through them like the rays of the sun...Here are seen the graceful robes of the prelates, here may be found gold and jewels, the tribute of the wealthy. Here also is the gold-adorned choir, the nave, the gilded tabernacle-work, the pinnacles, worthy of the three mystical fountains. Imperial arms distinctly may be seen on the glass; a ceiling resplendent with kingly bearings, and on the surrounding border the shields of princes, the arms of Neath, of a hundred ages; there is the white freestone; the arms of the best men under the crown of Harry; the church walls of grey marble. The vast and lofty roof is like the sparkling heavens on high, above are seen archangels' forms, the floor beneath is for the people of earth, all the tribes of Babel, for them it is wrought of variegated stone. The bells, the benedictions, and the peaceful songs of praise proclaim the frequent thanksgivings of the White Monks...Never was there such a fabric of mortal erection, nor roofed wall, nor vast habitation; never was there such a foundation nor splendid palace, nor oak of earthly growth; never was there and never will there be such workmanship in wood as this which will not perish whilst the day and wave continue... A temple of masterly construction, through gracious co-operation from the heavenly mansions. A building of regular construction, through skilfull workmanship, a house of piety for the fathers... Golden ceilings are over their heads, goodly canopies, in these splendid dwellings; masses, writings in books, all dignified and complete. Sacred is this dwelling by the cheerful sea... In this compact retreat will be found the warmth of hospitality and welcome banquets, and deer from the parks of yonder hill above, and salmon from the ocean, and wheat and every kind of wine.'

The medieval conventual buildings of the Cistercian abbey were first converted c.1500 into the abbot's house, and further modified by the Williams/Cromwell family and the Herberts after the Dissolution.

Remains of the Abbey Church at Neath

Neath Abbey possessed not only a considerable amount of land in its immediate neighbourhood but land also on the sea coast at Sker, Monknash, Marcross and Gower. In far off Devonshire the Abbey also owned several granges and houses at various times.

It seems to have been by far the most famous abbey in South Wales and the poems still extant give an indication of its patronage of Welsh literature. Although all but two of the manuscripts of Neath Abbey have now disappeared, there was a time when important Latin and Welsh manuscripts were kept and copied here. Among them were the *White Book of Rhydderch* and the *Red Book of Hergest*, the latter being one of the most important of Welsh medieval manuscripts, copied for Hopcyn ap Tomas ab Einion of Ynysdawy, one of the most cultivated Welsh literary patrons of the Middle Ages. It is likely that the *Red Book of Hergest*, a major collection of Welsh prose texts, was compiled at Neath or Margam. Also the manuscript known as *Y Cwta Cyfarwydd* belonged to Neath's scriptorium.

When the smaller monasteries were suppressed in 1536, Neath was deemed of sufficient importance, and wealth to escape being dissolved. Its Charter, or grant of continuance was tendered on 30 January 1537, upon payment of a fee of £66 13s 4d. By 1539, the year of its dissolution, there were only eight monks in its cloister and this number included Lleision Tomas, the Abbot, who subsequently became the rector of Llan Catwg (Cadoxton-juxta-Neath).[4]

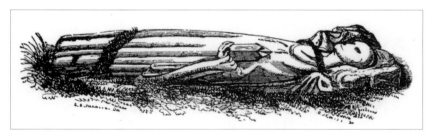

This recumbent effigy is believed to be that of Adam de Kaermerdyn, or Adam of Carmarthen, Abbot of Neath. He holds a model of the church in his left hand and the effigy is of 13th century period which coincides with his time. It is possible that the model signifies the rebuilding of the church of the Abbey and the earlier part of the church of Cadoxton, which was appropriated to the Abbey. Both these works were carried out during his abbacy. John Carter who visited Neath Abbey in the late eighteenth century described it as a 'statue lying in a field near the ruins of Neath Abbey.'

The Neath Abbey estate was granted by Henry VIII to Sir Richard Williams, a nephew of Thomas Cromwell and the great-grandfather of Oliver Cromwell. He purchased it in 1542 and he or his son built an impressive Tudor mansion in the south-eastern corner of the cloister. The house was enlarged in 1600 by Sir John Herbert, utilising stone from the abbey. By the early 1700s it was abandoned. This sacred site was then used for smelting copper during the eighteenth century and an adjoining ironworks later turned the abbey kitchen into a foundry, with ashes dumped in the cloisters.

The most important document ever held at Neath Abbey was the *Register of Neath*, for this manuscript contained material of particular significance concerning the history of Glamorgan.[5]

After the Dissolution, the *Register of Neath* was acquired by Sir Edward Stradling of St. Donat's Castle. This is confirmed by the fact that in a letter dated 18 December 1574 Rhys Meurig craved the loan of the Register of Neath from Sir Edward Stradling. In his *Morganiae Archaiographia*, [6] written between 1578 and 1584, Rhys Meurig acknowledges his indebtedness to this work.

Sir Edward Stradling's library was said to rival the vast collection of books at Raglan Castle in Gwent, held by his father-in-law, Sir William Herbert, the first Earl of Pembroke. Not only was Sir Edward Stradling an enthusiastic collector of books and manuscripts, but he also acquired considerable literary distinction as an author and patron of Welsh writers. Being a great linguist, he was the author of poems on the Holy Sepulchre in Latin, French, Welsh and Italian.

It is of interest that the distinguished and learned scholar Archbishop James Ussher spent twelve months at St Donat's Castle in 1646. Fearing the siege of Oxford during the Civil War, he had taken refuge with his son-in-law, Sir Timothy Tyrrel, Governor of Cardiff Castle. There he remained for many months, during which time he wrote a substantial portion of his *Annals*, and *Antiquities of the British Church*.

When the garrison was withdrawn from Cardiff, the Archbishop had to seek a new sanctuary. Lady Elizabeth Stradling immediately offered him shelter at St Donat's Castle. The Archbishop's party, which included his two daughters, was first escorted to Sir John Aubrey's castle at Llantrithyd, where they remained for one night. On their way to St Donat's the following day, they fell into the hands of the Parliamentary forces, but were soon rescued, and then under friendly escort proceeded to the home of the Stradlings.

St Donat's Castle stands on the site of an Early Iron Age Fort and the earliest parts were built by the Stradling family in about 1300. This distinguished family occupied the castle for about 400 years.

During his stay at St Donat's Castle, Archbishop Ussher spent most of his time in the library, where he consulted many interesting manuscripts, particularly those relating to the early history of Wales, which he said were 'ancient, rare and curious'.[7]

In 1572, Sir Edward Stradling compiled an account of *The Winning of the Lordship of Glamorgan out of the Welshmen's Hands*.[8] It was his account of the Norman invasion of Glamorgan which gave rise to the story of the 'Twelve Knights of Robert Fitzhamon'. This manuscript was later included by Dr David Powell in his edition of Humphrey Llwyd's *Historia of Cambria* (London,1584).

Sir Edward Stradling is also mentioned by Lewis Dwnn as among those who had written on the history and genealogies of the whole of Britain. His name and reputation would have given him easy access to old records and books held in the great religious houses such as Neath and Margam. Such manuscripts available to him would of course have included the *Register of Neath*, which in due course came into his possession.

During our research, we came to realise the considerable importance of the ancient *Register of Neath*, for it would contain an early history of Morgannwg and possibly provide the first identification of Athrwys ap Meurig as King Arthur, thus proving that such a statement was made several centuries before the time of Iolo Morgannwg, who is generally regarded as a forger of genealogies.

It is significant that the following antiquaries consulted the *Register of Neath*:-

(i) In a letter dated 18 December 1574, Rhys Meurig sought the loan of the Register of Neath from Sir Edward Stradling. It was then used as one of the sources for Rhys Meurig's *A Book of Glamorganshire Antiquities* published in 1578. In this book he names **Morgan as the son of Adras ap Meurig.**

(ii) Llywelyn ap Rhisiart (Lewys Morgannwg), who flourished 1520 - 1565, mentions **Arthur as king of the warlike land of Morgan.** Lewys Morgannwg had cultural connections with Lleision Tomas, the last abbot of Neath Abbey which was dissolved in 1539. It is significant that the chief patron of Neath Abbey was Sir Edward Stradling (d. 1535) of St Donat's Castle, who was also the patron of Lewys Morgannwg.

(iii) Llywelyn Sion of Llangewydd (1540-1615) in *Llyma Enwau a Hiliogaeth Brenhinoedd Morgannwg* ('These be the names and genealogies of the Kings of Glamorgan') mentions **Morgan succeeding** to the twelve hundreds of Gwent Essyllt **in the principalities of Arthur.** Elsewhere he records that **Adras ap Meurig was a very heroic sovereign** who frequently put the Saxons to flight.

(iv) In 1591 Sir Edward Mansel of Margam, in *Another Account of the coming of the Normans* mentions **Morgan as a prince who lived in the time of King Arthur and was his son as some would have it.**

V) In 1673 Sir William Dugdale in his *Monasticon Anglicanum* Vol III p. 190) mentions **Arthur as the son of Meurig.**

Rhys Meurig and Sir Edward Stradling were both associated with the Herberts of Raglan Castle, which, before its destruction in the Civil War, housed a library of valuable documents. The Harl Ms 2273 shows that the Register of Neath was in Sir Edward Stradling's possession in 1595.

History of the Stradling Family

The Stradlings were once one of the most important families in the Vale of Glamorgan. They owned thousands of acres of land, much of which came to them through inter-marriage with other landowners in the area. Not only did they hold numerous estates, including the four castles of St Donat's, Sully, East Orchard and Penlline, but they held twelve manors and the patronage and living of six churches.

Sir William Esterling, of Flemish descent, is said to be the first of the family to own the lordship and in the course of a century the name became gradually abbreviated to Stradling..[9] There were seventeen generations of the family in male descent, and they all resided at St Donat's. Five of them were named Edward and, for example, in 1340, a Sir Edward Stradling was Sheriff of Glamorgan and three years later MP for Somerset. He was a great patron of Neath Abbey and the Abbots of this convent gave him an undertaking that they would hold a memorial service for him on the anniversary of his death. This was probably in gratitude for his gift of 2 acres of land in the Vale to the Abbey.

Another Edward was Knight of the Sepulchre. He married the daughter of Roger Berkerolles of East Orchard, St Athan, in 1367. Through this marriage, the family obtained the large estates of East Orchard and Merthyr Mawr.

In 1422, a Sir William Stradling made the pilgrimage to the Holy Land, accompanied by his son, and was also made a Knight of the Sepulchre. His marriage to the daughter of Cardinal Beaufort brought into the family the estates of Holsway Manor in Somerset.

The most prominent member of this noble family was undoubtedly Sir Edward Stradling, who was born in 1529 and died in 1609. He was educated at Oxford, travelled widely and could speak seven languages. A keen antiquarian, he collected a number of valuable books and ancient manuscripts from many religious houses which had been written by the abbots and friars.

Between 1561 and 1566 he wrote his famous account of the *Winning of the lordship of Glamorgan and Morgannwg out of the Welshmen's hands by Robert Fitzhamon and his twelve knights*, of whom William le Esterling was reputed to have been Stradling's ancestor. The origins of Sir Edward's account were in fact current among the Glamorgan bards at least a century before his time, but historians have done their best to demolish such traditions.

Sir Edward Stradling worked hard for the continuation of Welsh culture and encouraged Dr John Dafydd Rhys to produce a Grammar of the Welsh language, which was the first ever published.

The church of St. Donat's is dedicated to St. Dunawd, who in conjunction with his sons, founded the monastery of Bangor Iscoed on the banks of the Dee in Flintshire

Sir Edward Stradling was proud of his family and commisioned three unusual memorials, painted on wood, which recount the exploits of his ancestors. It was he who also converted the Lady Chapel, built by his father, Sir Thomas Stradling, into a burial place for his ancestors, whose remains were reinterred here.

Memorial in the Stradling Chapel in St Donat's Church to Sir Edward Stradling (1529-1609) and his wife Agnes (d.1610). They are depicted kneeling on cushions on the opposite sides of a central altar.

Memorial to Morgan Stuart Williams, a wealthy coalowner of Aberpergwm, who purchased St Donat's Castle in 1901 and carried out extensive restoration and improvement of the buildings.

The last of the Stradling line was Sir Thomas Stradling, who met his death in a duel at Montpelier on 27 September 1738. A series of lawsuits followed his death, and finally St Donat's passed to a cousin, Sir John de la Fontaine Tyrwhitt, through whom it went to the Tyrwhitt-Drake family of Great Shardloes, Amersham, Bucks. They sold the estate in 1862 to John Whitlock Nicholl-Carne, a descendant of the Stradlings in the female line. He had a very romantic attachment to the castle, and his possession of it realised the dream of his boyhood. He assumed the surname of Stradling, repaired and restored the ancient castle and made it his permanent residence, remaining there until his death.

At the end of the 19th century Morgan Stuart Williams of Aberpergwm purchased the castle and estate from the Nicholl-Carne family. He was very proud of the fact that he was a descendant of Iestyn ap Gwrgan. The Williams family settled at Aberpergwm in about 1560, when they inherited the estate by marriage with the grand-daughter and heiress of John ap Rhys of Glyn Nêdd, which is the ancient name of that seat. In the male line the family came from Blaen-Baglan, where in the churchyard their ancient tombs are preserved.

Morgan Stuart Williams' son, Godfrey, sold the castle in 1922 to Lady Winifred Pennoyer, who shortly afterwards sold it to William Randolph Hearst, the American newspaper magnate. He used the castle to entertain film star guests. Following his financial downfall the castle changed hands again and in 1962 it became Atlantic College, the first international sixth-form.

But what happened to the *Register of Neath*?

We know that this manuscript was seen in Sir Edward Stradling's library at St Donat's Castle as late as 1657 when Thomas Wilkins referred to it in his *Analecta Glamorganica*, but then with the extinction of the Stradling line the contents of the library were scattered. This happened in 1755, when an Act of Parliament dispersed the Stradling estates among the claimants. St Donat's Castle and its contents fell to the lot of the Tyrwhitt-Drake family of Shardloes, in Buckinghamshire, with whom Sir Edward Stradling had been on his 'Grand Tour' at the time of his death in France.

There is no doubt that the bards Lewys Morgannwg and Llywelyn Sion had access to the Register of Neath Abbey and were therefore fully aware of King Arthur's true identity. This knowledge was passed down to the succeeding bards, but sometime in the mid 18th century, the Register of Neath disappeared from the library at St Donat's Castle and with it went the vital evidence confirming the identity of King Arthur.[10]

Seventeen

THE BLOODLINE OF KING ARTHUR

Following the dissolution of Neath Abbey in 1539, Lleision Tomas,[1] the last Abbot of Neath Abbey, became the rector of Llan Catwg (Cadoxton-juxta-Neath), a position he held for two years. Llan Catwg was founded by St Catwg in the sixth century and there is a tradition that he was walking along the banks of the River Nedd and 'he saw a white boar lying under a tree, which his companions killed; he saw secondly, bees coming and entering a hollow tree; and thirdly, the nest of a hawk at the top of the tree. Then he sent these gifts to **King Arthmael**, who gave to the blessed Catwg the liberty of dwelling and possessing that land.' This strange tale simply implies that Catwg found a quiet refuge on the right bank of the Nedd and sent a suitable tribute to the ruler of that territory.

Of the medieval church which was built here in Norman times, only the tower remains and this dates from the thirteenth century, when Abbot Adam of Carmarthen enlarged the neighbouring monastery.

Writing in 1803, the Rev J Evans comments that: 'Near Neath is the small neat church of Cadoxton, or St Cadoc's Town, where over a monument is a very singular epitaph: it is no less than the whole pedigree of the family of Williams.'

This 'singular epitaph' consists of sheets of copper on which is engraved a very long but fascinating pedigree of the Williams family of Dyffryn Clydach, which lies on the right bank of the river Neath. They can be seen on a wall inside the vestry and are of considerable interest for the members of this family were descended from Iestyn ap Gwrgan, the last Prince of Glamorgan, and were thus direct descendants of King Arthur:-

'Waiting for the second coming of our blessed Saviour lieth Llewelyn Williams, of Duffryn in this parish, Gent., whose soul departed this life the 11th day of Dec. 1625: and his body is interred with several of his ancestors in this church. He was, by paternal descent in issue male, son in the tenth degree to Rees, the son of Iestyn ap Gwrgan, the last Prince and Lord of Glamorgan of British blood, and by his maternal descent in issue male, he was son in the like degree to Prince Conan, the son of Jago, King of North Wales, by Ranulph, the daughter of Alfred, King of Dublin. His wife was Gwladis, the daughter of Evan ap William Sir Howel Goch, by his wife Mault Cadogan;

Llan Catwg (Cadoxton-juxta-Neath) was founded by St Catwg in the sixth century on the banks of the Afon Nedd in the territory of King Arthmael (Arthur)

by whom he had seven sons and four daughters, from whom are descended a numerous issue, now living in this parish and county, and in Monmouthshire and Caermarthenshire. All his sons, except the eldest, took his christian for their surname, according to the old British and Welsh method.

Here also lieth the body of William Williams, eldest son of the said Llewelyn and Gwladis, who departed this life the 14th day of August,1643. His wife was Bridget, daughter of Lewis Evans, of Montgomeryshire, Esq.

And also lieth the body of Charles Williams, eldest son of the said William and Bridget, who died the 29th day of March,1639. His wife was Joan, daughter of Sir Edward Aubrey, knight, by Dame Jane, his wife, daughter and heir to William Havard, of Tre' Domin, Esq.

And also lieth the body of Philip Williams, Esq., second son of the said William, who died the 24th day of April, 1658. He was first married to Margaret, daughter of David Powell of Landow, Gent. by Anne, the daughter of Lupon Evans, of Neath, Esq. by Margaret his wife, sister to Sir William Herbert, secretary of state to Queen Elizabeth; and by the said Margaret had William Williams, who died the 31st of January 1668, and lieth buried here.

The second wife of the said Philip was Rose, daughter to Morgan Craddock, of Cheriton, Esq. by Anne his wife, daughter of William Pritchard, of Caerwent, Esq. by his wife Jane, the daughter of Sir Thomas Stradling, of St. Donat's, Knight, by his wife Dame Catherine, the daughter of Sir Thomas Gamage, Knight, lord of Coyty, by dame Margaret his wife, daughter to Sir John St. John, knight; by whom he had issue Philip Williams, now living, anno 1707, at whose charge this inscription is now revived.

And here also lieth the body of the said Rose, wife of the said Philip, who departed this life the 24th day of March 1680. She was, by her said mother, descended from John of Gaunt, duke of Lancaster, king of Castile and Leon, and son to King Edward III, king of England.

The said Morgan Craddock, father of the said Rose, was descended, in issue male, from the valiant Caradock, well known in antiquity by the name of Cradock the puissant and strong; and by female extraction from the family of Sir Rhys ap Thomas, Knight of the Garter, and the Mansells, then of Scurlidge, Penrhys, and Oxwich castles, now of Margam.

Another descendant of the said Cradock the strong, was Sir Matthew Craddock, who lies interred in the Caradock's aisle, in the church of Swansea. This Sir Matthew was grandfather to Sir George Herbert, the first sheriff of Glamorgan; and to Black Will, the first Earl of Pembroke of the family now in being. The estate of the first Sir Matthew is now enjoyed by Fulke Greville, Lord Brooke, and by the family of Herberts, descended to them by a daughter of he said Sir Matthew.

The above-mentioned Iestyn ap Gwrgan was prince and lord of Glamorgan, and Morgannwg, and Gwentland, in the time of William Rufus, King of England; and was wrongfully and treacherously (by Sir Robert Fitz-Hammond, and the twelve Norman knights, whom Prince Iestyn had retained in his service to fight against his enemies, and who came into England with William the Conqueror) dispossessed of his ancient paternal inheritance, the castle of Cardiff, where he then kept his court; and of twelve other castles in this county, with all the lands thereunto belonging; besides the castle and lordship of Senghenith, or Cairfilly, which Einion ap Colwyn, who after the base action was called Eynon Tradwr, or Eynon the treacherous, for combining with the said strangers to betray the prince that had generously relieved him in his distress, took to his own share, and, by the assistance of the said Normans, possessed himself thereof. Prince Iestyn was lineally descended in issue male, by his ancestors Morgan Hen or Wlwyn Fawr, who married the daughter of Rodric the Great, King of all Wales, and by Ithel, King of Gwent and Morgannwg, from Brennus, who as some say, conquered Rome or Bran Fendigard, ancestor to Coelus or Cael Bodibog, king of Britain, father to Helena or Elen Weddog, mother o Constantine the Great, the first Christian emperor. His wife, or princess, the mother of the said Sir Rhys, was daughter to Elhestan or Elistan Clod Rhydd, prince of Terlex (Trelech?)

and lord of the lands between the Wye and Severn; descended from Casnar Wledig, the son of Leith or Leid, the son of Belimaur, or Belinus the Great, king of Britain. And his mother was Ancreda or Angharad, daughter to Ednowin, prince of Teyengl.

The said son of Hammond and his twelve Norman followers, thereafter named, took themselves, as aforesaid, the castles and manors following: himself, as chief of them, took the castle of Cardiff; Richard de Granvilli, Neath; William de Londres, Ogmore; Paganus de Turberville, Coyty; Robert de Quintin, Llanblethian; Richard de Syward, Talyfan; Gilbert de Humphrevill, Penmarch; Reginald de Sully, the castle of Sully; Roger de Berkralles, East Orchard; Peter le Soor, Peterston upon Ely; John le Fleming, that of St George; Oliver St. John, Fonmon; and William de Easterling, that of St Donat's.

The above-mentioned Sir Howel Gwch was ancestor, in the male line, to Sir Robert Thomas, late of Llanmianyl in this county, Baronett; and son in the eighth degree to Craddock, eldest son of the said Prince Iestyn, by his second venture of the said princes. The said Sir Howel was also ancestor to Judge Jenkins of Hensol, by his mother, sister to the above-mentioned Gwladys.

Here also lieth the body of the afore-mentioned Philip Williams, Esq. who departed this life, the 6th day of November, 1717.'

The descent of the Williams family is traced from Rees ap Iestyn ap Gwrgan on the paternal side and from Prince Conan, son of Iago, King of North Wales on the maternal side.

This memorial inscription is probably the longest to be found in any church in Britain. Not only is the pedigree of the Williams family given, but also of the wives of the several generations of Williams buried there; the families mentioned include Evans of Neath, Aubreys, Craddocks, Herberts of Swansea, Gamages of Coity and the Mansells of Margam.

Blaen Baglan, Plas Baglan and the descendants
of Caradoc ap Iestyn ap Gwrgan

In the sixth century St Baglan, a disciple of St Illtud, founded a small church at the place which is now known as Baglan. There is a legend that he was told to build a church on a spot where he would find a tree bearing three kinds of fruit. It was here that he found a tree with a sow and a litter of pigs rooting about underneath it; there was a hive of bees in the trunk, and in the branches a crow had made its nest. St Baglan did not care for this situation and began to build on what he considered to be a better spot, but what he put up by day fell down in the night, so he had to accept the place to which he had been guided.

Baglan is situated about 2 miles west of Aberavan and the original church was superseded by a 12th century building, which was last used in 1822 and destroyed by fire in 1954. The ruins can be seen in the upper part of the graveyard of the Victorian church dedicated to St Catherine.

Remains of the 12th century church which stands on the site of one founded in the sixth century by St Baglan, son of Dingad ab Nudd Hael, who became a disciple of St Illtud.

Morgan Fychan, the second son of Morgan Gam, possessed half a commote of land at Baglan and it was his descendant Jenkin ap William who gave the name Williams to the family.

In Cwm Baglan on a steep sided knoll are the remains of Plas Baglan, once the home of the Lords of Baglan who lived here in the fourteenth century. Low grass banks and remains of stone walling could be seen at one time, providing evidence of a rectangular building measuring about 20 metres by 16 metres.

Here was the court of Ieuan ap Lleision, descendant of Iestyn ap Gwrgan, which once attracted bards and minstrels from all over Wales and it held a high place in the story of Welsh Bardism.

A possible reconstruction of Plas Baglan by Paul Davis. All that remains are earthworks in a dingle about a quarter of a mile above the old church of Baglan. It is probably the first stronghold that was occupied by the Lords of Nedd-Afan, or their summer abode after the castle of Aberavan was built. It was certainly the home of Morgan Vychan, second son of the rebellious Morgan Gam, who held half a commote of land in Baglan and died in 1288. Some of his descendants lived at Neuadd Baglan (Baglan Hall) and the large farm of Blaen Baglan.

Blaen Baglan Farm, sometimes called Llan Baglan, stands about half-a-mile from Baglan Church. The house has been much altered since Tudor days, but it still retains several features which indicate its antiquity. The empty square recess above the main doorway probably displayed the family coat of arms at one time.

Blaen Baglan was the home of William ap Jenkin, who was descended from Caradoc ap Iestyn ap Gwrgan. His eldest son was George ap William who inherited the family property of Blaen Baglan. Another son was Jenkin ap William, who settled at Aberpergwm, which had been leased some time after 1530 from the last Abbot of Neath. Their father, William ap Jenkin, left Blaen Baglan in about 1545 and spent the remainder of his days at Thytegston Court at Loughor. He was made Sheriff of Glamorgan in 1565.

George ap William was the steward of the manors of Afan and Afan Wallia, held by the Earls of Pembroke, and he also served the office of Constable of Aberavan Castle in 1590. He was a patron of music and Welsh literature, as were successive members of the Baglan squirearchy.

George was succeeded at Blaen Baglan by his eldest son William, and on his death, the property passed to his half-brother Edward Williams. He died on August 8, 1658, and was buried at Baglan. The tombs of his five daughters and other members of the family can be found near the eastern end of the old church.

Edward Williams, the son of George, was the last representative of the main Baglan line of the family. He died on 17 January 1692 and his sister Margaret inherited the estate. The old mansion has been unoccupied since 1956.

In 1560 Jenkin ap William[2] of Blaen Baglan settled at Aberpergwm on land leased to him by Lleision, the rector of Cadoxton-juxta-Neath. The Williams family inherited the estate by marriage with the grand-daughter and heiress of John ap Rhys of Glyn-nedd, which is the ancient name of that seat. Jenkin ap William was a direct descendant of Morgan Vychan, whose great-great-grandfather was Iestyn ap Gwrgan. By marrying Angharad, the daughter of Llewelyn ap Gwilym of Garreg Fawr, he united the lines of Einion ap Collwyn and Iestyn ap Gwrgan.[3]

Aberpergwm House was in later years famous for its library of manuscripts and it became a centre of cultural activities where lavish hospitality was bestowed on the domestic and visiting bards, who in turn sang the praises of their descendants.

Iestyn ap Gwrgan	last Prince of Glamorgan, killed 1093
Caradoc ap Iestyn	Lord of Afan d. c.1148
Morgan ap Caradoc	Lord of Nedd-Afan d.1207/8
Morgan Gam	Lord of Afan d.1240
Morgan Fychan	Lord of Afan d.1288
Rhys ap Morgan	Lord of Baglan
Lleision ap Rhys	(Tad y Lleisioniaid)
Ievan ap Lleision	of Blaen Baglan
Hopkin ap Ievan	of Blaen Baglan
William ap Hopkin	of Blaen Baglan
Hopkin ap William	of Blaen Baglan
Jenkin ap Hopkin	of Blaen Baglan
William ap Jenkin	of Blaen Baglan
Jenkin ap William	settled at Aberpergwm in c.1560

'Even the common people know their family tree by heart and can readily recite from memory the list of their grandfathers, great-grandfathers, great-great grandfathers, back to the sixth or seventh generation; or beyond that, in this manner; Rhys son of Gruffydd, son of Rhys, son of Tewdwr, son of Einion, son of Hywel, son of Cadell, son of Rhodri Mawr and so on.'

Giraldus Cambrensis 1177

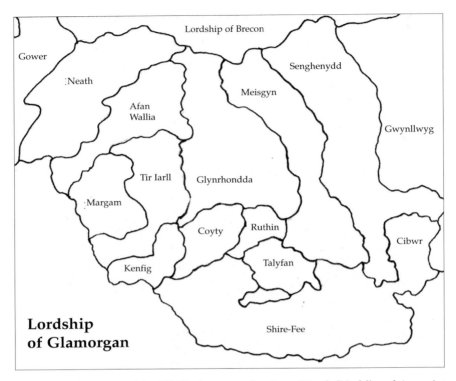

Lordship
of Glamorgan

The territory known as Afan Wallia, between the rivers Neath (Nedd) and Avan, juts out to the sea at Aberavan. It was possessed after the Fitzhamon conquest by Caradoc, eldest son of Iestyn ap Gwrgan, and his successors, in whose lineage was the house of Aberpergwm, whose patrimony extended along both banks of the river Nedd.

Afan Wallia was held for many generations by the descendants of Caradoc ap Iestyn. Its boundaries as shown on the map are taken from surveys of the 17th century, and there is no reason to doubt that they show the limits of the Lordship in the later medieval times, though its earlier Welsh Lords probably claimed a much more extensive rule.

Tir Iarll means 'the Earl's Land' and it was named after Robert, Earl of Gloucester and Lord of Glamorgan. It consisted of the two large parishes of Llangynwyd and Bettws. It is an area of approximately 90 square miles, bounded on the north and north-east by the River Afan and on the east by the River Garw from its source to Brynmenyn.

The ruined mansion of Aberpergwm is sadly now in danger of total collapse

The greater part of the building is Tudor with later additions in the 19th century. It was once famous for its library of Welsh manuscripts.

Aberpergwm House by William Weston Young

During the 1970s, Aberpergwm House was used as a venue for auctions, having been let to a Swansea businessman, but vandalism began to destroy the building and by 1979 it had been reduced to a dangerous ruin

The Williams family resided at Aberpergwm for about 380 years and there are several pedigrees of this family in the British Museum, while others exist in the Herald Office. Lewys Dwnn, in his *Heraldic Visitation of Wales*, makes frequent mention of them. They are descended by various intermarriages from Nest, the daughter of Iestyn ap Gwrgan, and wife of Einion ap Collwyn; from Rees, the son of Iestyn ap Gwrgan, who held territory between the rivers Neath and Towi; and from Caradog, the son of Iestyn ap Gwrgan. The name Williams was adopted during the reign of King Henry VIII, but, correctly, it should be De Afan, which, by different writers, has been variously given as De Aven and De Avene, with some deviations.

Not surprisingly, the Williams family of Aberpergwm were obsessively interested in their roots and the motto of Iestyn ap Gwrgan, 'Y ddioddefws y orfu' ('He who suffered, conquered') was adopted and cherished by them. It was carved on the wall above the main entrance to Aberpergwm House, with the family crest, the Lamb and Flag.

The Lamb and Flag represents 'the supreme sacrifice of Our Saviour for the redemption of mankind, and His glorious victory over sin and hell'. The crests of the lords of Afan contained, apart from the three chevrons, that beautiful emblem of Christianity the 'Agnus Dei' (Lamb of God).

The Williams Family at Aberpergwm

Jenkin ap William, the second son of William ap Jenkin, settled at Aberpergwm in about 1560 and married Angharad, the daughter of Llewelyn ap Gwilym of Garreg Fawr, thus uniting the lines of Einion ap Collwyn and Iestyn ap Gwrgan

William ap Jenkin ap William of Aberpergwm next inherited the estate. He died c.1598 and was succeeded by his eldest son, Lleision, who died in about 1669, and his son Richard Williams inherited the estate. His grave stone can be seen at Llangattock-juxta-Usk in Monmouthshire, where he died on 10 September, 1721, aged 67. His son and heir was George Williams, who died on 29 October, 1746.

George Williams, the second son and heir of the above George Williams died on 12 March, 1796. Interestingly, he was the owner of the *Book of Aberpergwm*, when the Rev. T. Richards of Llan Grallo copied it in 1764.

Rees Williams, son of George Williams, then succeeded and was the last man in Wales to employ a household bard (Dafydd Nicolas). In 1808 he commissioned the re-building of Aberpergwm Church. He was in poor health and died in London on 25 September 1812 at the age of 57. His marble memorial at St Cadoc's, Aberpergwm, reads:

> Sacred to the memory of
> REES WILLIAMS Esq.of Aberpergwm
> on whom providence had bestowed abilities
> of a superior order and a most benevolent
> heart
> He died at Fulham the XXV day of September
> MDCCCXII aged LVII

His famous daughter was Jane Williams (b.1793), who was a noted harp player and collected folk-songs and folk-lore and was a great friend of Lady Llanover, who frequently visited Aberpergwm House. In 1838, at the Abergavenny Eisteddfod, Jane Williams won the Lady Greenly prize for the best collection of the *Ancient Airs of Gwent and Morganwg* and the work was published in 1844. Jane lived to the age of 80 and died on 10 November 1873.

The portrait was purchased in London by Morgan Stuart Williams in 1886 and he claimed that it was of his ancestor Jenkin ap William of Blaen Baglan. However, it is in fact a portrait of Edward Morgan of Llantarnam Abbey, who died on 26 March 1633 and was probably buried in Llantarnam Church, near Newport in Gwent.

William Williams, eldest son of Rees Williams, succeeded to the estates on the death of his father in 1812. He was educated at Harrow and Oxford and spent sixteen years travelling abroad, before returning to his beloved Vale of Neath. He is mentioned in the *Cambrian Journal* (1863, p.272):-

'Fervently attached to his native vale, he was emphatically a Welshman, and a lover of Cambrian literature - was well known to Welsh poets and scholars under the name of *Gwladwr*. He married Matilda, the only daughter and heiress of Colonel Thomas Smith of Castellau, near Llantrisant, and they had four sons: Rees, Lleision, Morgan Stuart and George. William Williams carried out many improvements to Aberpergwm House, extending it and constructing walks in the grounds. He served as High Sheriff for Glamorgan in 1830 and for Breconshire in 1845. He was a generous donor of prizes at the Vale of Neath and Abergavenny Eisteddfodau. He died in 1855 and there is a memorial plaque to him in Aberpergwm Church:-

SACRED
TO THE MEMORY OF
WILLIAM WILLIAMS ESQ.
OF ABERPERGWM

A SCHOLAR AND A GENTLEMAN HIGHLY GIFTED WITH VARIOUS
TALENTS WHICH WERE CULTIVATED DURING EXTENSIVE TRAVELS
AMONG DISTANT NATIONS AND AFTER A LONG ABSENCE HE
RETURNED TO A HAPPY HOME, AMONG HIS OWN PEOPLE WHOSE
LANGUAGE AND LITERATURE HE LOVED WHOSE WELFARE AND
INCREASE OF KNOWLEDGE AND GOODNESS HE PROMOTED WITH
UNWEARIED ZEAL AND BY WHOM HE WAS DEEPLY LAMENTED
LEAVING BY HIS HUMILITY AND AFFABILITY ENDEARED HIMSELF TO
ALL BEING EVER READY TO ENLIGHTEN AND COMFORT THE POOR
AND THE DISTRESSED

HE WAS BORN THE VII OF DECEMBER
MDCCLXXXVIII (1788)
AND DIED XVII OF MARCH MDCCCLV (1855)

William Williams 1814

His son Rees Williams then succeeded to the estates. He was born in 1838 and educated at Harrow and Magdalen College, Cambridge. His brother Lleision died of pulmonary tuberculosis in Egypt in 1860 while travelling with Rees, who brought the body home to Aberpergwm to be buried. A marble tablet in Aberpergwm Church reads:-

LLEISION DE AVEN WILLIAMS
SECOND SON OF
THE LATE WILLIAM WILLIAMS
OF ABERPERGWM
NAT 22 SEPT 1839 OB: 20 JAN 1860
THIS TABLET IS ERECTED
AS A TOKEN OF THE SINCERE AFFECTION
OF HIS WHOLE FAMILY
BY HIS BROTHER REES WILLIAMS
OF ABERPERGWM

Rees died of consumption in London on 9 November 1863, and was buried on 17 November at Aberpergwm Church.

Morgan Stuart Williams was born in 1846 and succeeded to the estates on the death of his eldest brother Rees in 1863. On 22 July 1873, he married Josephine, the daughter of William Herbert of Clytha, Monmouthshire. He became J.P. for Breconshire and High Sheriff of Glamorgan in1875. During the next three years three sons were born to the couple and they were named Mervyn, Owain and Idris. From 1876-9, Morgan undertook extensive improvements to the mansion and these included a new stable block and laundry wing.

In 1899 St Donat's Castle, the ancient home of the Stradling family, was put up for sale and Morgan Stuart Williams, without hesitation, purchased the property and in due course Aberpergwm became his second home, with day to day management in the hands of his estate manager, Moir Ogilvy Spence. Morgan Stuart Williams was well known for his passion for acquiring armour and weaponry. Over many years, he amassed a huge collection which was displayed in the restored St Donat's Castle. He collapsed and died in London (Belgravia) on 13 December 1909.

Morgan Stuart Williams and his family 1886
From left to right: Godfrey, Josephine (Morgan's wife), Idris, Owain, Morgan holding the hand of Sybil, Mervyn, and Nest on the lap of the governess.

When St Donat's Castle was sold to the American newspaper magnate William Randolph Hearst in 1922, the Williams family decided to establish a new burial ground adjacent to Aberpergwm Church, for by this time the vault under the chancel where their ancestors were buried was now full. The new burial ground was consecrated on 27 July 1926 by the Bishop of Llandaff, the Right Reverend Joshua Pritchard.

Soon afterwards the bodies of Morgan Stuart Williams and Idris Havard Joseph Williams were removed from their resting places at St Donat's and re-interred in the new burial ground at Aberpergwm. Morgan was soon joined there by his wife Josephine, who lived to the age of 90, and in 1930 their son Owain Lloyd Joseph Williams was also buried there, to be joined in 1956 by their eldest son, Godfrey.

The grave of Morgan Stuart Williams

St Cadoc's, Aberpergwm, is possibly of late medieval origin, but was largely rebuilt 1808-9, as an estate church for the Williams family. It was remodelled for William Williams in 1840

A private burial ground adjacent to Aberpergwm Church was provided for family members in 1926, when the vault under the chancel, where previous members of the Williams family were interred, became full.

Interior of St Catwg's, Aberpergwm

Examples of the numerous memorials to members of the Williams family

These recumbent figures grace the corners of the chancel east wall. The inscription for the earlier of them claims the burial at this church of the Lords of Glyn Nedd, and mentions 'Rhys ap Sion 1460' and 'Sion ap Rhys'. However, it would seem that they were buried at Neath abbey from where these effigies were moved here during the nineteenth century.

Captain George Williams was killed in the Zulu war. His body was brought back from South Africa and interred in the family vault.

Godfrey Williams at the age of seven in 1882. He was the eldest son and heir of Morgan Stuart Williams and the last Squire of Aberpergwm.

Godfrey Herbert J. Williams was born in 1875. He was the eldest son and heir of Morgan Stuart Williams. In 1901 he married the Hon. Miriam Isabel, daughter of the 5th Lord Rendlesham, and they had four daughters. The marriage was dissolved in 1923. Godfrey purchased an estate on Jersey in 1938 and left Aberpergwm. He then bought another estate at East Grinstead, and from that time onwards no member of the Williams family was to reside at Aberpergwm House, which had been their home for about 380 years.

During the Second World War the house was used as a sanctuary for children from a special school at East Grinstead, near Godfrey's estate. The grounds were utilised to grow food produced by women of the Land Army.

Godfrey Williams died at the age of 81 in Jersey on Saturday, 7 April 1956, and his ashes were interred at Aberpergwm. He was the last squire to be buried there. His obituary was published in the *Aberdare Leader* on 28 April 1956:-

'The small St Cadoc's Church, Aberpergwm, which dates back to the early 16th century was filled to overflowing on Wednesday week, when the ashes of the late Mr Godfrey Herbert Joseph Williams came home for internment in the family's private burial ground at Aberpergwm.

Mr Godfrey Williams was the last of the Williams family to occupy the manorial residence of Aberpergwm House, a family seat which dates back to Cromwellian days and round which practically the whole history of the Neath Valley turns.

To many, Mr Williams was known as 'the Squire of Aberpergwm,' and, as such, he administered the huge estates and former collieries which abound in the Vale.

He last resided at Aberpergwm in 1926, and many of the older folk who attended the service were former estate or colliery workmen employed under him.

Many who failed to gain admittance to the church service stood in silent groups under the huge oaks which border the drive, all paying their last respects to a master *friend*, who had controlled the destiny of the Vale for so long.

To many of the younger generation, who stood in silent tribute in the fields outside the church, this was history being unfolded, as many of the family mourners had been familiar figures about whom their parents had often spoken when the revered name of Aberpergwm had been mentioned in the home.'

Godfrey's brother Mervyn was 80 years of age when he inherited the estate and was in poor health. He had made his home in England where he served as a Justice of the Peace, a member of Berkshire County Council from 1928-34, and as a member of Basingstoke Rural District Council from 1941-63. After his death in 1963, his elder son Major Idris Morgan Williams then inherited the Aberpergwm estate.

Mervyn's nephew George Williams was interested in leasing Aberpergwm House but his offer was declined and he then purchased Llanharan House in the Vale of Glamorgan where he lived for many years. In the footsteps of his ancestors he was appointed Sheriff of Glamorgan in 1966 and his son Owain was subsequently appointed to this position in 1985.

George Williams,	Owain Williams
Sheriff of Glamorgan in 1966	Sheriff of Glamorgan in 1985

The first Sheriff of Glamorgan was George Herbert, a member of the most powerful family of sixteenth century Glamorgan, which had risen to power with the house of Tudor. He was followed in office by Sir Rice Mansell of Oxwich and Margam, the head of the second most prominent family.

The Williams family has produced several Sheriffs over the centuries, the first to serve being William ap Jenkin who held office in 1566, exactly four hundred years before George Williams.

Robert Morgan Williams
inherited the Aberpergwm estate in 1992

The Williams family of Aberpergwm are very proud of their family history and in particular the fact that they are descended from Iestyn ap Gwrgan. The publication of this book has revealed to them that they are also descendants of Athrwys ap Meurig, who is also known as King Arthmael and can be identified with the King Arthur of history and legend.

The Arms of the
Williams family with
their motto:

'Y Ddiodefws-y-orfu'

'He who suffered
conquered'.

The Bloodline of King Arthur

Our research into the history of the Williams family of Aberpergwm enabled us to trace the male line of Iestyn ap Gwrgan (c.1093) down to Robert Morgan Williams who was born in 1963.

The Williams family ensured that the male line was preserved through the centuries. If the son and heir died without issue or had only daughters then his brother would inherit and his son became the heir.

Macsen Wledig (Maximus 'the Imperator') d. 388
Anhun Dunawd (Antonius Donatus) b.c.365 d.388
Tathal, king of Garth Madryn
Teithrin, king of Garth Madryn
Teithfallt, king of Garth Madryn and Gwent *
Tewdrig Fendigaid ('the Blessed'), king of Garth Madryn and Gwent, b.c. 400 d. 470.
Meurig, king of Gwent
Athrwys(ARTHUR), king of Gwent b.482 d.562
Morgan Mwynfawr (Morcant 'the Most Courteous', king of Morgannwg and Gwent
Rhyhawd or Rahawd (Rahaut), Eil Morgan
Einydd
Morgan Morgannwg d. 665
Ithel
Rhys
Brochmael
Gwriad
Arthmael
Rhys
Hywel d. 885
Owain d. 931
Morgan Mawr ('the Great') also known as Morgan Hen ('the Aged') d. 974
Ithel
Gwrgan d. c.1042
Iestyn, the last independent Welsh prince of Glamorgan, killed 1092/3
Caradog, 'The Warlike', Lord of Afan, d.c.1148.
Morgan Arglwydd ('the Lord'), Lord of Nedd-Afan, d.c.1207/8
Morgan Gam, ('the Crooked') Lord of Afan, d. 1240
Morgan Vychan, ('the Younger') Lord of Afan, d. 1288

Rhys, Lord of Baglan
Lleision (Tad y Lleisionaid)
Ievan ap Lleision of Blaen Baglan
Hopkin of Blaen Baglan
William of Blaen Baglan
Hopkin of Blaen Baglan
Jenkin of Blaen Baglan
William ap Jenkin ap Hopkin of Blaen Baglan
Jenkin ap William, settled at Aberpergwm c. 1560
William ap Jenkin ap William of Aberpergwm d. c. 1598
Lleision Williams of Aberpergwm d. 1669
Richard Williams d. 1721
George Williams b. 1683 d. 1746
George Williams b. 1714 d. 1796
Rees Williams b. 1755 d. 1812
William Williams b. 1788 d. 1855
Morgan Stuart Williams b. 1846 d. 1909
Owain Lloyd Joseph Williams b. 1877 d. 1930
Mervyn Gwynne Joseph Williams b.1876 d.1963
Idris Morgan Williams b.1922 d.1992
Robert Morgan Williams b.1963

N.B. There are 47 generations between and including Anhun Dunawd (Antonius Donatus), who was born c.365, and Idris Williams, who died in 1992. 1992-365 = 1627 divided by 47 = 34.6 years per generation. Genealogists allow 30 years per generation, as a standard.

*The Union of Gwent and Garth Madryn

Llyr LLedieth ('Half-Speech')
Bran Fendigaid ('The Blessed')
Caradog
Meurig   Macsen Wledig
Erbig   Anhun Dunawd
Erb   Tathal, king of Garth Madryn
Nynniaw, king of Gwent = Welsh Princes = Teithrin, king of Garth Madryn
                              |
                   Teithfallt, king of Gwent and Garth Madryn

EPILOGUE

The mass of Arthurian connections in South Wales confirm, without doubt, that this was the true realm of the historical King Arthur. At the time of the Roman invasion the Silures were the most powerful tribe in Britain and their reputation as brave warriors attracted to them the Catuvellauni chieftain Caractacus, who became their leader in a series of battles against the Romans.

The Silures were never fully subjugated by the Romans and the result was that they were able to maintain a semi-independent rule under their tribal king. In his book *Welsh Christian Orgins*, the Rev Arthur W. Wade-Evans concluded that Arthur was allied by family ties to the Silurian reguli. Arthur was in fact more than that. He was the hereditary king of the Silures, and the Silurian reguli had married into the powerful Romano-British family of the Aurelii, who held the last vestiges of Roman power.

It is relevant that the historians Bernard Merdrignac (*The British Settlements of Brittany*) and H. P. R. Finberg (*The Formation of England* 550-1042) have both located the seat of power of the Aurelii in the territory of the ancient Silures. This included large parts of Monmouthshire and Herefordshire, and its capital Venta Silurum (Caerwent) gave its name to the British kingdom of Gwent.

Under the Aurelii, the Romano-British elite were in a sufficiently strong position to maintain political ties with the Eastern Roman Empire and trade with Byzantium continued uninterrupted. The Eastern Roman Emperor Justinian I (527-565) had good reason for regarding Britain as the last enclave of the Western Roman Empire.

The latest archaeological evidence confirms that there never was a Saxon conquest as such. What actually took place was incursion, in filtration and integration which happened over several generations. This was a direct result of Arthur's overwhelming victory over the the Saxons in 517 at the Battle of Mount Badon, which gave a temporary check to Saxon encroachment.

About six hundred years after the time of Arthur, his descendants were once more involved in a struggle against determined invaders who had their work cut out to defeat and subdue the native population. Iestyn ap Gwrgan, a direct descendant of King Arthur, was defeated in a battle just north of Cardiff, but his son Caradoc was allowed to retain all the territory in Glamorgan between the rivers Neath and Afan. His descendants through the centuries continued to live and have influence in that area.

Robert, Earl of Gloucester and Lord of Glamorgan, residing in Cardiff Castle, took a keen interest in the legends and history of Wales, and this was probably owing to the fact that his mother, Princess Nest, was the daughter of Rhys ap Tewdwr. It was no doubt on Robert's request that Geoffrey of Monmouth produced his famous *Historia Regum Britanniae*, which ensured that Arthur would be remembered for posterity.

Within two centuries the legend of Arthur and his knights had spread all over Europe and even into parts of Asia. His great deeds were celebrated by the finest medieval poets in Germany, and his name was familiar in Scandinavia, Switzerland, Spain, Portugal, Cyprus and Sicily.

London, the chief city of the Norman kings, claimed Arthur as its own; but so did Winchester, Lincoln, York, Chester and Carlisle. It seems ironic that a British hero, famous for fighting the ancestors of the English, has been adopted as a King of England, but more realistically he is also associated with Caerleon-upon-Usk, the 'metropolitan' city where Geoffrey of Monmouth located his court in Wales.

Even today, all the Celts from Scotland to Brittany lay claim to Arthur; he lived at a time when they were in close contact with each other, and he remains through the centuries a link between them. Of all the great men who have defended and enriched our tradition, he is the most famous but also the most mysterious.

The true legacy of King Arthur, with his victory at Mount Badon, is that the Welsh, the true British, were able to preserve their proud identity and among his descendants there are those who have continued to hold high office.

> 'Lives of great men all remind us
> We can make our lives sublime,
> And, departing, leave behind us
> footprints on the sands of time.'

> Henry Wadsworth Longfellow
> *A Psalm of Life*

APPENDIX I
NOTES

Introduction

1 The exodus of the British gentry to Armorica started soon after the failure of their appeal to Aetius in 446. Large numbers of the British landowners along with their independents fled to Armorica in and after 446. The Breton kingdom of Dumonée in the north is named after Dumonii of the Severn Sea and the name survives in Britain as Devon. By the sixth century, Gregory of Tours refers to Armorica as Britannia and in the lives of the Breton saints the area is known as Britannia Minor.

2 *A Historical Essay on the Bards, Jonleurs, and Trouveres, Norman and Anglo-Normans* by Abbe de la Rue (quoted from a translation in the *Athenaeum* No 425 for 1835, p.842). This quotation can be found in *The Literature of the Kymru* by Thomas Stephens (Longmans, Green & Co., London, 1876).

Chapter One

1 *The Life of St Cadoc* contained in *The Lives of the Bfritish Saints* by Sabine Baring Gould and John Fisher, *The Honourable Society of Cymmrodorion*, London, 1907-1913.

2 *Genealogies and Texts*, Vol5 of *Arthurian Period Source*s, (Phillimore, London 1995), Lists XXVIII and XXiX, Harleian MS 3859.

3 Thomas Carte, *A General History of England* Vol I, Book III, p.202

4 *The Llancarfan Charters* by the Rev Arthur Wade-Evans in *Archaeologia Cambrensis* Vol LXXXVII, 192, (pp.151 and 165).

5 J. W. James (*Chronology in the Book of Llandav 500-900* by The National Library of Wales Journal XVI 91968/70), determined that there is a gap of approximately a hundred years in the Charters of Llandaff. This anomaly has not been recognised by the compiler of the *Book of Llandaff,* and he consequently made one 'King Morgan' out of two men bearing the same name - Morgan ap Athrwys and Morgan the father of Ithael. The gap between the two kings Morgan may be due to the loss of a document, possibly a book of the Gospels, which contained memoranda coveering the entire seventh century. As soon as the two Morgans are separated by a century, the chronological difficulty disappears.

Chapter Two

1 It is interesting that there is a village by the name of Glewyston, situated in Herefordshire, four miles from Ross-on-Wye on the A40. The chapel in the village is dedicated to St Glywys, the son of Gwynlliw Filwr and the grandson of King

Glywys. The latter was the father of Gwynlliw Filwr, Paul of Penychen, Meirchion Vesanus, Mar, Gwrae and Petroc. It was during the time of Morgan Mwynfawr that the name Glywysing was replaced by that of Morgannwg, the land of Morgan, although it is also associated with the reign of Morgan Hen, son of Owain, who died in 974.

2 Hywel ap Rhys, king of Glywysing, is mentioned by Asser in his Life of Alfred (880) , where he is called 'Houil filius Ris, rex Gleguising': 'Hywel ap Rhys, King of Glywysing, and Brochwel and Ffernfael, sons of Meurig, kings of Gwent, compelled by the violence and tyranny of Earl Ethelred and of the Mercians, of their own accord sought King Alfred that they might enjoy his government, and his protection from their enemies.'

Hywel ap Rhys is mentioned several times in the *Book of Llandaff* as a contemporary of bishops Cerenhir (BLD 212), Nudd (BLD 227-231) and Cyfeiliog (BLD 236). In the later charter we are told that his wife was Lleucu, his sons were Owain and Arthfael, and his daughters Ermithridd and Nest.

3 The *Antonine Itinerary* is thought to have been written during the late Second or early Third century. It gives details of the Roman Empire as it then was, with routes from one place to another and the distances between the forts and towns.

4 The various and successive names under which Boverton appears in old records and documents of the 11th and 12th centuries are: Tref Beferad, Tref Byfferad, Tref Byfered, Treberfayadd and Tre Brenin . In the 13th century the Welsh call the place Treberfedd and Treberferad, while the Normans refer to it as Bovyarton. In the 16th century Leland describes it as being known to the inhabitants as Trebrenin.

5 In the tale of *Culhwch and Olwen* in *The Mabinogion*, Peibio and his brother Nynnio are mentioned as two ychen (as in Penychen) Bannawc, 'Horned Oxen', whom God had transformed into oxen on account of their sins. This indicated that Peibio and Nynnio originated in the cantref of Penychen.

6 The *Life of St Cadoc* tells us that Paul Penychen ruled over a marshy district of which Llancarfan also formed a part (Fisher, British Saints, 'Cyngar and Cadoc'). Penychen is mentioned in a Bull of Honorius II to Urban, Bishop of Llandaff in 1128. It was an ancient Ecclesiastical Deanery, and down to the thirteenth century the name continues to occur in the charters. For example; Isuac, dean of Pennechen, witnesses one of the earliest of the Margam charters (M.M. i.6), and among the witnesses of Elias, Bishop of Llandaff, about 1240, are William de Lanmays, dean of Goronoid, and Master Adam, dean of Penhecen (M.M. i. 48).

7 Richard de Clare was born at Boverton and he became a Crusader. When he returned from the Holy Land in 1244, he immediately took a very prominent part in the series of battles waged between Henry III and the Welsh.

8 It is interesting that when Henry VII held the lordship of Glamorgan, he styled himself, 'Rex Anglia,' etc.. and 'Dominus Glamorganie et Morganie' (King of England etc.. and Lord of Glamorgan and Morgannwg).

9 The earliest account we have of St Illtud's monastic college is contained in the early seventh century *Life of St Samson* of Dol in Brittany.

'Now this Illtud was the most learned of all the Britons in his knowledge of the scriptures, both Old and New Testaments, and in every branch of philosophy, and rhetoric, grammar and arithmetic, and he was the most sagacious and gifted with the power of fortelling future events.'

10 llltud was of a military family. His father Bicanys is described as 'a soldier, illustrious in race and military prowess'. Before he settled at Llanilltud, Illtud served for a time as a the military magistrate under the Glamorgan prince, Paul of Penychen (a cantref in Mid Glamorgan). - uncle of St Cadoc and brother of Gwynllyw, King of Gwynllywg.

Illtud's name occurs under a variety of forms: Iltutus, Ildutus, Hildutus, Eldutus, Ulltyd, Illtyd, Illtud, Elltyd. Iolo Morganwg, in Llanover MS. 2, p.93, observes that it 'is a name still pretty common in the Parish of Llantwit, particularly in the ancient family there of the Nicholls, who generally give that name to the eldest son.'

11 In the *Horae Britannicae* it is recorded that the monastery had as habitations, seven halls and four hundred houses. Another account states that the establishment comprised seven churches, each with seven companies and seven colleges in each company, having seven saints in each college, making in all 2,401 students.

12 In the 18th century the ruins of the ancient college were said to be in a garden north of the churchyard, and fragments of hewn and carved stone were strewn around the area, incorporated into garden walls, fences and various buildings. The site was offered in the 19th century by its owner Dr. Nicholl-Carne of St Donat's Castle as a free gift of six acres of land on which to build a University College for South Wales. It was decided, however, to erect a central college for Wales at Aberystwyth, and the Castle House premises were purchased for this purpose.

13 The *Life of St Samson* by Tigernomail (of St Pol de Leon in Brittany) infers that Samson died at Dol and the *Liber Landavensis* also states that he was attacked by severe illness at that place, and passed away surrounded by his sorrowing disciples. The Welsh accounts, however, say that he returned from Armorica to the college at Llanilltud Fawr, where he died at the age of 79 in 565 and was buried in the graveyard there and the spot marked by a stone cross. In the 'Life of St Illtud' it is said that the monastic brothers interred the body 'in the centre of quadrangular stones', (i.e. stones set in a square or rectangle, standing upright).

14 Urien can also be identified with Urbgennius, the Consul de Badon of Geoffrey of Monmouth's *Historia*, and it is of interest that the Rev. Arthur Wade Evans also identified Urien of Gorre with Gwrgant Mawr, King of Erging, whose daughter Onbrawst married Meurig, the father of Arthur.

15 According to the *Brut y Brenhinedd*, Urien of Caer Badon attended the crown-wearing ceremony of King Arthur held at Caerleon-upon-Usk, where a great celebration was held on the feast day of St Aaron..

16 A place called Caer Gynydd at Waunarlwydd, a few miles from Loughor, may preserve the name of the place where St Cenydd was born.

Chapter Three

1 Geoffrey tells us that 'He (Arthur) handed over the crown of Britain to his cousin Constantine, the son of Cador Duke of Cornwall; this in the year 542 after our Lord's Incarnation.'

Chapter Four

1 Tewdwr Mawr was the son of Einion ab Owen ab Hywel Dda ab Cadell ab Rhodri Mawr. He was slain in 997 while fighting under his uncle Meredydd, Prince of South Wales, against Idwal, King of North Wales.

2 The kingdom of Deheubarth was founded during the reign of Hywel Dda when the Vale of Tywi, Ceredigion and Dyfed were combined to be ruled by a royal line which remained in power until the death of Rhys ap Tewdwr in 1093. Deheubarth, with its fifteen cantrefs, extended from the mouth of the river Dyfi in old Cardiganshire to the Severn. It was ruled from Dinefwr Castle which was listed with Mathrafal in Powys and Aberffraw in Gwynedd as one of the chief royal courts in Wales.

3 The battle of Mynydd Carn (1081) has often been confused with a battles fought at Carno in Montgomeryshire and also one on Mynydd Cyrn, near Crickhowell in Powys. Its exact site is not known, but it was at the end of a day's march from St. David's and probably took place on the lower slopes of Carn Ingli, above Dinas in Pembrokeshire.

4 The story of Rhys ap Tewdwr's death at Penrhys is recorded in the mistrusted *Gwentian Brut*, which cannot be older than 1550 and is of little historical value compared with the *Brut y Twysogion,* which states that Rhys ap Tewdwr died in 1091 at Brecon. This is virtually a contemporary account.

5 The Penrhys foundation was not in fact a monastery but a monastic cell belonging to the abbeys of Llantarnam and Margam. It stood on a hill above Ffynnon Fair (St. Mary's Well), which was surrounded by oak and hawthorn trees and, according to legend, a statue of the Virgin had miraculously appeared here. It was claimed the

statue had resisted all attempts to remove it to a spot further up the hillside, and it was said that 'eight oxen could not have drawn it from this place.' Penrhys Monastery was endowed with adjacent lands, and it existed for three centuries as a house of Franciscans. This Order of Friars (in Wales) in later years were supporters of Owain Glyndwr. It is reputed that Owain visited this house and presided at an Eisteddfod that took place there

The monastery was later dissolved by Henry V and its possessions sold in 1415, as a punishment for the crime of supporting Glyndwr. Although the destruction by Henry V is credible it is considered that such a tradition of an eisteddfod here is an invention of Iolo Morganwg which was later repeated by William Llywellyn. The first reference to the monastery is in the Harley Charter of 1203 and it was in fact a monastic cell which belonged to the abbeys of Llantarnam and Margam. The farm house of Pen Rhys used to stand on the site of the monastic cell and was built of the stone from the ancient building. Medieval Penrhys also had a hostelry or guest house standing on the site later occupied by the barn of Penrhys Uchaf. When the site was examined by the Cambrian Archaeological Association in 1912, little remained of the chapel above ground, but in the old farmhouse several oak beams and a door lintel 'obviously came from a medieval building of some distinction.'

6 Not long after the battle near Brecon a chapel of Brecon Priory was established at 'Battle'and may mark the site of the death of Rhys ap Tewdwr.

7 Bernard of Newmarche by the advice of his confessor Robert, a monk of Battle Abbey (in Sussex), made atonement for his sins by founding and liberally endowing the Benedictine Priory of St. John the Evangelist, which he constituted a cell of Battle Abbey. From his castle at Brecon, he ruled over the the the four cantrefs of old King Brychan. For the next four hundred years the area of Brycheiniog and Buellt (which later became known as Breconshire) became part of the marcher land which extended in a broad band of border country from the mouth of the Dee to the estuary of the Severn.

8 Rhys ap Tewdwr had married Gwladys, a daughter of Rhiwallon, brother to Bleddyn ap Cynfyn, and by whom he had a daughter Nest, who was the future grandmother of Giraldus Cambrensis (Gerald of Wales). His three sons were Goronwy, Cynon and Gruffydd.

9 Gruffydd was just a youngster and he was taken to Ireland where he remained until 1112, when he was invited by his countrymen to assist them in their fight against the Normans. He returned to Wales and continued for 24 years to oppose the Normans until he died in 1136. An inscribed stone bearing Gruffydd's name was discovered in Ireland in 1873, No date is recorded on the stone, but it is inscribed with the pedigree of one Robert Carrec, through thirteen generations back to Gruffydd, son of Rhys ap Tewdwr, Prince of South Wales. The stone was found at St. Augustine's Chapel-of-Ease, Londonderry.

10. In 1104 Owain was killed by an arrow fired by Gerald de Windsor. Six years later, Cadwgan was assasinated by Madoc at Welshpool.

Chapter Five

1 Giraldus Cambrensis, writing later that century, said: 'She marched like the Queen of the Amazons and a second Penthesileia leading her army.'

2 Gruffydd ap Cynan died at the advanced age of 82 and was buried on the south side of the great altar in Bangor Cathedral. He had three legitimate sons and five daughters by his wife, Angharad, the daughter of Owen ab Edwin. The sons were named Owen, Cadwaladr and Cadwallawn, the youngest of whom was slain before the death of his father.

Gruffydd ap Rhys ap Tewdwr died in 1137 and was greatly lamented. 'The bravest, the wisest, the most merciful, the most generous, the most just, of all the princes of Wales.' (*Brut y Tywysogion*)

3 William de Londres was so-called because he was born in London. He married a Welsh heiress and his father-in-law was Caradoc ap Iestyn. William was more than likely dead by 1126, as his son, Maurice, is among the witnesses to an agreement between Bishop Urban and Robert Consul, of that date.

4 Rhys ap Gruffydd was the nephew of Owain Gwynedd and also of Robert, Earl, of Gloucester. One of his sisters, Gwladus, married Caradog ap Iestyn of Aberafan and then Seitsyllt ap Dyfnwal of Gwent-uth-chcoed, who was murdered by William de Braose in 1175. A decade later, Gruffydd, the eldest son of Rhys ap Gruffydd, married Matilda, a grand-daughter of William de Braose. Gerald of Wales was Rhys's first cousin, once removed, which made Rhys the nephew of Princess Nest, the daughter of Rhys ap Tewdwr.

5 The name 'The Lord Rhys' (Yr Arglwydd Rhys) was first used by the chroniclers when writing of the year 1165, but the title was apparently due to the position of 'Justice' which he held under Henry II from 1172.

Chapter Six

1 Ieuan Rudd (fl. c.1470), a Glamorgan bard from Glyn Rhondda, refers to the discord between Rhys ap Tewdwr and Iestyn ap Gwrgan in a *'cywydd '* which he sang on the occasion of the marriage feast of Sir Rhys ap Tomas and Sioned (Janet), daughter of Thomas Matthew of Radyr and widow of Thomas

2 For Gwent read Gower for this was probably Llangenydd which is mentioned as Llangenni in the *Liber Landavensis*, which records a gift by King Meuric ap Tewdric of land there to the church of Llandaff. Roger de Beaumont, second Earl of Warwick, who died in 1153, is the reputed founder of a small priory here in 1135, dedicated to St Cenydd, and annexed to the great French Abbey of St Taurinus of Evreux, in Normandy. The *Iolo MSS* (p.391) states that Iestyn ap Gwrgan died in the Priory of Llangenydd in Gower.

3 Iestyn ap Gwrgan is mentioned twice in the 12th century *Liber Landavensis*. In the first case he features as a contemporary of Bishop Herewald of Llandaff, who died in 1104. In the second instance, as a ruler, with a warband for whose misdeeds, he makes amends to Bishop Herewald, by the gift of a manor in the Ely Valley.

4 Neither in the *Brut* nor in the *Annales Cambriae* is there any reference to the conquest of Glamorgan; but in the so-called Gwentian *Brut* the story of the conquest is given with some pomp and circumstance. It is evident that the story cannot be accepted completely, but there is no reason for rejecting it out of hand. Robert Fitzhamon undoubtedly conquered Glamorgan and Iestyn ap Gwrgan was lord of the whole or at least part of Morgannwg.

5 Robert Fitzhamon's full titles recorded in the various charters are:- 'Sir Robert Fitzhamon, Earl of Corbeil, Baron Thorigny and Granville, Lord of Gloucester, Bristol, Tewkesbury and Cardiff, Conqueror of Wales, near kinsman to the king, and General of his Highness's army in France.'

6 Robert Fitzhamon's widow was Sybil, the daughter of Roger de Montgomery, and there were four daughters but no sons. Following his death, the King himself arranged the future of Fitzhamon's daughters. Cicely and Hawise became abbesses; Amice married the Earl of Bretagne but died young and childless. Mabel, the fourth daughter, was thus the sole heiress of Fitzhamon's vast estates. In 1109, Henry's choice for her husband was Robert, the eldest of his many illegitimate sons, whose mother in this case was Nest, the daughter of Rhys ap Tewdwr. She is said to have been a very beautiful lady and is popularly remembered as the 'Helen of Wales'. On the death of her father Rhys ap Tewdwr she was captured by Bleddyn of Powys, the father-in-law of Iestyn ap Gwrgan, and subsequently held prisoner in Cardiff Castle. It is said that here in the Lion Tower in 1090 she gave birth to a son by Prince Henry (who became Henry I), and also a later son Henry, named after his father. The first born was called Robert and this no doubt was intended as a compliment to Sir Robert Fitzhamon.

Chapter Seven

1 Henry I was William the Conqueror's youngest son and he was born at Selby in Yorkshire in September 1068, when Queen Matilda had accompanied William on his expedition to subjugate the north. Henry was the only one of the Conqueror's sons to be born in England and he acceded on 2 August 1100 and was crowned in Westminster Abbey, four days later. It would seem that he was quite a philanderer for he had numerous mistresses including Sibil, the daughter of Sir Robert Corbet of Alcester, Edith, a daughter of a northern gentleman; Elizabeth, sister of the Earl of Mellent; the widow of Anskil of Oxford, and Nest, the daughter of Rhys ap Tewdwr. He seemed to have found a paramour wherever he kept court and as a result he had nineteen illegitimate children, a greater number than any other king of England.

2 If only Henry I had nominated his natural son Robert as his successor, then this much respected grandson of of William the Conqueror and of Rhys ap Tewdwr, would have united England and Wales more than a century earlier than their nominal union by Edward I in 1284, by the Statute of Rhuddlan, having the effect of making Wales a crown colony under its own laws.

3 There was also a son, mentioned by William of Jumieges, who was probably the 'Richard, son of Robert, Earl of Gloucester', who, says Orderic, received in 1135 the Bishopric of Bayeux. As bishop, in 1138, he witnessed a deed of commution, between Roger, Abbot of Fecamp, and Earl Robert, concerning the priory of Gilves.

4 Earl William commenced his rule with a charter dated 1148 which alludes to the foundation of the churches of St Mary and St Thomas at Cardiff. By another charter he confirmed certain gifts to Tewkesbury. In 1153 his name as 'William Earl of Gloucester' is attached to the convention between Stephen and Matilda.

5 Ifor Bach's dominions extended from the river Rhymney to the River Taff and from the seaboard to Morlais Castle and the Brecon Beacons, including the village of Merthyr Tydfil. The district around Morlais is known as Pant Coed Ifor or Pant Cad Ifor. In old parish records it is given as Cad Ifor, which would identify the district with the father of Ifor Bach. Pant Cad Ifor is the wooded hollow of Ifor and tradition states that here he fell in battle and was slain. It appears that he came in possession of the mountain district extending from Dowlais to Cardiff by marriage to Nest, daughter of Madoc ap Caradoc ap Einion. (i.e. great-grand daughter of Einion ap Collwyn who quarrelled with Iestyn ap Gwrgan). Ifor ap Meurig (Ifor Bach) was succeeded as Lord of Senghenydd by his son Gruffydd ab Ifor (d.1211), then by his grandson, Rhys ap Gruffydd (d. 1256), and lastly by his great-grandson, Gruffydd ap Rhys, who was deposed by the Normans in 1266.

6 Through Earl William's daughter, Amica, the lordship of Glamorgan passed to the line of De Clare. Four of her sons followed in succession, of whom the last, Gilbert, fell at Bannockburn 1314, when the lordship descended to his three sisters. The eldest sister married Sir Hugh Despencer, who claimed the lordship of Glamorgan in her right. Edward III made the Despencers his favourites, but when the barons confederated against the Court, they ravaged Despencer's manors and in 1321 drove him into banishment.

Chapter Eight

1 Queen Eleanor of Aquitaine was first married to Louis VII of France, whom she found ineffective both in war and politics and became scornful of him. They were divorced in March 1152. Her daughter by her first marriage was the Countess Marie de Champagne. Count Henry visited the court of Paris to do homage for Normandy and Eleanor saw in this dynamic young man that he was destined by fate and character to be a great king. Two months after her divorce, they were married; Henry a youth of nineteen and Eleanor by now nearly thirty years of age.

2 The heir of Henry II's great Angevin empire was christened Arthur in 1187. A contemporary register recorded that, 'Arthur, son of Geoffrey, Duke of Brittany, is born, the one hoped for by his people.' In 1190, Prince Arthur was recognised by Richard I as heir to the exclusion of Prince John. It had been Henry II's hope that Prince Arthur of Brittany would become King Arthur the Second.

3 Eleanor of Aquitaine was Queen for seventy years, first of France, and then of England. She was undoubtedly used as a model for the Queen Guinevere of many of the Arthurian romances. Giraldus Cambrensis claims that while Eleanor was still married to Louis VII, she had amorous relations with Henry Plantaganet's father, Geoffrey, then seneschal of France. Here we have an obvious similarity with the fabled romance of Lancelot and Guinevere.

4 Even though John had divorced Hawise, his first wife, he still clung to her lands and kept her from marrying for thirteen years in order to retain the Lordship and Honour of Gloucester and Glamorgan in his hands. This is shown by an order of 5 March, 1208, to the barons and knights of the Honour of Cardiff and the Honour of Gloucester, to put in repair his houses in the ballium of Cardiff Castle. Again, on 1 November, 1208, he freed the English and Welsh of Gower from certain burdens, connected with the Castle of Swansea. There is evidence that King John assumed the titles of Lord of Glamorgan and Earl of Gloucester but rarely used them. King Richard sent him a letter from Messina, while on his way to the Holy Land, written about 25 January, 1191, which was addressed to John, Earl of Gloucester; and John so describes himself when he forwarded the letter to Archbishop Baldwin. In a Charter of Glamorgan, dated at Cardiff, in 1193, John's seal appears as Lord of Glamorgan.

In 1213, Hawise, the divorced wife of King John, and the real owner of the Lordship, married Geoffrey de Mangnaville, Earl of Essex, and was fined by the king to the extent of 20,000 marks for the privilege. This second husband died childless in 1216, in the same year that John died. Hawise immediately married Hubert de Burgh, the Justiciary, but she died childless the following year. The inheritance then passed to the son of Mabel, the eldest sister, who married Aymar de Montford, Earl of Evreux, but it seems more than likely that the Earl of Evreux held only the title of Earl. The Lordship then passed to the son of Amice, the second sister. Amice and her husband, Richard de Clare, Earl of Hereford, were both dead; hence their son, Gilbert de Clare, became Lord of Glamorgan and Earl of Gloucester and Hereford. Thus, there came to the Lordship the great De Clares, whose name stands high in the annals of the marcher Lordship of Glamorgan.

Chapter Nine

1 Before removing the remains of Bishop Dyfrig from Bardsey Island, Urban had to seek the favour of Radulphus, Archbishop of Canterbury, and the permission of David, Bishop of Bangor, and Gruffydd, Prince of North Wales. The remains were apparently discovered with great difficulty. Inquiry was made into a number of monuments in order to ascertain where, by whom, how and when, the body was

buried. The saint had been lying there unshrined for six centuries and his remains were so little regarded that other bodies were buried over him.

2 The *Liber Landavensis* has thrice been published, first edited by W. J. Rees in 1840, but this was from the transcripts, as the editor did not have access to the original. A far superior edition is that of Drs. J. Gwenogfryn Evans and J. Rhys. It is a diplomatic reproduction from the twelfth-century original MS at Gwysaney, published at Oxford in 1893. A facsimile edition appeared in 1979.

Chapter Ten

1 The lordship remained with William Fitz Baderon's family for the next four generationsup until1 256.

2 In his writings Geoffrey of Monmouth refers to himself by name on three occasions and each time indicates that he has some connection with Monmouth. The use of his chosen epithet 'Monumutensis' indicates that he was either born in Monmouth or brought up in the priory.

3 During the period that Geoffrey used the prefix 'magister' in his signature it is possible that he may have had a teaching appointment at St George's college. He retained his father's name Arthur in his signature until he was in his fifties and became a bishop elect.

4 There are more manuscript copies extant of the *Historia Regum Britanniae* than any other medieval work. The British Museum alone has thirty-four, and the Bodleian has sixteen. In total it survives in two hundred manuscripts, and this is not surprising for by the end of the twelfth century the story of Arthur was known in France, Spain, Poland and Byzantium.

5 There can be no doubt that there is a link between the *Book of Llandaff* and Geoffrey of Monmouth's *Historia Regum Britanniae* for St Dubricius is made archbishop in both. He was undoubtedly a historical figure and features in the earliest surviving 'life' of a Celtic saint, the seventh-century *Vita Samsonis*, as the bishop who ordained St Samson deacon and consecrated him bishop on the Festival of St Peter's Chair, 22 February, 521.

6 In his edition of the *Liber Landavensis*, Gwenogfryn Evans states: 'In the rubric to the late 12th century work of the Life of Teilo, which is part of that work, the author's name appears as 'Galfrid the brother of Urban, Bishop of Llan Dav.' Gwenogfryn Evans admits that the words 'brother of Urban' present a difficulty here and explains it by the suggestion that the 'Vespasian copyist hearing that Geoffrey was a near relative of the Bishop of Llan Dav, without staying to inquire to what bishop or in what degree he was related, 'put him down' as brother of Urban.

7 It is of interest that Geoffrey was called Bishop of Llandaff in the *Red Book of Hergest* and *Peniarth* 20 versions, and in *Brenhinedd y Saesson*. It is possible that Geoffrey of Monmouth has been confounded with Godfrey or Geoffrey ap Arthur, who was consecrated bishop of St Asaph 24 February 1152. This bishop was appointed to the abbey of Abingdon in 1165, which was held in commendom with his bishopric until 11 July 1175, when in a general council at London his clergy complained that he was constantly absenting himself from his diocese, and he was compelled to resign his bishopric.

8 Like most of the Welsh clergy, Uchtryd was a family man; and his daughter Angharad was married to Iorwerth, who succeeded his father, Owen ap Caradoc, as lord of Caerleon-upon-Usk. Owen lost and regained his lordship more than once, but in his latter years he was finally confirmed in it by Henry II in about 1177. It is interesting to find Geoffrey thus closely connected with the lords of Caerleon, a place established through his *Historia* as the favourite resort of King Arthur.

9 'Calenius' probably meant 'of Oxford' as Calena was the Latin name sometimes given to Oxford.

10 The confusion of Walter Calenius with Walter Mapes, who were both archdeacons of Oxford, is due to Leland (*Commentarii de Scriptoribus Britannicus* P.187).

11 The greater part of our information relating to to Walter Mapes is contained in *Speculum Ecclesiae*, an unedited work of Giraldus Cambrensis, who was his close friend. From Giraldus, we learn that Mapes was a great favourite of Henry II who respected him greatly for his extensive learning and courtly manners. He obtained, by this high favour various ecclesiastical dignities, being canon of the churches of Salisbury and of St. Paul's in London, precentor of Lincoln, incumbent of Westbury in Gloucestershire, with many other benefices, and finally archdeacon of Oxford. We learn from Thomas of Walsingham that he obtained the latter dignity in 1197, and he probably held it as well as the parsonage of Westbury to the end of his life. He visited Rome at the time of the great dispute between his friend Giraldus and Hubert, Archbishop of Canterbury, relating to the rights of the Church of St. David's. We have no certain indication of the date of his death, but it is supposed to have occurred towards the year 1210. He was no longer alive when Giraldus Cambrensis wrote the preface to the second edition of his *Hibernia Expugnata*, which was dedicated to King John.

Walter Mapes is well known as the composer of an important portion of the cycle of King Arthur and his knights, but he was, above all other things, remarkable for his bitter enmity to the Cistercian order of monks, and he showed his hostility towards them in numerous satirical writings both in prose and verse.

12 Lifris is mentioned three times in the *Liber Landavensis* as archdeacon of Glamorgan and son of Herewald, bishop of 'Gwlad Morgan' (later Llandaff) from 1065 to 1104. He is described in the *Liber Landavensis* in three charters granted

Bishop Herewald (d.1104), as 'son of the Bishop, Archdeacon of Gulat Morcant and Master of Saint Catoc of Llancarfan.'

13 The *Vita Cadoci* by Lifris represents the nucleus or core of the collection of the Lives of the Saints. It had as its source another important manuscript. A charter by Merchiaun, witnessed by Bishop Gwrgan, who died in 982, mentions 'Abbas totius dignitatus ecclesiae sancti Cattoci Lancarvanie', and it was held at Llancarfan towards the middle of the twelfth century. It would seem possible that the vital manuscript was transferred from Llancarfan to Neath Abbey, and information from this document was later incorporated into the 15th century Register of Neath Abbey.

14 The islands referred to would have been Echni, (Steepholm), where Gildas built a chapel and lived on sea birds' eggs and fish; and Ronech (Flatholm). Caradoc of Llancarfan's 'Life of Gildas' contrasts Echni, 'that lies over against England' with Ronech, 'near to Wales'.

15 The date of Caradoc's death is usually placed in the year 1156, although a chronicle in the *Red Book of Hergest* places it about three years later, but, according to the writings of Geoffrey of Monmouth, he must have died prior to the year of Geoffrey's death in 1155.

Chapter Eleven

1 Gerald called himself Cambrensis for as an educated man he used the international language of Latin. In spite of his Welsh descent and his antipathy to alien appointments, Gerald was a Norman to his fingertips. He represented a Norman culture and was steeped in Norman traditions. In no way was he a Welsh scholar and he had no acquaintance with the native literature, but Gerald spoke of Manorbier as his birthplace with considerable fondness:

'As Dyfed, linked in seven cantrefs, is the fairest part of the land of Wales, as Pembroke is the chief and fairest part of the land of Dyfed, and this spot Manorbier is the sweetest of all Pembroke, it follows that Manorbier is the sweetest spot in Wales.'

2 The De Barri family took their name from one of their conquests - Barry Island on the Glamorgan coast. William de Barri and Angharad gave the name Gerald to their youngest son in honour of Angharad's father, Gerald de Windsor.

3 Baldwin was consecrated Bishop of Worcester on 10 August 1180. He succeeded Thomas a' Becket as Archbishop of Canterbury and was enthroned on 19 May 1185. He was a Cornishman who knew no Welsh and preached entirely in Latin. He died in the siege of Acre on 19 November, 1190.

4 The tour lasted about seven weeks and the route was a follows: Hereford, Radnor, Brecon, Abergavenny, Caerleon, Newport, Cardiff, Llandaff, Ewenny, Margam, Swansea, Kidwelly, Carmarthen, Haverford, St David's, Cardigan, Strata Florida;

then keeping close to the coast to Bangor and Chester, then south to Oswestry, Shrewsbury, Ludlow, and so back to Hereford.

5 Gerald in fact refused a bishopric four times - twice in Ireland and twice in Wales. He had set his heart on St David's and that was all that he wanted. He rejected the other offers 'because of the poverty of the land and the wickedness of the people.'

6 Gerald wrote seventeen books in total and he was one of the foremost scholars of his time. The three greatest writers of that period were all men of South Wales - Gruffydd ap Arthur (Geoffrey of Monmouth), Walter Map and Gerald of Wales. They had no equal in England, Scotland, Ireland or indeed Europe. Gerald's books were written in tolerable Latin and were works of considerable extent, couched in a graphic style, full of fact and anecdote, but marred by occasional exaggerations and frequent displays of excessive credulity. He wrote at least five saints' 'Lives' including those of St David and Caradoc of Rhos (d.1124), a holy Pembrokeshire hermit who was enshrined in St David's Cathedral. This work was compiled in an endeavour to see Caradoc officially canonised in 1199. When Gerald visited Pope Innocent in Rome he read the work to him and persuaded him to set the process in motion.

7 Independence of the Welsh Church from Canterbury was finally achieved in 1920, when, with the Disestablishment of the Welsh dioceses, they were made into a separate Province with its own Archbishop. In 1944 the Bishop of St David's was raised to that high office.

Chapter Twelve

1 Adam was writing a hundred years after the monks' 'discovery' of the remains of Arthur, and according to him the dark age king had been buried for 648 years. He no doubt based this time period on Geoffrey of Monmouth's date of 542 for the battle of Camlan, which of course suggests that the discovery was made in 1190.

2 The depth of the excavation (16 feet) is explained by an account that St Dunstan, the Abbot of Glastonbury in the tenth century, had the existing graveyard covered with a substantial layer of earth. Stow, in his 'Chronicle,' declares that King Arthur was buried sixteen feet underground to prevent the Saxons from 'offering any dignity to his corpse.'

3 *De Principis Instructione* was not published as a whole until 1217, but the first book in which the narrative occurs was probably composed between 1193 and 1199. About 25 years later, Giraldus gives a similar account in his *Speculum Ecclesiae* but adds confusion to the matter by dating the discovery in the reign of Henry II, who died on 6 July 1189.

4 Montacue, four and a-half miles from Yeovil, built on the point of a hill, hence the name.

5 This extract can be found in *The Quest for Arthur's Britain* edited by Geoffrey Ashe.

6 Quoted in *The Life of King Arthur* by Joseph Ritson, London 1825.

Chapter Thirteen

1 The term Aberafan, as applied to the town is, relatively modern, and does not go back to the time of the Charter. The 'ancient borough' is variously designated in the chronicles of the past, and appears as Avan, Aven, Avene, Afan, Avon, Avana, Avena and even Avyne. Aberavan was officially renamed Port Talbot in 1836 in honour of the Talbot family of Margam Castle, who owned most of the land on which the town and docks were built.

2 Morgan, the son and heir of Caradoc, is often called Morgan Arglwydd (Lord Morgan) because of his relationship to Rhys ap Tewdwr. His first wife was Wenllian, daughter of Ifor bach of Senghenydd, the second Gwyrfil, daughter of Idnerth ap Cadwgan.

3 We have a grant of Morgan ap Caradog's land to Margam from the Penrice MSS dated 1208 (Clarke, C.M.G. ii,282). He died probably between 1208 and the 6th July 1213, which is the date of the 'Confirmatio' by Lleision ap Morgan of all his father's grants to Margam (Clarke, iii,297).

4 Morgan Gam married a Norman heiress - Matilda de Braose. Their daughter Matilda married a Turberville of Coity Castle.

5 At the beginning of 1240, Morgan Gam must have yielded to the influence of the Church for he granted land to Margam, and had as witness to his deed 'Gregory', chaplain of Avene. (Margam MS 115) Evidence that he repented for his misdoings is also shown by another deed setting forth that he has sworn upon the Holy Reliques at Margam, that he will for the future observe all the charters and confirmations of his father and brother, and his own to Margam Abbey. (Birch, *Margam Abbey* p.229).

6 Lleision is mentioned among the Neath benefactors in King John's confirmation charter of 1208 to that abbey. He confirms the considerable gifts of his father Morgan; thus showing that he was the head of the family, and in possession of the property.

7 Sir Rice Mansell was Sheriff of Glamorgan in 1533 and 1541. He died before 1589. The Mansel family by intermarriage with leading Gower families, such as the Langtons, Scurlages, Penrices and Turbervilles, became considerable landowners.

Chapter Fourteen

1 It is of interest that Geoffrey states that Caerleon was in the principality of Glamorgan and during the 1130s the Lord of Glamorgan was his patron Robert, Earl of Gloucester. Morgan and Iowerth both referred to Robert of Gloucester as his lord and the Anglo-Norman lords of Caerleon, whom they ousted, were followers of Stephen. It would thus appear likely that there was a political significance in Geoffrey's comment that Caerleon lay in the principality of Glamorgan. It is particularly relevant that when Geoffrey was writing his 'Historia' there was a King once more in South Wales, based at Caerleon.

2 Henry of Huntingdon saw a copy of Geoffrey of Monmouth's *Historia Regum Britanniae* at Goldcliff Priory in January 1139. Morgan ap Owen was a patron of that priory.

3 Sitsyllt ap Dynfwal, who governed Gwent-uth-Coed, was twice married. By his first wife Angharad, daughter of Owain ap Caradoc and sister of Iorwerth of Caerleon, he had a son Morgan. Some time later, before 1167, he married Gwladus, widow of Caradoc ap Iestyn of Aberafan, and thus connected himself with the powerful Rhys ap Gruffydd.

4 During the reign of King Stephen, Robert Consul prevailed upon Iorwerth of Caerleon to assist him in supporting the cause of his sister Matilda. The 'Brut' records that Iorwerth, with his men of Gwent, took a very prominent part in the battle of Lincoln in which Stephen was defeated and taken prisoner.

5 Sir Morgan ap Meredydd, the Lord of Tredegar, was sixth in descent from Rhys ap Tewdwr.

6 For several generations the Morgans of Tredegar House intermarried with the Vaughans, the Stradlings, the Herberts, the Somersets, etc. until the line of Morgan ended in an heiress, Jane Morgan, eldest daughter of Thomas Morgan, Esq. of Ruperra and niece of Sir William Morgan of Tredegar. She married Dr Charles Gould, judge advocate and member of the Privy Council, knighted in 1779 and made a baronet in 1792, who assumed the surname Morgan. He was succeeded by his eldest son, Sir Charles Morgan, bart. (1760-1846). He was Member of Parliament to the Borough of Brecon, 1787-96, and for Monmouthshire 1796-1831. Among his children by his first wife were Charles Morgan Robinson Morgan (1792-1875), the first baron of Tredegar, Charles Augustus Samuel Morgan (1800-75), the rector of Machen and chancellor of Llandaff Cathedral, and Charles Octavius Swinnerton Morgan. The sons of Charles Robinson Morgan (Lord Tredegar) were Charles Rodney Morgan (1828-54), who was Member of Parliament for the Borough of Brecon, 1852-4, Godfrey Charles Morgan (1831-1913), the 2nd Baron, and Frederick Courtenay Morgan of Rhiwpera Castle (1834-1909). The two younger sons served in the Crimean War, and the 2nd Lord Tredegar, then a captain in the 17th lancers, took part in the famous cavalry charge at Balaclava. He was Member of Parliament for

Brecknock from 1858 till he succeeded to the title in 1875. He was created Viscount Tredegar, 28 Dec 1905. He died unmarried in March 1913, when the viscountcy became extinct, but the barony devolved on his nephew, Courtenay Charles Evan Morgan (1867-1934), the eldest son of F.C. Morgan, as 3rd baron. He was created Viscount Tredegar on 4 August 1926. He was succeeded by his only son, Evan Frederick Morgan (1893-1949), as 4th baron and 2nd viscount. Evan died of a throat infection in 1949. He had no children to succeed him, so the estate and title passed to his uncle, Colonel Frederick George Morgan. The estate was immediately handed over to his son, John, who sold the mansion in 1951 and the agricultural part in 1956. He was the sixth and last Lord Tredegar and he died in 1962, leaving no heirs.

Chapter Fifteen

1 *The Literature of the Kymry* by Thomas Stephens, 1876, p. 405.

2 *The Literature of the Kymry* by Thomas Stephens, 1876, p. 322.

3 It is of utmost significance that Geoffrey of Monmouth was involved with the writers of the *Book of Llandaff* and he may well have seen the original charter naming Arthurus, king of Gwent, as the grantor of Llan Cinmarch. It is also significant that Dafydd Ddu had a first-hand knowledge of the *Book of Llandaff*.

4 It is very likely that Dafydd Ddu's translation of *Y Seint Greal* was from the very manuscript written by Bledri Latimer in the early 12th century. If this is the case then Bledri may well have copied it from the original manuscript of *Y Seint Greal* which was brought back from Brittany by Rhys ap Tewdwr in the late 11th century.

Chapter Sixteen

1 After founding Neath Abbey in 1129, Richard de Granville retired to Bideford in his Devon lordship to become the progenitor of one of the famous families of the West Country. The Welsh occupation of Gower must have rendered his position on the Nedd one of great danger and under the constant threat of attack he decided to leave the area.

2 The name Laleston is more likely to be derived from the family of Lageles, resident there in the twelfth and thirteenth centuries. They held lands in Llangenydd for one Laheles sold it to a local magnate, a De Penris of Penrice Castle.

3 Lleision ap Tomas (fl.1513-41), last abbot of Neath, was a man of great influence in the days of Henry VIII. The earliest record we have of him is that he was one of the commissioners of the peace appointed to assemble at Cardiff, a position he occupied again in 1534. He was held in great respect by the Cistercians, for he was one of the five members of that order appointed by the king in 1532 to visit the Cistercian houses throughout the kingdom and to revive the College of St Bernard of Clairvaux at Oxford for the promotion of learning and virtue.

4 When the dissolution of the lesser monasteries occurred in 1536, Neath Abbey had its life prolonged on payment of £150, but Lleision ap Tomas was forced to give up his position as Abbot on 9 February 1539 and to hand over all the abbey's possessions to the king. Sir John Price, the Crown deputy, made an earnest appeal to Thomas Cromwell to treat the abbot generously and he was duly given a pension of £48 and the rectory of Llangattock.

5 The only other one of Neath's former manuscripts which has survived is a copy of the *Digestum Novum,* which is now held at Hereford.

6 Rhys Meurig's *Morganiae Archaiographia* is preserved at Queen's College, Oxford. Rhys Meurig compiled other works, including a history of Wales, a history of Glamorgan (lost when Thomas Johne's library at Hafod was destroyed by fire in 1807), a history of the bishopric of Llandaff and a collection of manuscripts known as the *Cottrell Book*. The volume of pedigrees termed the *Cottrell Book* was in the possession of the late John C. Earl of Clarendon (see *Stradling Correspondence* edited by the Rev John Montgomery Traherne - William Bird, Cardiff, 1840, p.169).

7 Dr Parr, the biographer of Archbishop Ussher, states that in 1645-6 the archbishop spent twelve months at St Donat's Castle, where he made 'choice collections of the British or Welsh antiquities.' It would seem that Archbishop Ussher's studies were interrupted by a serious illness, which left him so weak from haemorrhage that his death was reported. On his recovery in 1646, he went to Reigate as the guest of Elizabeth Mordaunt, dowager countess of Peterborough. From 1647 to 1654 he was preacher at Lincoln's Inn, London. He died at Reigate on 21 March 1656 and was buried in Westminster Abbey. Ussher in his *Britannicarum Ecclesiarum Antiquitates* (Dublin 1639) refers to an old Welsh history in the Cottonian library, which, he says, some thought to be the very one which Geoffrey of Monmouth copied.

8 A manuscript copy of Sir Edward Stradling's *Winning of Glamorgan* can be seen in Cardiff Central Library (MS.4.943).

9 It is generally considered that in the late years of the 16th century, the Stradlings compiled a fictitious pedigree, tracing it to an imaginary William le Esterling, contemporary with Fitzhamon. At the same time they perhaps invented the legend of the twelve knights of Glamorgan, of which Le Esterling was numbered. Sir Edward Stradling claimed that his ancestor, William de Esterling, was a close friend of Robert Fitzhamon, but in fact his family did not arrive in Glamorgan until more than 200 years after the invasion.

10 This proves that Iolo Morganwg drew on genuine Welsh literary traditions dating back to the 15th century. Therefore, it is not appropriate to dismiss all his manuscripts as forgeries. Admittedly, he was an embellisher but not an outright fabricator. The traditions upon which he drew date back to the time of Rhys ap Siankyn, Lord of Glyn Neath, who flourished 1430-50 and was therefore contemporary with the compilation of the Register of Neath Abbey. His grandson was Rhys ap Sion, Lord of Glyn Neath, to whom his grandson Lewys Morgannwg composed an elegy in praise of his grandfather, Rhys ap Sion. It is more than likely

that Lewys Morgannwg consulted the manuscripts in the library at his grandfather's home at Aberpergwm, and thus ascertained the true identity of King Arthur.

Chapter Seventeen

1 Lleision, the Rector of Cadoxton-juxta-Neath, was the son of Richard ap Tomas ap Griffith Goch of Ynys Arwed, who was buried at Llangatwg Church, where his son was vicar.
The Williams family of Dyffryn Clydach are descended from Rhys ap Iestyn ap Gwrgan, whereas the Williams family of Aberpergwm are descended from Caradog ap Iestyn ap Gwrgan.

2 By his will, 1598 (now at Llandaff), Jenkin ap William shows that he was in possession of Aberpergwm, under a lease granted by Lleision Tomas, the late Abbot of Neath Abbey; and this farm and all the tithes he now leaves to his son William ap Jenkin William of Aberpergwm (Ref: *The History of the Vale of Neath* by David Rhys Phillips (1925).

The *Gwentian Chronicle*, also known as the *Gwentian Brut* or *Llyfr Aberpergwm* or *Brut Aberpergwm* is the work of a 16th century bard who had access to earlier material but made his own unreliable additions. Its chronology is worse than useless for it often compresses the events of several years into one. The original manuscript has been lost.

According to Edward Williams, the *Brut Aberpergwm* was made from a text copied in 1764 by Thomas Richards from a manuscript belonging to George Williams, a member of the Williams family of Aberpergwm. It records events from the year 660 down to 1196 and was published in *The Myvyrian Archaeology of Wales* (1801).

APPENDIX II
The Origins of the Arthmael/Arthur Theory

c.530 - The grant of Cadoxton-juxta-Neath by King Arthmael to St Cadoc (Catwg)

c.1073-1086 - *The Vita Cadoci* ('Life of St Cadoc', written by Lifris, attached to which are the Llancarfan Charters. Mention is made of the grant of Cadoxton-juxta-Neath to St Cadoc by King Arthmael in c.530.

The 11th-century stone found buried in the floor of Ogmore Castle mentions a grant of land by King Arthmael to Glywys, Nertat and Bishop Fili, who all belong to the 6th century. The inscription reads 'Sciendum est omnibus quot dedit Arthmail agrum do et Gligws et Nertat et Fili epi.' - 'Be it known to all that Arthmael has given this field to God and to Glywys and to Nertat and to Bishop Fili.' The particular usage of 'Sciendum est quod' is rare elsewhere and it is extremely significant that it can also be found in the charters attached to the *Vita Cadoci* from Llancarfan.

The 15th-century Register of Neath, the cartulary of Neath Abbey, which contains an early history of Morgannwg (Glamorgan) and mentions King Arthur as ruling over the 'Land of Morgan' in the 6th century.

c.1560 - Llywelyn ap Rhisiart (Lewys Morgannwg), who flourished 1520-1565, mentions Arthur as the king of the warlike land of Morgan. Lewys Morgannwg had cultural connections with Lleision Tomas, the last abbot of Neath Abbey, which was dissolved in 1539. The chief patron of Neath Abbey was Sir Edward Stradling (d.1535) of St Donat's Castle, who was also the first patron of Lewys Morgannwg.

1572-91 - Llywelyn Sion of Llangewydd (1540-1615), in *Llyma Enwau a Hiliogaeth Brenhinoed Morgannwg* ('These be the names and genealogies of the Kings of Glamorgan), mentions Morgan succeeding to the twelve hundreds of Gwent Essyllt in the principalities of Arthur. Elsewhere he records that Adras ap Meurig was a very brave heroic sovereign who frequently put the Saxons to flight.
Adras = Athrwys = Arthmael = Arthur

1578-1584 - Rhys Meurig (1520-1587), in *A Book of Glamorgan Antiquities*, refers directly to the Register of Neath, which was held in the library of St Donat's Castle, and names Morgan as the son of Adras ap Meurig. Adras = Athrwys.

1591 - Sir Edward Mansel of Margam, in *Another Account of the Coming of the Normans*, mentions Morgan as a prince who lived in the time of Arthur and was his son as some would have it.

1673 - Sir William Dugdale, in *Monasticon Anglcanum* Vol. III p.190, mentions Arthur as the son of Meurig. He also used as a principal source the *Book of Llandaff*

The Grand Alliance of Arfon, Gwent and Erging

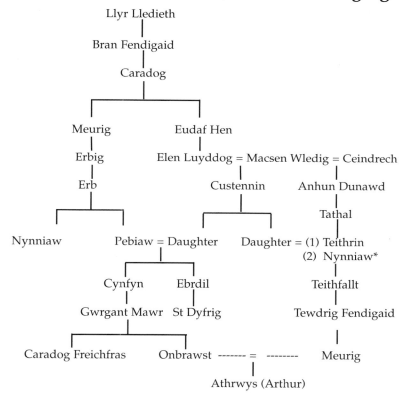

```
                    Llyr Lledieth
                          |
                    Bran Fendigaid
                          |
                       Caradog
                          |
          ┌───────────────────────────────┐
       Meurig                         Eudaf Hen
          |                               |
       Erbig          Elen Luyddog = Macsen Wledig = Ceindrech
          |                          |                  |
        Erb                      Custennin        Anhun Dunawd
          |                          |                  |
    ┌──────────┐            ┌──────────────┐         Tathal
 Nynniaw    Pebiau = Daughter      Daughter = (1) Teithrin
               |                              (2) Nynniaw*
         ┌──────────┐                             |
      Cynfyn     Ebrdil                        Teithfallt
         |                                         |
   Gwrgant Mawr   St Dyfrig                Tewdrig Fendigaid
         |                                         |
   ┌──────────────┐                             Meurig
Caradog Freichfras   Onbrawst ------- = -------- 
                              |
                      Athrwys (Arthur)
```

The rulers of Arfon, Domnonia, Gwent, Morgannwg and Erging all claimed descent from Llyr Lledieith ('Half Speech'), the father of Bran Fendigaid ('the Blessed'), whilst the rulers of Glywysing, Garth Madryn and Tredegar claimed descent from Macsen Wledig (Maximus 'the Imperator').

Eudaf Hen (Octavius 'the Aged'), prince of Arfon, was the great grandson of Llyr Lledieith. His brother Meurig ruled Gwent and Erging. Eudaf's daughter Elen Luyddog (Helen 'of the Hosts') married Macsen Wledig. Macsen's son Anhun Dunaws (Antonius Donatus), by his previous marriage to Ceindrech, was the ancestor of the kings of Garth Madryn. Macsen and Elen's son Custennin (Constantine) had two daughters - one married Pebiau Clavorauc, king of Erging, whilst the other daughter first married Teithrin, king of Garth Madryn, who died, and then Nynniaw, king of Gwent, who thus became the step-father of Teithrin's infant son Teithfallt.

The result of these marriages was an important alliance between the principality of Arfon and the kingdoms of Gwent and Erging, and the union of Garth Madryn with Gwent under one ruler Teithfallt, who was the father of Tewdrig Fendigaid. Tewdrig later surrendered the rule of Garth Madryn to his son-in-law Anlach, who became the father of Brychan, founder of Brycheiniog.

The Positive Dating of Arthmael/Athrwys ap Meurig

Modern day historians have refused to recognise Athrwys, the son of Meurig ap Tewdrig, as the King Arthur of legend and history for, according to their interpretation of the early Welsh genealogies, he lived in the wrong century.

This misunderstanding is due to serious errors made by several respected academics, which has resulted in Athrwys ap Meurig being pushed into the seventh century, thus disassociating him completely from Arthur and his contemporaries. Until these mistakes are recognised the truth of the matter will continue to be ignored. The following statement is given as a very simple way of placing Athrwys ap Meurig in his correct time period.

> Arthmael and Athrwys ap Meurig (Arthur) may be positively dated by the seventh-century Vita Samsonis. St Samson was the son of Anna of Gwent, who was the daughter of Meurig and the sister of Athrwys. Therefore, St Samson was the nephew of Athrwys ap Meurig.
>
> St Samson was the witness of a grant, listed in the Llancarfan Charters, made by Meurig ap Tewdrig to St Catwg and his family. The witness of St Samson whilst Abbot of Llanilltud Fawr, makes the original of this charter to have been composed prior to the 22nd February 521, when he was consecrated bishop by St Dyfrig.
>
> Saints Samson and Arthmael were involved in the negotiations with the Frankish king Childebert (d.558) for the release of Judwal, the rightful king of Armorican Domnonia, in order to raise an insurrection against the usurper Marcus Conomorus. An army was gathered and Conomorus was defeated and killed in 555.
>
> In 557 St Samson attended the third Council of Paris where he signed his name 'Samson peccator episcopus' on the acts of the Council among the names of the other bishops. He died in 565.

A Church in Gwent founded by St Arthmael

The now disused church at Peterstone in Gwent was re-dedicated to St Peter in the time of William of Gloucester, but its original dedicatee, and perhaps the founder of the clas attached to it, must have been a Celtic saint. It seems probable that the saint was a St Arthmael. In the 1535 valuation of all church property, the revenues of the parish church of Rumney were stated to be £5 10s 8d beyond reprises, one mark of 13s 4d of these revenues being derived from capella de Sancti Armigilo.

Sir Joseph Bradney notes that at the time of the suppression of Bristol Abbey the church at Rumney had a chapel of Armagillus attached to it and suggests from this that the saint was the original dedicatee of Rumney Church (*Valor Ecclesiasticus*, 6 volumes, Record Commission, 1810-34, iv. 364; Sir Joseph Bradney, 87). An attached chapel, however, is more likely to be the church at Peterstone, which is the only church in the deanery of Newport not mentioned in the *Valor* of 1535 and which is often referred to as a chapelry of Rumney rather than part of Rumney Church.

The name Armagillus is probably a sixteenth-century rendering of the Old Welsh name Arthmael, assuming that migilo or magillus is a form of maglos, a British word thought to lie behind the Welsh name Mael. He is not known to have had any other churches in Wales dedicated to him, but, in common with many of the 'Letavian' saints of the littoral of south-east Wales, he was celebrated in Cornwall as well as in Brittany. The 'Letavian' saints under the leadership of St Cynllo, St Cadfan and St Tydecho, and including St Padarn, left the Gwent area for West Wales and Ceredigion in the time of Caradog Freichfras. From there they passed through Cornwall on their way to Brittany.

We shall probably never know why the dedicatee was changed to St Peter, but Arthmael must have retained his popularity among the local Welsh people and that ensured the preservation of his name in association with the church until the sixteenth century.

APPENDIX III
SIGNIFICANT DATES

43	The beginning of the Roman Conquest of Britain.
383c.	The first British settlement of Armorica (Brittany)
449	Vortigern invites the German tribes (Anglo-Saxons), into Britain to fight the Picts and Scots
460-64	Ambrosius Aurelianus leads the British resistance against the Anglo-Saxons
465	Overthrow of Vortigern by Ambrosius and St Garmon
470c	Death of King Tewdrig at Mathern
482	Birth of Arthur at Boverton in the Vale of Glamorgan
486	Birth of St Samson in the Vale of Glamorgan
487	Birth of St Paul Aurelian at Boverton in the Vale of Glamorgan
497	Ambrosius dies and Arthur becomes 'dux bellorum,' leader of battles, fighting with the kings of the Britons
517c.	Battle of Mount Badon
521	Consecration of St Samson by St Dubricius
524	Death of Riwal Mawr, the nephew of Arthur
530	Death of Count Gwythyr, the father of Gwenhwyfar (Guinevere)
537.	Battle of Camlan, abdication of Arthur
544	Death of St David at his monastery at Mynyw (St David's)
545c.	Gildas writes his *De Excidio Brittaniae*
546	Death of St Dubricius on Bardsey Island
547	Death of Maelgwyn Gwynedd
555	Death of Marcus Conomorus in Brittany
562	Death of St Armel (Arthur) at St Armel des Boschaux in Brittany
565	Death of St Samson at Dol in Brittany
570	Death of St Gildas in his monastery at Rhuys in Brittany
573	Death of St Paul Aurelian at his monastery in Brittany
574	Battle of Arfderydd (Arthuret)
577	Battle of Dyrham (Deorham)
	The epic poem *Y Gododdin* is composed by Aneurin
613	Battle of Chester
642c.	The Mercians attack the kingdom of Powys.
664	Death of Cadwaladr, the last Welsh 'King of Britain'
665	Second Battle of Mount Badon, death of Morgan Morgannwg
800c.	Nennius completes his *Historia Brittonum*.
855	Death of Hywel ap Rhys.
918	Ethelfleda, Queen of Mercia, attacks Morgannwg
900-50	Reign of Hywel Dda
c960	*Annales Cambriae* are written
974	Death of Maredudd ab Owain, grandson of Hywel Dda
	Death of Morgan Morganwg
997	Tewdwr Mawr, grandson of Hywel Dda, is killed in battle

1042	Death of Gwrgan, Prince of Morgannwg
1043	Death of Hywel ap Morgan Hen
	Iestyn ap Gwrgan becomes Prince of Morgannwg
1056	Consecration of Herewald, Bishop of Llandaff
1066	Death of Edward the Confessor
	Conquest of England by William of Normandy
1067	The Normans begin to penetrate Wales and the lordships of the Marches are created
1068	Birth of Henry I
1077	Rhys ap Tewdwr returns from Brittany to reclaim his kingdom of Deheubarth
1081	Caradog ap Gruffydd is killed in the Battle of Mynydd Carn.
	William the Conqueror visits the shrine of St David
1087	Death of William the Conqueror
	Accession of William Rufus
1090	The Normans begin to conquer south and west Wales
	Birth of Geoffrey of Monmouth
	Birth of Robert, Earl of Gloucester
	Birth of William of Malmesbury
1092	Defeat of Iestyn ap Gwrgan at Mynydd Bychan
1093	Death of Rhys ap Tewdwr in a battle near Brecon
1096	First Crusade: Robert of Normandy takes the Cross
1098	Cistercian Order founded
1100	Death of William Rufus in hunting accident
	Accession of Henry I
1104	Bishop Herewald of Llandaff dies
1106	Death of Robert Fitzhamon
1107	Robert, Earl of Gloucester, becomes Lord of Glamorgan
1112	Gruffydd ap Rhys returns to Wales from Ireland
1114	Henry I invades Gwynedd.
1120	Dewi Sant is canonized by Rome as St David
	The remains of St Dubricius (Dyfrig) are brought to Llandaff
1120-40	The Book of Llandaff is compiled
1121	Bishop Urban commences rebuilding Llandaff Cathedral
1129	Foundation of Neath Abbey.
1134	Death of Robert Curthouse, Duke of Normandy
	Death of Bishop Urban of Llandaff
1135	Death of Henry I after a reign of 35 years
	Accession of King Stephen.
	Princess Gwenllian is killed at Cydweli
1136	Death of Gruffydd ap Rhys
	Geoffrey of Monmouth's *Historia Regum Britanniae* is published
1137	Death of Gruffudd ap Cynan
1137-70	The reign of Owain Gwynedd
1140	Foundation of Whitland Abbey by the Cistercians
	The Book of Llandaff is completed

1141	Battle of Lincoln
1143	William of Malmesbury's *Historia Regum Anglorum* is published
1145	Morgan ap Caradoc is recognised as King of Gwent
1147	Birth of Giraldus Cambrensis (Gerald of Wales)
	Robert, Earl of Gloucester, founds Margam Abbey
	Death of Robert, Earl of Gloucester, Lord of Glamorgan
1148	Death of Caradoc ap Iestyn, 'The Warlike', Lord of Afan
	Geoffrey of Monmouth writes *Vita Merlini*
1150	Geoffrey of Anjou dies
1152	The future Henry II marries Eleanor of Aquitaine
1153	Treaty of Wallingford.
1154	Death of King Stephen at the age of 57
	Accession of Henry II
1155	Death of Geoffrey of Monmouth
1157	Death of Mabel, wife of Robert, Earl of Gloucester
	Birth of Richard I at Beaumont Palace, Oxford
1158	Morgan of Caerleon is murdered by Ifor Meurig
	Ifor Bach, Lord of Senghenydd, abducts William, Earl of Gloucester, his wife and son
1160	Death of Madog ap Maredudd, the last ruler of a united Powys
1163	Henry II invades Wales to subdue Rhys ap Gruffydd
1170	Death of Owain Gwynedd
1170-97	Rhys ap Gruffydd (The Lord Rhys) rules south Wales
1170	Rhys ap Gruffydd holds an eisteddfod at Cardigan Castle.
1171	Rhys ap Gruffydd becomes the Lord Rhys, Justicar of South Wales
1175	Massacre of Welshmen at Abergavenny Castle by William de Braose
1178	Death of Hywel ap Iorwerth of Caerleon
1180	Giraldus Cambrensis is appointed Archdeacon of Brecon
1183	Death of William, Earl of Gloucester
1184	Baldwin becomes Archbishop of Canterbury
	Glastonbury Abbey is destroyed in a fire
1185	Giraldus Cambrensis is made Court Chaplain and adviser to Prince John
1187	Capture of Jerusalem by Saladin
	Birth of Arthur of Brittany
1188	Giraldus Cambrensis and Archbishop Baldwin tour Wales, preaching the Third Crusade
1189	Death of Henry II
	Accession of Richard I
	Prince John becomes Lord of Glamorgan
1190	Arthur of Brittany is recognised by Richard I as his heir
1191	'Discovery' of Arthur's grave at Glastonbury
1192/3	Giraldus Cambrensis visits Glastonbury
1196	Accession of Llywelyn ap Iorwerth (Llywelyn Fawr)
1197	Death of the Lord Rhys
1199	Death of Richard I in Aquitaine
	Accession of King John

1202	Murder of Arthur of Brittany
1208	Death of Morgan ap Caradoc
1209	Excommunication of King John
1215	King John signs the Magna Carta
1216	Death of King John
	Accession of Henry III
	Death of Lleision ap Morgan
1223	Death of Giraldus Cambrensis
1240	Death of Morgan Gam, who is buried at Margam Abbey
	Death of Llywelyn Fawr
1246	Death of Dafydd ap Llywelyn Fawr
1246	Commencement of the reign of Llywelyn ap Gruffudd
1272	Death of Henry III
	Accession of Edward I
1278	Edward I and Queen Eleanor visit Glastonbury Abbey
1283	Death of Llywelyn ap Gruffudd, the last Prince of Wales
1284	The Statute of Rhuddlan
1288	Death of Morgan Vychan
1331	Edward III and Queen Philippa visit Glastonbury Abbey
1344	Edward III decides to create a Round Table for his knights
1351	The Order of the Garter is established
1377	Death of Edward III
1457	Birth of Henry Tudor in Pembroke Castle
1471	Henry and Jasper Tudor seek sanctuary in Brittany
1485	Battle of Bosworth and Accession of Henry VII
1486	Birth of Arthur, Prince of Wales
1502	Death of Arthur, Prince of Wales, at Ludlow Castle
1529	Birth of Sir Edward Stradling
1536	Dissolution of Glastonbury Abbey
1539	Dissolution of Neath Abbey
1537	Dissolution of Margam Abbey
1560	Jenkin ap William settles at Aberpergwm
1598	Death of William ap Jenkin
1669	Death of Lleision ap William
1721	Death of Richard Williams
1746	Death of George Williams
1796	Death of George Williams
1812	Death of Rees Williams
1855	Death of William Williams
1909	Death of Morgan Stuart Williams
1956	Death of Godfrey Williams, the last member of the family to occupy Aberpergwm House
1966	George Williams is appointed as Sheriff of Glamorgan
1985	Owain Williams is appointed Sheriff of Glamorgan
1992	Robert Morgan Williams inherits the Aberpergwm estate

APPENDIX IV
EVENTS IN THE LIFE OF KING ARTHUR

482   Birth of Arthur at Boverton in South Glamorgan

497   Ambrosius (Emrys Wledig) nominates Arthur as his successor and appoints his brother Uthyr and his nephew Geraint Llyngesog ('the Fleet Owner') as Pendragons to head the British forces against the Saxons. The death of Ambrosius coincides with the appearance of a comet which is described by Geoffrey of Monmouth. Arthur is crowned leader of the Britons at Caer Vudei, 'the Camp in the Wood', by St. Dyfrig (Dubricius). Geoffrey of Monmouth identifies this place with Silchester, but it is in fact Woodchester in Gloucestershire, where, significantly, Ambrosius had his headquarters.

501   A war-band of Jutes from Kent and Gewissei from south-east Hampshire land at Portsmouth Harbour and pillage Portus Adurni (Portchester).

508   The Gewissei and their Jutish allies make a piratical raid up the Severn Sea but their advance is checked by the western Britons led by Geraint Llyngesog. In the Battle of Llongborth (War-ship port) Geraint is slain. He is buried at Merthyr Gerein (Martyrium of Geraint) on the Gwentian shore of the Severn Estuary.

510   Arthur gives assistance to his kinsman Riwal Mawr, king of Armorican Domnonia (509-524) against an invasion of the Visigoths. The united armies of Riwal and Arthur succeed in repelling a seaborne attack by the Visigoths at Baden, situated south-west of Vannes. The Venetians of Vannes appoint Arthur (Arthmael) as their Dux. Armel (Arzel) is Breton for Arth (Arz) mael, meaning 'Bear Prince'. Arzon and the Ille de Arz, south of Vannes, are both named after a mighty warrior prince called Arzur, who utilized a fortress in the Sarzeau Forest, near to which stands St. Gildas's monastery of Rhuys. There are dedications to St. Armel at Ploermel and St. Armel, situated west and south of Vannes respectively and near to the site of Arthur's victory over the Visigoths.

512   Uthyr Pendragon comes out of retirement to fight a battle against the Teutonic alliance and avenge the death of his nephew Geraint at the Battle of Llongborth. The Saxon Chronicle tells us that a British Pendragon is killed at Dragon Hill (near Uffington) with five thousand of his men.

        Arthur takes over as battle commander and fights a series of twelve important battles. Five of them are fought to subjugate the settlements of the Middle and East Angles. Another is fought against the northern Angles followed by one against the Picts. The remaining five battles are

	fought in south-west Britain against the Gewissei and their allies.
517	The final battle is fought at Mount Badon, just outside Bath, and Arthur's decisive victory results in a fifty year period of peace for the Britons and enables them to become a united nation, but sadly on Arthur's abdication in 537 the unity quickly disintegrates.
522	St. Dubricius (Dyfrig), Archbishop of Wales, resigns his see and retires to Bardsey Island.
524	Riwal Mawr, the nephew of Arthur, dies. It is reputed that he was buried at Llanilltyd Fawr (Llantwit Major) in the Vale of Glamorgan.
530	Count Gwythyr (Victor), the father of Gwenhwyfar (Guinevere), dies and she inherits his estates. Her husband, Arthur, thus gains control of the principality of Leon in Armorica (Brittany). Leon is absorbed into the Armorican kingdom of Domnonia under the joint rule of Arthur and Riwal Mawr's son and successor Deroch (King of Armorican Domnonia 524-535).
533	Deroch requests help against an invasion of the Visigoths, and Arthur, as a result, is away from his own kingdom for four years. Medraut seizes Arthur's realm and Queen.
537	News of the uprising reaches Arthur, who has now moved on to Ireland to defeat Llwch Llawinawg, and he returns with all that survives of his army. He lands at the little harbour (now called Cadlan -'Place of Battle') on the Lleyn Peninsula, where the family of Medraut have territory. During the ensuing Battle of Camlan Medraut is slain and Arthur is critically injured. He is taken to Ynys Afallach (Bardsey Island) to have his wounds tended. After recovering from his injuries, he abdicates, handing over his crown to Constantine, the son of Cadwy. Following the fall of Arthur, the great confederacy of British kingdoms, which has been so effective in keeping the Saxon invaders at bay, disintegrates into its component parts.
544	St. David dies, aged 82, in his monastery at Mynyw (Menevia), where the impressive cathedral of St. David's now stands and his bones are kept in a casket.
546	Death of St. Dubricius (Dyfrig) in retirement on Bardsey Island (Isle of Avalon).
547	Maelgwyn Gwynedd dies of the bubonic plague.
549	Marcus Conomorus (King Mark), who has now settled in Armorica, assassinates Jonas, the son of Deroch. In order to obtain the regency, Conomorus marries Jonas's widow, and Judwal, the rightful heir, is forced to flee to the court of the Frankish King Childebert in Paris.

554   Arthur quarrels with the usurper Conomorus and goes to Paris, where he does his best to persuade Childebert to displace Conomorus and restore Judwal. Arthur's nephew, Samson, arrives and together they manage to break down Childebert's opposition. They then return to Armorica to organise an insurrection on behalf of Judwal.

555   The combined forces of Samson, Judwal and Arthur, together with reinforcements provided by King Childebert, meet the forces of Conomorus near Brank Aleg at the foot of Montagnes d' Aree and fight three fierce battles over three days. Finally, Judwal runs the usurper through with a javelin. Conomorus falls wounded from his horse and is trampled to death in the press of the charge.

Judwal, now King of Armorican Domnonia, rewards Arthur for his services by granting him land on the River Seiche, where today stands the village of St. Armel des Boschaux. Here he establishes a monastery. It is signifcant that the whole region of the Ille et Villaine, which was granted to St Armel (Arthur) by Judwal for services rendered, is the area in Brittany most associated with the legends of King Arthur and his Knights of the Round Table and here their memory still lingers.

562   Death of Arthur (St. Armel) at St. Armel des Boschaux, where he is buried in a stone sarcophagus. He lived to be 80 years of age. The true identity of this highly venerated soldier saint from Glamorgan was previously unknown to the Bretons.

During the next eleven years the death occurs of three of King Arthur's most important contemporaries and it is significant that they also spent their final years in Armorica.

565   Death of St. Samson, the nephew of Arthur, at his monastery in Dol, Armorica, where his shrine used to attract large numbers of pilgrims.

570   Death of St. Gildas, aged 94 at St. Gildas du Rhuys, where his tomb and bones in a casket can be seen.

573   Death of St. Paul Aurelian (a contemporary of Arthur who was also born at Boverton in South Glamorgan) at his monastery, St. Pol de Leon in Armorica. He was aged 86.

APPENDIX V

EARLY HISTORICAL SOURCES AND ARTHURIAN LITERATURE

548c.   *De Excidio Conquesta Britanniae* ('On the Ruin and Conquest of Britain') by Gildas

600c.   *The Gododdin,* an epic poem by Aneurin

731c.   *Historia Ecclesiastica Gentis Anglorum (The History of the English Church and People)* by the Venerable Bede

800c.   *Historia Brittonum* ("History of the Britons') attributed to Nennius

960c.   *Annales Cambriae* (Annals of Wales) is first written, but the original manuscript has not survived

1136   Geoffrey of Monmouth's *Historia Regum Britanniae* published

1148   *Vita Merlini* (The Life of Merlin) by Geoffrey of Monmouth

1155   *Roman de Brut* ('Romance of Brutus') by Wace

1165c.   *Tristan* by Thomas de Britagne

1172   *Lancelot* or *Le Chevalier a la cherrete* by Chrétien de Troyes

1182   *Perceval* or *Le Conte du Graal* by Chrétien de Troyes

1200-10 *Brut* by Layamon

1230   *Vulgate Cycle* by anonymous author

1250c.   Llyfr Du Caerfyrddin ('The Black Book of Carmarthen')

1275c.   Llyfr Taliesin ('The Book of Taliesin';) attributed to the 6th century poet Taliesin.

1400   Llyr Coch Hergest ('The Red Book of Hergest')
(Arthur is mentioned in two of the stories)

?   *Trioedd Ynys Prydain* ('Triads of Britain')

1470   *Le Morte d' Arthur* is completed by Thomas Malory

1485   Publication of Malory's *Le Morte d' Arthur* by William Caxton

1582   *The Assertion of the Most Noble Arthur* by John Leland

1825   *Life of King Arthur* by Joseph Ritson

1832   *The Lady of Shalott* by Alfred Lord Tennyson

1842   *Idylls of the King* by Alfred Lord Tennyson (first volume)

1846   The *Mabinogion* by Lady Charlotte Guest

1868   *Four Ancient Books of Wales* edited by W. F. Skene

1888   Final Volume of *Idylls of the King* by Alfred Lord Tennyson

BIBLIOGRAPHY

Allen, Rosamund, *Lawman's Brut*, J.M. Dent & Sons Ltd, London 1992.

Ashe, Geoffrey, *All About King Arthur*, Carousel Books, London 1973.

    A Guidebook to Arthurian Britain, Aquarian, Wellingborough, 1983.

    Kings and Queens of Early Britain, Methuen, London 1982.

Barber, Richard, *King Arthur - Hero and Legend*, Boydell & Brewer, Woodbridge, 1986.

Baring-Gould, Sabine and Fisher, John, *St Brychan - King Confessor*, Archaeologia Cambrensis, 1903.

    The Lives of the British Saints, (4 volumes), The Honourable Society of Cymmrodorion, London, 1907-13.

Bartrum, Peter Clement, *Early Welsh Genealogical Tracts*, University of Wales Press, Cardiff, 1966.

    A Welsh Classical Dictionary, The National Library of Wales, Aberystwyth, 1993.

    Welsh Genealogies AD 300-1400, University of Wales Press, Cardiff, 1974.

Breeze, Andrew, *Welsh Medieval Literature*, Four Courts Press, Dublin, 1997.

Bromwich, Rachel, *The Arthur of the Welsh*, University of Wales Press, Cardiff, 1991.

    Trioedd Ynys Prydein, University of Wales Press, Cardiff 1978.

Brooke, Christopher, *The Archbishops of St David's, Llandaff and Caerleon-upon-Usk*, contained in *Studies in the Early British Church*, edited by Nora Kershaw Chadwick, Cambridge University Press, 1958.

Cambrensis, Giraldus, *The Journey through Wales* and *The Description of Wales*, London, Penguin, 1978

Camden, William, *Britannia* (1695), John Stockdale, London, 1806.

Carte, Thomas, *General History of England* Vol I, (1747).

Chadwick, Nora Kershaw, *Studies in the Early British Church* , Cambridge University Press, 1954.

    Studies in Early British History, Cambridge University Press, 1954.

Chambers, E. K., *Arthur of Britain*, Sidgwick & Jackson, London 1947.

Clark, George Thomas, *Limbus Patrum Morganiae et Glamorganiae*, (The Genealogies of Morgan and Glamorgan), 1886.

    The Land of Morgan, Journal of the Archaeological Institute, London 1883

Coxe, William, *An Historical Tour of Monmouthshire*, Merton Press, 1995

Davis, Wendy, *The Llandaff Charters*, The National Library of Wales, Aberystwyth, 1979.

Dicks, Brian, *Portrait of Cardiff and its Valleys*, Robert Hale, London, 1984.

Dugdale, William, *Monasticon Anglicanum*, (3 volumes), 1655-73.

Eaton, George, *The Williams Family of Aberpergwm*, Neath Antiquarian Society Transactions, 1979.

Evans, A. L. *The Story of Baglan*, 1970

Evans, C. J. O., *Glamorgan - Its History and Topography*, William Lewis, Cardiff, 1938.

Evans, Gwynfor, *Land of My Fathers*, Swansea, John Penry Press, 1978

Evans, J. Gwenogvryn and Rhys, John, *The Text of the Book of Llan Dav*, Oxford at the Clarendon Press, 1893.

Evans, T. C., *History of Llangynwyd Parish,* 1887

Finberg, H.P.R., *The Early Charters of the West Midlands,* contained in *Studies in Early English History,* Leicester University Press, 1961.

Gillingham, John, *The Context and Purpose of Geoffrey of Monmouth's History of the Kings of Britain,* Anglo-Norman Studies XIII, 1990.

Goodrich, Norma Lorre, *King Arthur,* Franklin Watts, New York, 1986.

James, J.W., *Chronology in the Book of Llan Dav 500-900,* The National Library of Wales Journal, XVI, 1969/70

James, J. W.,*The Book of Llan Dav and Canon G. H. Doble,* National Library of Wales Journal, XVIII, i ,1973.

Jones, E., *Baglan and The Llewelyns of Baglan Hall,* 1987.

Lacy, Norris J., *The Arhurian Encyclopaedia, Boydell Press,* Woodbridge, 1988.

Lloyd J.E., *A History of Wales from earliest times to the Edwardian Conquest* (2 vols, London, 1911

Loomis, R. S., *Wales and the Arthurian Legend,* Cardiff University Press, 1956

Matthews, John and Stewart, Bob, *Legends of King Arthur and his Warriors,* Bookmart, Leicester, 1993

Matthews, John, *Gawain: Knight of the Goddess,* The Aquarian Press, Wellingborough, 1990

Morgan, Owen 'Morien', *A History of Wales,* Edward Howell, Liverpool, 1911

Morris, A., *Glamorgan,* John Southhall, Newport, 1907

Morris, John, *The Age of Arthur - A History of the British Isles from 350-650,* Weidenfeld and Nicolson, London 1973

Nicholl, David, *The Antiquities of Llantwit Majo*r (1729) contained in *The History of Monmouthshire* by David Williams, Tudor & Hall, Monmouth 1796

O' Brien. J. *Old Afan and Margam,* 1926

Phillips, David Rhys, *The History of the Vale of Neath,* Swansea, 1925

Rhys, John, *Celtic Folklore,* Oxford at the Clarendon Press, 1891

Ritson, Joseph, *The Life of King Arthur from Ancient Historians and Authentic Documents,* William Nicol, St James's, London, 1825

Roberts, Brynley F., *Brut y Brenhinedd,* Dublin Institute of Advanced Studies, 1971

Stephens, Meic, *The Oxford Companion to the Literature of Wales,* Oxford University Press, 1986

Stephens, Thomas, *The Literature of the Kymry,* Longmans, Green & Co., London, 1876

Tatlock, John Strong Perry, *The Legendary History of Britain - Geoffrey of Monmouth's 'Historia Regum Britanniae' and its Vernacular Versions,* University of California Press,   Berkeley, 1950

Thomas, Charles, *And Shall These Mute Stones Speak?,* University of Wales Press, Cardiff, 1994

Thomas, Hugh, *An Essay towards the History of Brecknockshire,* 1698

Thorpe, Lewis, *Geoffrey of Monmouth - 'The History of the Kings of Britain,'* Penguin Books, Harmondsworth, 1966
Gerald of Wales - The Journey through Wales and *The Description of Wales,* Penguin Books, Harmondsworth, 1978

Treharne, R.F., *The Glastonbury Legends,* London, 1967

Trevelyan, Marie, *The Land of Arthur - Its Heroes and Heroines*, John Hogg, London, 1895

Wade-Evans, Arthur, *The Brychan Documents*, Y Cymmrodor, XIX, 1906

Wade-Evans, Arthur, *The Llancarfan Charters*, Archaeologia Cambrensis, LXXXVII, 1932

Wade-Evans, Arthur, *Welsh Christian Origins*, Alden Press, Oxford, 1934

Williams, David, *The History of Monmouthshire*, Tudor & Hall, Monmouth, 1796

Williams, Glanmor, *Neath Abbey*, contained in *Neath and District - a Symposium*, edited by Elis Jenkins, Neath, 1974

Williams, Griffith John, *Traddodiad Llenyddol Morgannwg*, Cardiff, 1948

Williams, Gwyn, A., *Excalibur - The Search for Arthur*, BBC Books, London 1994

Williams, John, *The Ecclesiastical Antiquity of the Cymry*, W. J. Cleaver, London, 1844

Williams, Stewart, *Glamorgan Historians*, D. Brown & Sons, Cowbridge, 1963

INDEX

OTHER TITLES BY CHRIS BARBER

Walks in the Brecon Beacons
Exploring the Waterfall Country
Ghosts of Wales
Exploring the Brecon Beacons National Park
Exploring Gwent
Mysterious Wales
More Mysterious Wales
Cordell Country
The Romance of the Welsh Mountains
Hando's Gwent (Volume I)
Hando's Gwent (Volume II)
The Ancient Stones of Wales (Jointly with J. G. Williams)
The Seven Hills of Abergavenny
Journey to Avalon (Jointly with David Pykitt)
Arthurian Caerleon
Abergavenny in Old Picture Postcards
Portraits of the Past (Jointly with Michael Blackmore)
Classic Walks in the Brecon Beacons
Walks in Cordell Country
In Search of Owain Glyndwr
Eastern Valley – The Story of Torfaen
Exploring Blaenavon Industrial Landscape World Heritage Site
Exploring Kilvert Country
Llanover Country
In Search of Owain Glyndwr (Revised Edition)